TEXAS FIELD GUIDE SERIES

A FIELD GUIDE TO
BIRDS
OF THE BIG BEND
SECOND EDITION

ROLAND WAUER
ILLUSTRATIONS BY NANCY McGOWAN

Gulf Publishing Company
Houston, Texas

Dedication

*To the more than 1,200 birders
who have submitted their sightings
to the National Park Service.*

Gulf Publishing Company
Book Division
P.O. Box 2608 ☐ Houston, Texas 77252-2608

10 9 8 7 6 5 4 3 2 1

Printed in the United States of America.

Illustrations by Nancy McGowan

Library of Congress Cataloging-in-Publication Data
Wauer, Roland H.
   A field guide to birds of the Big Bend / by Roland H. Wauer. –
2nd ed.
      p.   cm. – (The Texas field guide series)
   Includes bibliographical references (p.   ) and index.
   ISBN 0-87719-271-5
   1. Birds–Texas–Big Bend National Park–Identification.   2. Big
Bend National Park (Tex.)   I. Title.   II. Series.
QL684.T4W39   1996
598.29764'932–dc20   95-38033
                                                          CIP

CONTENTS

ACKNOWLEDGMENTS

More than 1,200 birders have participated in the development of this book. Without that multitude of birders who have visited Big Bend National Park over the years, such a book would be impossible. Every one of the more than 1,200 birders have submitted a bird sighting report ("Natural History Field Observation" card) to the National Park Service; some individuals submitted up to four dozen reports. The majority of these folks are mentioned at pertinent places throughout the text, and the complete list of birders (all those who have submitted reports) are listed alphabetically in Appendix B. All are gratefully acknowledged.

Also while preparing this book, I received special assistance from a number of friends and colleagues. Foremost of those was Greg Lasley, who reviewed the complete list of annotated species and made several valuable suggestions. Greg also has kept me aware of birds being reviewed by the Texas Bird Records Committee when they had been reported for Big Bend National Park. His concern, enthusiasm, professionalism, and friendship are much appreciated. And in addition, Greg kindly agreed to write the foreword to this book.

I also received special assistance or advice from Carl Robinson, of the Big Bend Natural History Association, who helped with the initial planning for this revision; Jeff Selleck provided me with numerous comments about various species and observers; Ray Skiles helped with the review of the park's Bird Record File; Carl Fleming and Jeff Marcus assisted with obtaining pertinent references; Bryan Hale provided me with current Christmas Bird Count data; and Betty Alex, Anne Bellamy, Sarah Bourbon, Bonnie McKinney, and Judy Townsend provided advice regarding certain bird sightings. However, any mistakes that might still exist are my full responsibility.

Thanks also are due Nancy McGowan for her excellent illustrations that give personality to this otherwise rather esoteric book. Nancy revised five of the earlier illustrations, and added ten entire new ones.

And finally, Betty, my wife, has given me considerable support and encouragement during the development of this new book. She is much appreciated.

FOREWORD

Big Bend! To an avid birder, just saying those two words out loud brings up magical feelings. Big Bend! The national park with more bird species recorded than any other in the entire United States. When I think of Big Bend, my mind wanders through the cottonwood groves along the Rio Grande, up into Green Gulch and the Basin, and along the Window Trail. I can visualize myself walking up the Pinnacles Trail to Boot Canyon, and I can hear Colima Warblers singing among the oaks and maples at Boot Spring. Big Bend is truly magic.

I clearly remember my first trip to Big Bend 20 years ago. I was a relatively inexperienced birdwatcher, and I had purchased a copy of *Birds of Big Bend National Park and Vicinity* by a man named Roland Wauer. I remember following Ro's advice on where to look for many of the species I sought and how accurate his descriptions were. Big Bend quickly became a favorite destination for me, and I began to make many trips there, sometimes three or four per year. On each of these visits I relied on Ro's book to help me find birds and to better understand the park and its bird life.

In 1982, I was fortunate enough to find and photograph one of the first Red-faced Warblers documented in Texas while I was in Boot Canyon. This lead me into correspondence with Ro as he was preparing his second edition of the Big Bend bird book, which was published in 1985 as *A Field Guide to Birds of the Big Bend*. This second edition was similar to the first, but with updated information. My trips to Big Bend continued, and my love for the park grew. By the late 1980s, I knew the park very well, and there were few places there I had not visited. Ro's books were my constant companions as I hiked and drove along nearly every trail and road in the park. In 1989, Ro and I finally met in person and became good friends. We have been able to be in the field together in Mexico, in various areas of Texas, and yes, in Big Bend. Ro's love for Big Bend is like mine, and we feel a kinship known only to those who have experienced this magical place.

I can think of no person better qualified than Ro Wauer to write about the birds of Big Bend National Park. Ro has 30 years of experience in Big Bend and knows the park like few others. He has made considerable efforts to seek the most reliable and accurate data concerning the bird records from the park, and his continued personal observations and involvement with the park staff allow him to be abreast of changes in bird status and distribution in the Big Bend country. This third edition of the birds of Big Bend is the best yet and is an important addition to any birder's library. Whether you are a new visitor to the park or an experienced Big Bend birder, Ro's book will be your companion and guide through your avian adventures. Experience Big Bend and its bird life. Walk the cool mountain canyons at dawn or explore a desert flat; at either place special birds await the explorer. Let Big Bend and its bird life become a part of you while you are there—but, I warn you, it's a relationship that can become a habit. For some of us it is more than a habit. Big Bend is, simply, my favorite place on earth.

Greg W. Lasley

In addition to serving as editor of the Texas region for the Audubon Society's Field Notes *magazine for 15 years, Greg W. Lasley is secretary of the Texas Bird Records Committee, is a member of the American Birding Association Check List Committee, and leads tours for Victor Emanuel Nature Tours, Inc.*

INTRODUCTION

The Big Bend Country is one of those special "must visit" places for birders. It is one of a handful of localities in North America that represent birding at its best. Places like Florida's Everglades, the Lower Rio Grande Valley of Texas, Arizona's Ramsey Canyon, and Big Bend National Park sooner or later will show up on every birder's calendar. Big Bend offers at least one species—Colima Warbler—that cannot be found anywhere else in the United States; several Mexican species have been discovered within the park in recent years—Ruddy Ground-Dove, Elegant Trogon, Tufted Flycatcher, Rufous-backed Robin, Aztec Thrush, Slate-throated Redstart, Rufous-capped Warbler, and Black-vented Oriole—that provide considerable interest to birders; and a number of species, including the Zone-tailed Hawk, Peregrine Falcon, Elf Owl, Lucifer Hummingbird, Hepatic Tanager, and Varied Bunting, often difficult to find anywhere else, are reasonably common in spring and summer at Big Bend. More bird species (444) have been recorded at Big Bend National Park than in any other national park in North America.

The intent of this book is to help the Big Bend visitor find the particular birds he or she may want to see. It is a where-to-go-to-find-what-book, not a bird identification guide. *A Field Guide to Birds of the Big Bend* should be a companion to the popular identification guides that more than likely are already part of your library. This book also is written to satisfy two worlds: that of the ornithologist, who may be especially interested in statistics and records, and that of the birder, who may watch birds simply for the thrill of seeing an old friend or making a new one.

A Field Guide to Birds of the Big Bend includes all the known birds that have been recorded for Big Bend National Park. The first edition of this book, *Birds of Big Bend National Park and Vicinity,* appeared in 1973. It contained an annotated list of 385 species; 359 of those were included in the regular list of "accepted" species, and 26 hypothetical species were included in a list of "Birds of Uncertain Occurrence."

A revised book, *A Field Guide to Birds of the Big Bend,* appeared in 1985. That book contained 423 species, 38 more than the original version. Of those 423 species, 372 were included on the regular list, and 51 were listed as uncertain. Most interesting were the new discoveries (from 1973 to 1985) that became part of the regular list: Ross' Goose, Wild Turkey, Forster's Tern, Varied Thrush, Aztec Thrush, Tennessee Warbler, and Common Grackle. Eleven additional species were elevated from uncertain to accepted status: White-tailed Kite, Elegant Trogon, Rose-throated Becard, Steller's Jay, Veery, Cape May Warbler, Golden-cheeked Warbler, Yellow-throated Warbler, Red-faced Warbler, Purple Finch, and Evening Grosbeak.

The current revision, reflecting the extensive amount of birding activity that occurs year-round at Big Bend National Park, includes a total of 444 species, 21 more than were reported in 1985, and numerous status changes. Four of the 21 new species were adequately documented and appear on the regular list—Double-crested Cormorant, Ruddy Ground-Dove, Tufted Flycatcher, and Smith's Longspur—and the remainder are listed as uncertain.

New uncertain species include the Western Grebe, Brown Pelican, Reddish Egret, Roseate Spoonbill, Black-bellied Whistling-Duck, Muscovy Duck, White-rumped Sandpiper, Herring Gull, White-collared Swift, Berylline Hummingbird, Violet-crowned Hummingbird, Nutting's Flycatcher, Crescent-chested Warbler, Prairie Warbler, Swainson's Warbler, Connecticut Warbler, Yellow Grosbeak, Blue Bunting, Lapland Longspur, Snow Bunting, and Bobolink.

Ten previously uncertain species were moved to accepted status: Red-breasted Merganser, Black Tern, Black-billed Cuckoo, American Dipper, Tropical Parula, Pine Warbler, Cerulean Warbler, Slate-throated Redstart, Yellow-eyed Junco, and Altamira Oriole.

Also for this revision, all the records of species not verified by a specimen or photograph were reassessed; a number of these were questionable, even though they may have been reported on numerous occasions. For example, although Bendire's Thrasher has been reported in the park on nine occasions, it has never been verified by a specimen or photograph in Big Bend or anywhere else in Texas. It, therefore, was moved from the regular list to uncertain status.

These kinds of determinations are difficult at best, especially because I am no longer able to assess fresh reports, including on-site visits, as I did while I was working and living in the park. I, therefore, subjected each species to rather stringent rules as to which category it best fit. All species included in the regular list must be verified by a specimen or a photograph, or have been reported at least five times by unimpeachable sources. Even probable but unverified species will remain in the uncertain category. I also decided to take greater advantage of the very effective Texas Bird Records Committee (TBRC), a standing committee of the Texas Ornithological Society. TBRC evaluates all first occurrence or rare bird sightings for Texas, including those at Big Bend National Park, for possible inclusion on the official list of Texas birds. Therefore, all new or extremely unusual Texas records (see Appendix A for a list of requested species) should, along with being reported to the National Park Service, be submitted to Greg Lasley, Secretary for the TBRC, 305 Loganberry Court, Austin, TX 78745, OR to Dr. Keith Arnold, Dept. of Wildlife and Fisheries Sciences, Texas A&M University, College Station, TX 77843-2258. A sample Report Form is included in Appendix A.

During the reassessment/assessment process, there were a few species that did not fit either accepted or uncertain status, but their presence, though remote, is possible. I therefore developed a third category—"Questionable Reports"—for species considered extremely unlikely but not altogether impossible. Birds included in this category are not part of the park's total species count.

Also in the process of reassessing the various reports, I moved eight species from accepted (Wauer 1985) to uncertain status: American Black Duck, American Woodcock, Least Tern, White-tipped Dove, Allen's Hummingbird, Rufous-backed Robin, Bendire's Thrasher, and Bay-breasted Warbler. Even though I had personally observed five of the eight species, they will remain in the uncertain category until they have been fully verified. And also in keeping with the stricter rules for listing, I moved four species from the official lists (accepted and/or uncertain) to the questionable category: Spotted Rail, Three-toed Woodpecker, Bohemian Waxwing, and Hooded Grosbeak. Some of these may later be verified and be moved into one of the higher categories. And three species that were listed as uncertain in the 1985 book were eliminated altogether: Squirrel Cuckoo, White-necked Jacobin, and Blue-black Grassquit. I also eliminated Chukar, which was listed because it had been introduced years ago at

Black Gap Wildlife Management Area; it now appears that those have not survived or at least have not moved into the park.

Also as part of the current revision, all but about a dozen of the 1985 annotations were revised due to new (additional) reports that changed the earlier description in some way. And a few changes were necessary because of changes in common and/or scientific names initiated by the American Ornithologists' Union (AOU supplements in 1985, 1989, or 1993). But the majority of changes were necessary because of the tremendous volume of reports, primarily by observers reporting their sightings to the National Park Service. Those reports are first placed in a notebook that is maintained at the Panther Junction Visitor Center; they are available for perusal upon request. The cards eventually are deposited in a permanent NPS file.

BIRD STUDY IN THE BIG BEND

The first ornithological investigation within the Texas Big Bend Country was by a party from the United States Biological Survey in 1901. During May, June, and July of that year, Harry C. Oberholser, Vernon Bailey, and Louis Agassiz Fuertes did extensive field work throughout the area. Oberholser summarized their more important findings in 1902, Fuertes published on the Harlequin (Montezuma) Quail in 1903, and Bailey reported on the expedition's total findings in 1905. In 1904, Thomas H. Montgomery collected birds around Alpine and southward to the Chisos Mountains between June 13 and July 6. He reported his findings in a paper on the "summer resident" birds of Brewster County in 1905. And the following year, John K. Stecker briefly visited the Big Bend area in April and May.

This early period of activity was followed by one in which expeditions to this remote section of the United States was discouraged. The Mexican Revolution caused considerable unrest along the Mexican border. For the next 20 years, except for Austin Paul Smith's visit to the Davis Mountains from September 2 to October 6, 1916, the only ornithologists to visit the Texas Big Bend area were those associated with the military. Frank B. Armstrong was one of those who collected birds for Col. John E. Thayer in May 1913 and in January and February 1914. George E. Maxon, a member of the Texas National Guard, was stationed at Boquillas, Terlingua, and Lajitas, and collected bird eggs throughout the region during 1916. Maxon published his findings in two papers that same year.

It was not until 1928 that additional ornithological research was instigated within the Big Bend. That year, Josselyn Van Tyne and Frederick M. and Helen T. Gaige surveyed the bird life from Alpine to the top of Emory Peak between June 8 and August 7. The Van Tyne-Gaige party spent considerable time at Glenn Springs, San Vicente, Hot Springs, and Boquillas. They even reached Boot Canyon, where Frederick Gaige collected a Colima Warbler on July 20. That specimen represented the first for the United States and only the twelfth known specimen of this warbler. Van Tyne reported the most important data obtained by this expedition in 1929. The opportunity to find a new breeding bird for the United States prompted Van Tyne to return in 1932. His second visit, in which he was accompanied by Max M. Peet and Edouard C. Jacot, lasted from April 26 through June 22. Their success was published in Van Tyne's 1936 paper, "The Discovery of the Nest of the Colima Warbler (*Vermivora crissalis*)."

News of their ornithological discoveries soon attracted other biologists to the area. In the spring of 1933, George Miksch Sutton, John B. Semple, and Albert C. Lloyd spent more than a month within the Big Bend Country. Several days were spent around Marathon, Castolon, Hot Springs, and Boquillas, but visits to Juniper and Pine canyons also were undertaken before they turned north to the Del Norte and Glass mountains. Sutton published a fascinating account of this trip, "An Expedition to the Big Bend Country," in 1935, and a chapter of his 1936 book, *Birds in the Wilderness,* is devoted to this and a second trip to the Big Bend in 1935.

At about the same time, considerable interest was being expressed by concerned Texans about a national park within the lower Big Bend Country. This interest prompted the National Park Service to send biologists to the area to investigate its potential. Ben H. Thompson surveyed the wildlife for the Park Service in 1934, and several additional biologists were sent into the area during 1935 and 1936: James O. Stevenson, Walter A. Weber, Tarleton F. Smith, and Adrey E. Borell. Stevenson, accompanied by Van Tyne, who was returning for his third visit, reported his findings in 1935. Smith submitted a report on his studies in 1936, and Borell reported on her findings in 1936 and 1938. In addition, Roy W. Quillin, an independent ornithologist, published a note on his visit to the lower Big Bend Country in 1935. And in 1937, Herbert Brandt and associates spent the first half of May studying birds in the Chisos Mountains. Brandt reported on new races of the White-breasted Nuthatch and Hutton's Vireo in 1938, and he summarized his Big Bend experiences in *Texas Bird Adventures* in 1940. This book offers interesting accounts of his birding as well as an early description of the country itself.

By 1937, sufficient information on the bird life of the area was available for Van Tyne and Sutton to collaborate on a comprehensive analysis of the avifauna in "The Birds of Brewster County, Texas." This 120-page paper, published by the University of Michigan, was based on 425 days of field work by the authors and the combined information of earlier researchers. They reported a total of 215 species of birds for Brewster County.

Big Bend National Park was established on June 12, 1944. That congressional act resulted in the protection of all animals and plants and the historic and geographic features within the 708,221-acre park. It began a new era of land protection in Texas. For the first time since cattle were driven into the lush grasslands of the Chisos Mountains in 1885, the plant life was allowed to begin a slow recovery. More than 40,000 head of stock, mostly goats and sheep, had been removed from the area in 1943 and 1944.

In an attempt to monitor the natural recovery of the park's plant communities, vegetative transects were established during the mid-1940s. Walter P. Taylor, Walter B. McDougall, and William B. Davis completed a "Preliminary Report on an Ecological Survey of Big Bend National Park" in 1944, and by the mid-1950s an ecological survey team from Texas A&M University was stationed in the park. Team member Richard D. Porter resided there from June 1957 through early August 1959. During that time he collected a large series of birds, many of which were deposited in the Big Bend National Park study collection or at Texas A&M. Several of the members of this team kept records of the park's bird life, and a number of reports were eventually published; Keith L. Dixon and O. Charles Wallmo published a series of bird records in 1956, and Dixon reported on desert shrub birds in 1959.

In 1956, Col. L. R. Wolfe summarized all the state's bird records in his *Checklist of the Birds of Texas*. That publication was replaced by later checklists. The most recent (1995) is *Checklist of the Birds of Texas* Third Edition, prepared by the Texas Bird Records Committee of the Texas Ornithological Society.

Also in the mid-1950s, several National Park Service employees began to record their bird observations. Park Ranger Dick Youse recorded several important observations from May 1955 through September 1956. Harold Brodrick became the first park naturalist in December 1955, and until his departure in October 1961, he maintained an excellent series of bird records. Brodrick prepared a "Check-list of the Birds of Big Bend National Park" in 1960. This mimeographed list included 236 species of birds. It incorporated the records of other Big Bend Park residents—especially those of Pete Koch, John Palmer, Harold Schaafsma, Rod Broyles, and Pat Miller—as well as many park visitors who had thoughtfully sent their sightings to the park naturalist for the park files. Brodrick's checklist was revised in 1966 by C. Philip Allen and Anne LeSassier, who added several important records, increasing the list to 241 species. Additional park checklists have appeared every five to ten years; the 1995 checklist, edited by Jeff Selleck, includes a total of nearly 450 species.

My arrival in Big Bend National Park in August 1966 allowed me the opportunity to visit several strategic locations many times throughout the year. During a period from August 1966 through October 1971, field trips were taken one to four times a week to Rio Grande Village and the Chisos Basin. Boot Canyon, Castolon, and Laguna Meadow were surveyed regularly, and occasional visits to numerous other places were also made. I spent 3,589 hours of field research and more than 400 hours of analysis of avian records and the park's vegetation during that five-year period. For the first time, the study of birds of the Big Bend area began to show some continuity. In spite of the fact that the area had visits from some of the finest field ornithologists in the world, their records had not been thoroughly analyzed for a comprehensive publication on the birds.

The product of those investigations, along with the abundant reports of visiting birders, resulted in the first edition of this book: *Birds of Big Bend National Park and Vicinity,* that was published by the University of Texas Press in 1973. That book was updated and published as *A Field Guide to Birds of the Big Bend* by Texas Monthly Press in 1985. This is the third revision, and is being published by Gulf Publishing Company of Houston, Texas.

Since 1973, field research by numerous ornithologists, as well as reports from more than 1,300 birders, have contributed to Big Bend's avian database. I incorporated all of those records (through May 1995) into a central file that became the working database for this latest revision. It includes a total of 445 species, of which 62 (14%) are permanent or full-time residents and an additional 50 species (11%) are summer residents only; a total of 112 species (25%) are known to nest within the park. Approximately 131 (30%) are strictly migratory, and approximately 100 (23%) of the 445 species spend their winters in Big Bend National Park.

BIRD FINDING

Finding a maximum number of birds can best be accomplished by visiting all the different habitats within all the park's plant and animal communities. If you wish to find particular species of birds, however, it is more profitable to search within appropriate habitats at the proper time of year. Each species utilizes preferred sites that fulfill that individual's ecological requirements. Black-throated Sparrows, for instance, reside in the arid lowlands, while Mexican Jays occur in the mountain woodlands. Searching for a Painted Bunting at Boot Spring in December or a Townsend's Solitaire at Rio Grande Village in July would be an utter waste of time. The text contains clues to where and when to find the birds desired.

There are several locations in the park that a birder should visit if he or she is interested in a maximum number of species. Rio Grande Village is the best place I know for consistently finding a large number of birds. The principal areas to search at Rio Grande Village include the nature trail in the southeastern corner of the campground; the campground proper and the mesquite thickets just across the roadway to the north; the cottonwood groves and floodplain thickets behind the store and trailer court; the area west of the trailer court to the turnaround; and the area along the river, cottonwood groves, and the silt ponds beyond the cottonwoods to the north of the turnaround.

The second most important area is the Chisos Basin. This area includes the campground and the entire Oak Creek drainage below the campground, including the Window Trail and sewage lagoons. A most productive birding walk would include the Window Trail and a return to the campground via the Oak Creek drainage to a point below the lower loop of the campground. From there, you can return to the campground via a service road.

There are several other localities within the park where many of the same species can be found. Cottonwood Campground has come into its own in recent years, especially because of nesting Thick-billed Kingbirds (sporadic) and Lucy's Warblers. Green Gulch sometimes can be quite productive, particularly during the fall migration. Lower Blue Creek Canyon is best in spring. And lower Pine Canyon can be a good area for birds any time except in midsummer.

In late spring and summer, a visit to Boot Canyon is a must. Although the Colima Warbler usually can be found below Pinnacles Pass, at Laguna Meadow, and along the Colima Trail, Boot Canyon, between Boot Spring and the South Rim, can be very rewarding. One of the best localities for consistently finding highland birds, including the Colima Warbler from April 15 to early September, is about 200 yards beyond the Juniper Canyon sidetrail, a quarter-mile above Boot Spring. However, birders who are not able to hike to Boot Spring usually can find most of the same birds at Laguna Meadow, which is one mile closer to the Chisos Basin. Another area that can be very good in spring, summer, and fall is the Lost Mine Trail. This trail starts at 5,600 feet in elevation, and a two-mile walk offers some high-country exposure for a minimum of time and effort. The Lost Mine Trail, however, is never as productive, bird-wise, as Boot Canyon.

In late fall and early winter, you can hardly go wrong with a visit to the Castolon area. The weedy fields adjacent to the roadway to Santa Elena Crossing and along Alamo Creek can produce more sparrows than anywhere else in the park. Dugout Wells, located below Panther Junction along the road to Rio Grande Village, can be very productive during the spring migration.

For birders who like to find a bench and sit and wait for feathered friends to happen by, two places are suggested: the Old Ranch (Sam Nail Ranch) and the Rio Grande Village nature trail. The nature trail already has been mentioned. The Old Ranch is located along the Ross Maxwell Scenic Drive (Castolon Road) and is situated on Cottonwood Creek. Although the creek is dry some years, birds gather at the old ranch site because of the water available from a working windmill. A bench located beneath the walnuts and willows is a relaxing place to bird with a minimum of effort.

Fewer than 15% of Big Bend's birds are permanent residents. Only about 85% of the park's birds spend only a few hours to a few months in the area as either migrants or as summer or winter residents. As a result, Big Bend's avian composition and density fluctuate considerably. The seasonal variation of bird species at Rio Grande Village and the Chisos Basin are illustrated in Figure 1, which is based on three-to five-hour field trips throughout the year from August 1, 1966, to June 30, 1971. A total of 293 field trips were made to Rio Grande Village and 109 to the Chisos Basin during that period.

The Migration. Spring can arrive early in the Big Bend. The spring migration usually begins before the end of February with the arrival of Violet-green Swallows along the Rio Grande. Black dalea and blackbrush acacia begin to bloom in lowland arroyos by early March, and their aromatic flowers may attract Lucifer and Black-chinned Hummingbirds. By

Bird Finding

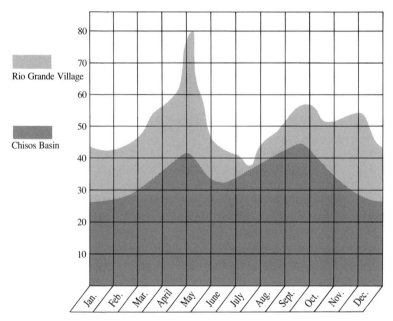

Figure 1. Seasonal variation of bird species averaged over a five-year period.

mid-March, spring migrants are evident throughout the desert. Numbers of the northbound migrants increase gradually during late March, accelerate rapidly in April, and reach a peak during the last days of April and the first week of May. That peak is followed by a swift decline in numbers of species, but fewer numbers of migrants can be detected during the rest of May and early June.

Spring migrants are far more numerous in the lowlands, particularly along the river, than in the mountains. The highest number of migrants move through the north-south "valleys," such as the rather broad Tornillo Creek drainage area. Dugout Wells and adjacent wetlands a short distance to the north, Hannold Draw, and the extensive areas of riparian vegetation along the Rio Grande provide convenient stopover sites for a wide variety of northbound migrants. For example, 52 species is the highest number of birds I recorded in the Chisos Basin (in five hours on April 27, 1969), versus 93 species at Rio Grande Village (in six hours on May 3, 1970).

The list of 93 species recorded at Rio Grande Village, an example of a maximum number of possible species, included: Least Grebe, Pied-billed Grebe, American Bittern, Green-winged Teal, Blue-winged Teal, Northern Shoveler, Gadwall, American Wigeon, Black Vulture, Turkey Vulture, Sharp-shinned Hawk, Red-tailed Hawk, American Kestrel, Common Moorhen, American Coot, Killdeer, Solitary Sandpiper, Spotted Sandpiper, White-winged Dove, Mourning Dove, Inca Dove, Common Ground-Dove, Yellow-billed Cuckoo, Greater Roadrunner, Groove-billed Ani, Great Horned Owl, Lesser Nighthawk, White-throated Swift, Black-chinned Hummingbird, Ladder-backed Woodpecker, Olive-sided Flycatcher, Vermilion Flycatcher, Ash-throated Flycatcher, Western Wood-Pewee, Say's Phoebe, Western Kingbird, Violet-green Swallow, Northern Rough-winged Swallow, Cliff Swallow, Barn Swallow, Common Raven, Verdin, House Wren, Marsh Wren, Ruby-crowned Kinglet, Blue-gray Gnatcatcher, Hermit Thrush, Northern Mockingbird, Curve-billed Thrasher, American Pipit, Cedar Waxwing, Bell's Vireo, Solitary Vireo, Warbling Vireo, Lucy's Warbler, Northern Parula, Yellow Warbler, Yellow-rumped Warbler, Townsend's Warbler, American Redstart, Northern Waterthrush, MacGillivray's Warbler, Common Yellowthroat, Hooded Warbler, Wilson's Warbler, Yellow-breasted Chat, Summer Tanager, Western Tanager, Northern Cardinal, Pyrrhuloxia, Blue Grosbeak, Indigo Bunting, Painted Bunting, Dickcissel, Black-throated Sparrow, Lincoln's Sparrow, Swamp Sparrow, White-throated Sparrow, Brewer's Blackbird, Brown-headed

Cowbird, Black-vented Oriole, Orchard Oriole, Hooded Oriole, Scott's Oriole, House Finch, Lesser Goldfinch, and House Sparrow.

Many of the birds found at Rio Grande Village also were recorded in the Chisos Basin on April 27, 1969. The following 19 species were recorded only in the Basin: Scaled Quail, Blue-throated Hummingbird, Acorn Woodpecker, Hammond's Flycatcher, Dusky Flycatcher, Gray Flycatcher, Mexican Jay, Tufted Titmouse, Bushtit, Cactus Wren, Rock Wren, Canyon Wren, Bewick's Wren, Gray Vireo, Rufous-sided Towhee, Rufous-crowned Sparrow, Black-chinned Sparrow, Dark-eyed Junco, and Pine Siskin.

Fall migration in the lowlands is only a shadow of the spring movement. Although post-nesting herons and shorebirds may reach the Rio Grande area in mid-July, the majority of the southbound birds do not begin to appear until the end of July or early August. A gradual buildup continues throughout August, reaches a peak in mid-September, and drops off during October. There is a second, less extensive influx of migrants during late November and the first few days of December.

In the mountains, birds begin to increase immediately after the spring movement subsides. Some post-nesting birds of the Rio Grande floodplain and desert move into the mountain canyons and slopes in June. And the first of the northern migrants, such as male Rufous Hummingbirds, reach the flowering slopes of the Chisos Mountains by the second week of July. Fall migrants reach a peak in mid-September, and the movement continues at a slower pace until the first cold front arrives in early winter. In general, the migration in the mountains is far more extensive in fall than it is in spring.

The differences in spring and fall movements of birds through the park area may be explained in two ways. First, the spring migration is shorter, lasting only about two months. It is characterized by a rather moderate buildup, but ends with a sharp decline. Conversely, the fall movement is gradual and scattered out over four months. Second, the number of southbound birds passing through the park is less than it is in spring. This is at least in part due to the topography of the Big Bend Country. Spring migrants follow the north-south desert valleys and ridges and are naturally funneled into the lower Big Bend along the western edge of the Sierra del Carmen, which forms the eastern edge of the park and runs south into Mexico for almost 100 miles. Fall migrants, on the other hand, are often diverted east of the park by the Santiago Mountains, which form a barrier to lowland migrants just north of the park. I have watched flocks of black-birds and individual hawks and gulls change their course to the southeast, toward Black Gap Wildlife Management Area and the eastern slopes of the Sierra del Carmen, as they approach the ridges just north of Persimmon Gap.

Figure 2 illustrates the relative abundance of five groups of birds that are regular migrants through Big Bend National Park. Ducks begin to move through the area during late February and early March. They become common along the Rio Grande and at adjacent ponds from mid-

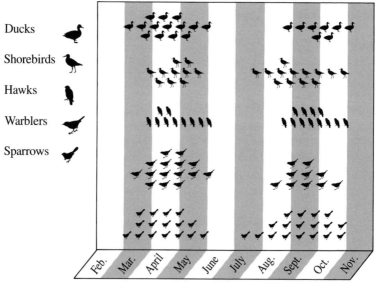

Figure 2. Relative abundance of five groups of migratory birds.

March through mid-May, and stragglers continue to pass through the area until mid-June. Fall migrants are less numerous; early birds may reach the Big Bend during the second week of August, but the peak of the fall movement does not occur until late September and lasts through October. Southbound waterfowl continue to pass through the area in small numbers until early November, and stragglers can usually be found along the river until late November. During very mild winters, the fall migration may be only half as great as that of normal years. Late winters may result in a movement of waterfowl through the park as much as three to five weeks later.

Although the Rio Grande would seem to be a physical pathway for migrating water birds, they are never common in the Big Bend; less than two dozen shorebirds have been recorded within the park. These birds do not reach the area until mid-March. They become most numerous from mid-April to early May, numbers decline considerably by mid-May, and stragglers continue to move through the area until the end of the month. The Killdeer is the park's only nesting shorebird. Fall migrants reach the Big Bend quite early; Solitary, Spotted, Baird's, and Least Sandpipers may appear by mid-July. The whole of the southward movement is stretched out from mid-July through early November, with a minor peak evident from August 20 to September 12.

Migrant hawks are sporadic within Big Bend National Park. They usually are found alone or in twos or threes; there are no waves of hawks like those that occur along the Texas Gulf Coast. The exception may be southbound Swainson's Hawks north of the park, that, for the most part, remain along the eastern slopes of the Sierra del Carmen. Early spring migrants arrive in the park in mid-March, a peak is reached during the last three weeks of April and early May, and stragglers continue to pass through the Big Bend until the first of June. Fall migrants begin to appear in mid-August and reach a peak from late August to mid-October. Migrant hawks usually can be found until about November 12.

The movement of wood warblers through Big Bend National Park produces the largest number of birds of any single group. Some early spring migrants can be found the second week of March; their numbers increase dramatically during the last of April and the first half of May, and they remain fairly common until late May. Stragglers often can be found to mid-June. Some fall migrants, such as Black-and-white Warblers, have been recorded in early July, but most of the early southbound migrants do not reach the Big Bend until the first part of August. The early birds have been found only in the mountains; lowland migrants are rarely detected until mid-August. The fall movement is not as dramatic as that in the spring, and a population peak is reached from late August through late September. Southbound birds appear throughout October, although only two or three species can be found by the end of the month.

Big Bend's sparrows are sporadic in migration and generally are restricted to the areas below approximately 5,500 feet elevation. Some movement of northbound sparrows is evident during the last days of February, but the main spring migration does not get under way until mid-March. Sparrows continue to be fairly common until late May, and stragglers occur until early June. Southbound Chipping and Lark Sparrows may reach the park as early as the last half of July, and Lark Buntings usually appear during the first days of August. The bulk of the southward sparrow migration does not become evident until September, but lasts through October. Fall migrants continue to move through the area until late November. The extent of the fall sparrow migration depends upon the summer rains producing sufficient seed-crops to attract the migrants. Some years can be characterized as "good sparrow years."

Weather conditions in West Texas are vitally important for finding birds year-round. Periods of drought can seriously affect migrants, breeders, post-nesters, and even wintering birds. Populations can be very different from one year to another. If winter rains produce an abundance of perennials, providing nectar, seeds, and insects, northbound migrants can be expected in abundance. Sparrows will be numerous along the roadsides following rainy periods, but can be practically nonexistent when the rains do not occur. Even in the fall, migrants take advantage of flowering areas when possible, but remain for shorter periods or pass over altogether during dry seasons. Late summer growth that produces an abundance of flowering mountain sage tends to hold the migrants for longer periods of time.

The Breeding Season. More than 100 species of birds have been found to nest within Big Bend National Park in recent years. Lowland residents are first to begin their territorial defense and nest-building. Some of the desert species may be incubating before the first of April, and some mountain birds may not arrive on their breeding grounds until late April.

Nesting birds of the *floodplain* include a few permanent residents, but the majority are neotropical migrants that reside within the park only during the spring and summer months. Most of these birds arrive in late March and April. The last of the summer residents to reach their breeding grounds are the Yellow-billed Cuckoo and Blue Grosbeak. The most conspicuous breeding birds of the floodplain include the White-winged and Mourning Doves, Greater Roadrunner, Black-chinned Hummingbird, Golden-fronted Woodpecker, Bell's Vireo, Yellow-breasted Chat, Summer Tanager, Painted Bunting, Northern Cardinal, Blue Grosbeak, and Brown-headed Cowbird. Other birds that are regular nesters within the floodplain are the Yellow-billed Cuckoo, Eastern and Western Screech-Owls, Elf Owl, Ladder-backed Woodpecker, Black Phoebe, Ash-throated Flycatcher, Verdin, Northern Mockingbird, Black-tailed Gnatcatcher, Orchard and Hooded Orioles, Pyrrhuloxia, and House Finch.

Typical floodplain habitat is most accessible at Rio Grande Village, Cottonwood Campground, Boquillas and Santa Elena crossings, and the Santa Elena Canyon picnic area. If sufficient water is present to form ponds or marshy areas, as at Rio Grande Village, a few water birds may find suitable nesting sites. These include the Pied-billed Grebe, Sora, American Coot, Killdeer, and Common Yellowthroat.

The *arroyos* offer a drier environment where many of the same birds often can be found nesting. The most conspicuous breeding birds of this community are the Verdin, Cactus Wren, Northern Mockingbird, Black-tailed Gnatcatcher, Pyrrhuloxia, and House Finch. Scaled Quail and Lesser Nighthawks are ground-nesters that find suitable conditions under the shrubby thickets of mesquite and acacia, and the larger shrubs may offer suitable holes and crevices for the nesting Eastern and Western Screech-Owls, Elf Owl, Ladder-backed Woodpecker, and Ash-throated Flycatcher.

Dugout Wells, Government Spring, and the Old Ranch and Cottonwood Creek contain permanent water and large cottonwoods, willows, and other trees; these areas serve as oases in an otherwise arid environment. They attract a number of nesting birds, including the White-winged and Mourning Doves, Yellow-billed Cuckoo, Bell's Vireo, Yellow-breasted Chat, Summer Tanager, Blue Grosbeak, Painted Bunting, House Finch, and Lesser Goldfinch. And the surrounding shrubbery also may attract the Scaled Quail, Curve-billed and Crissal Thrashers, and Varied Bunting.

The *shrub desert* is the most expansive of Big Bend's six plant communities, but contains the fewest nesting birds. Vitally important to nesting birds in this area are the high rocky cliffs and ledges that support the Black and Turkey Vultures, Zone-tailed and Red-tailed Hawks, Golden Eagle, American Kestrel, Peregrine and Prairie Falcons, Great Horned Owl, White-throated Swift, Say's Phoebe, Cliff Swallow, Common Raven, and Rock and Canyon Wrens. The Cliff Swallow also nests under concrete bridges, such as those over Tornillo Creek.

The plants of the open desert support only a few breeding birds; the majority nest within the brushy arroyos. These include the Scaled Quail, Greater Roadrunner, Ash-throated Flycatcher, Cactus Wren, Black-tailed Gnatcatcher, Northern Mockingbird, Pyrrhuloxia, Black-throated Sparrow, and House Finch. The Black-throated Sparrow is the only species that is more numerous in this community than in any of the others.

The *grasslands,* the transition zone between the desert and arroyos and the mountain woodlands, are used by a large number of birds from both of the adjacent communities. Yet in spite of the overlap, there are several that are unique or especially common in this community. Conspicuous grassland birds include Loggerhead Shrike, Blue Grosbeak, Varied Bunting, Canyon Towhee, Rufous-crowned and Black-chinned Sparrows, and Scott's Oriole. Other regular grassland breeders include the Scaled Quail, Common Poorwill, Ladder-backed Woodpecker, Ash-throated Flycatcher, Verdin, Cactus Wren, Black-tailed Gnatcatcher, Northern Mockingbird, Pyrrhuloxia, Black-throated Sparrow, Brown-headed Cowbird, and House Finch.

Some of the best localities to find grassland birds include lower Green Gulch, lower Pine Canyon, and the middle elevations along the Window Trail. The latter area is one of the park's better birding areas because of the combined habitats of grasslands and deciduous woodlands.

The *pinyon-juniper-oak woodlands* in the Chisos Mountains may be divided into two rather distinct associations, deciduous and pinyon-juniper woodlands. For the most part, these zones of vegetation often overlap and can usually be regarded as a single unit, even though various nesting species may prefer one area over the other. Boulder Meadow and Laguna Meadow are excellent places to find typical breeding birds of this woodland community, which include the Eastern and Western Screech-Owls, Broad-tailed Hummingbird, Acorn Woodpecker, Ash-throated Flycatcher, Mexican Jay, Tufted Titmouse, Bushtit, Bewick's Wren, Blue-gray Gnatcatcher, Hepatic Tanager, Black-headed Grosbeak, Rufous-sided and Canyon Towhees, and Rufous-crowned Sparrow.

Several species nest within the lower parts of the pinyon-juniper-oak woodlands and rarely, if ever, nest above 5,000 feet. Examples include the White-winged and Mourning Doves, Great Horned and Elf Owls, Black-chinned Hummingbird, Ladder-backed Woodpecker, Gray Vireo, Summer Tanager, Scott's Oriole, Brown-headed Cowbird, and House Finch. Species that rarely occur in the lower parts of this zone but are fairly common nesting birds in the highlands include the Zone-tailed Hawk, Band-tailed Pigeon, Whip-poor-will, White-breasted Nuthatch, and Hutton's Vireo.

The *cypress-pine-oak woodlands* are restricted to only a few localities within the Chisos Mountains. Boot Canyon contains the best example of this community, but Pine Canyon offers all of the same birds during most summers. The most conspicuous breeding birds to be found in Boot Canyon are the Band-tailed Pigeon, Blue-throated and Broad-tailed Hummingbirds, Acorn Woodpecker, Northern Flicker, Cordilleran Flycatcher, Mexican Jay, Tufted Titmouse, Canyon Wren, Hutton's Vireo, Colima Warbler, Black-headed Grosbeak, and Rufous-sided Towhee. Less conspicuous but regular nesters in this woodland environment are the Flammulated Owl, Whip-poor-will, Bushtit, White-breasted Nuthatch, Bewick's Wren, and Rufous-crowned Sparrow.

The Winter Months. It is reasonably safe to consider the period from mid-November to late February as wintertime in Big Bend National Park. During autumns that are warmer than normal, however, some southward movement may continue until mid-December. Conversely, colder-than-normal fall months may send the majority of migrants south of the border before early November.

Wintering bird populations vary considerably from wet years to dry ones. Sparrows are common following summer and fall periods of above-average precipitation, but are usually rare after dry ones. A few groups of birds and individual species, such as the Williamson's Sapsucker, Red-breasted Nuthatch, Pygmy Nuthatch, Brown Creeper, Cassin's Finch, and Red Crossbill, may be present during some winters and completely absent in others. During warmer winters, Dusky and Ash-throated Flycatchers, Bewick's Wrens, and Blue-gray Gnatcatchers are more numerous than in colder winters.

The best possible long-term indexes to wintering birds are the Christmas Bird Counts. These counts are part of a national bird census sponsored by the National Audubon Society and the U. S. Fish and Wildlife

Service and are taken on one day during the last two weeks of each year. The counts provide information on locations of wintering populations and are valuable tools for detecting increases and decreases in avian populations. Three different counts were taken annually within Big Bend National Park from 1966 through 1971: in the Rio Grande Village area, the Chisos Mountains, and the Santa Elena Canyon area. After 1971, Frances Williams continued the Rio Grande Village count in 1972; it and the Chisos Mountain count were dropped in 1973 and 1974, but C. C. Wiedenfeld coordinated counts at Rio Grande Village and the Chisos Mountains from 1976 through 1984. Bonnie McKinney was coordinator from 1985 through 1988, and Bryan Hale continued the two counts from 1989 through 1994.

THE ANNOTATED LIST OF SPECIES

The following is an annotated list of 445 species of birds that have been reported for Big Bend National Park and vicinity. The majority of these—377—are included in the regular list of species that follows, but 68 are regarded as hypothetical and are included in a second list, "Birds of Uncertain Occurrence." This second list includes all the species that are not adequately documented by either a specimen or photograph, or by five or more sight records by unimpeachable sources.

All common and scientific names used are those suggested by the American Ornithologists' Union's *Check-list of North American Birds*, sixth edition (1983), and supplements (1985, 1989 & 1993), hereafter referred to as the AOU Checklist. Also, I have attempted to identify pertinent observers when giving details of specific sightings; in some cases, however, full names are unknown.

The terms used to describe the status of the various birds are defined as follows:

Abundant: Can be found in sizeable numbers (50+ per day), without any particular search, in the proper habitat at the right time of year.

Common: Can usually be found in moderate numbers (10–50 per day), in the proper habitat at the right time of year.

Fairly Common: Can usually be found in small numbers (5–10 per day), in the proper habitat at the right time of year.

Uncommon: Can usually be found in low numbers (1–5 per day), in the proper habitat at the right time of year.

Rare: Not expected, but 1 to 5 individuals occur annually.

Casual: Totally unexpected; only a few sightings each decade.

Sporadic: May be present in numbers some years, and totally absent other years.

Permanent Resident: A bird that remains in the area throughout the year and does not migrate.

Summer Resident: A bird that breeds in the area; it may arrive as early as March and remain as late as October.

Post-nesting Visitor: A bird that visits the area in summer but does not breed there; one that wanders to the Big Bend after nesting.

Migrant: A bird that passes through the area only in spring and/or fall, from March to May and/or August to November, sometimes lingering for a few days to a few weeks.

Winter Resident: A bird that remains in the area during winter; it may arrive as early as September and remain as late as April.

Also, all locations mentioned in the text were derived from the *Big Bend Official Map and Guide* (1994) or the "Terlingua-Chisos Mountains, Texas" topographic map (scale 1:130,000). And, because a number of sites are mentioned numerous times, a few will be abbreviated as follows:

BBNP = Big Bend National Park
Black Gap WMA = Black Gap Wildlife Management Area
CC = Cottonwood Campground
NPS = National Park Service
PJ = Panther Junction
RGV = Rio Grande Village
SEC = Santa Elena Canyon

In addition to these place names, Christmas Bird Counts will be abbreviated to the commonly used term: CBCs; and Texas Bird Records Committee: TBRC.

BIRDS OF REGULAR OCCURRENCE

FAMILY GAVIIDAE: LOONS
Common Loon *Gavia immer*

Casual in fall and winter.

A specimen, collected on the Rio Grande near Solis by A. G. Clark on October 17, 1937 (Borell 1938), represents the first park record of this large water bird. It was not reported again until October 30, 1988, when Jim Burr, of Far Flung Adventures of Terlingua, discovered one at mile 190 in SEC. This loon occurs regularly at Lake Balmorhea (35 miles north of the Davis Mountains) and also on Amistad Reservoir, below the Lower Canyons. Additional records are expected.

FAMILY PODICIPEDIDAE: GREBES
Least Grebe. *Tachybaptus dominicus*

Rare in spring and fall, but it can occur at any time.

The majority of records are from ponds along the Rio Grande, where it usually remains for some time. For instance, the first park record was of a lone bird at RGV that I monitored for eleven months, from August 5, 1969 until July 1970. It was seen by numerous birders and photographed

Least Grebe, *Tachybaptus dominicus*

by Ty Hotchkiss. And Rick LoBello recorded one at RGV that remained from December 12, 1978, through April 1, 1979. Although this little grebe has been reported for every month, the majority of records are from late February through early May, and from mid-August through September.

Pied-billed Grebe *Podilymbus podiceps*

Rare summer resident; uncommon migrant and winter visitor.

The scarcity of water areas throughout the Big Bend limits the Pied-billed Grebe as a nesting species. Even at suitable habitats, such as the cat-tail-filled silt pond at RGV, it does not nest every year. Roger Siglin observed an adult with young on its back there on July 28, 1967, and I found four free-swimming fledglings on August 1. On May 17, 1970, I again heard and observed two birds courting at the same pond. They remained there throughout the summer and presumedly nested.

Pied-billed Grebes are most often seen on open, quiet stretches of the river and on adjacent ponds during migration from early March through May and mid-August through November. The only record of this bird away from the general vicinity of the Rio Grande is a lone bird that landed on the highway near PJ on September 16, 1975, apparently mistaking the road for water. It was rescued by Carol Kruse, who released it unharmed at RGV.

Eared Grebe. *Podiceps nigricollis*

Rare migrant and winter visitor.

All sightings of this water bird are from the Rio Grande and adjacent ponds. Records range from a specimen taken at San Vicente on October 26, 1957, by Harold Broderick and Richard D. Porter, to a lone bird at Stillwell Crossing on April 20, 1989 (Jeff Selleck). Except for a December 22, 1983, sighting of three birds at Hot Springs by Cynthia Simmons, all of the park reports are of solitary individuals.

FAMILY PELECANIDAE: PELICANS
American White Pelican. *Pelecanus erythrorhynchos*

Casual in spring and early summer.

Records range from three birds circling over Boquillas on March 17, 1991 (NPS files), to a lone bird found in the Rio Grande below Boquillas

Canyon Overlook on June 16, 1983, by Rich Simmons and Jay Liggett. The largest flock recorded was 13 birds at RGV, "flying in a rough V formation over the river in a westerly direction," on April 16, 1994, by Napier Shelton. The only sighting away from the immediate vicinity of the river was of four birds flying over Study Butte on April 5, 1992 (NPS files).

The first park record is from a bird band that Park Ranger Lloyd Whitt acquired from a Mexican boy (in 1961) who had taken it "from a large white bird" found dead in the Rio Grande near Castolon. The boy had carried the band in his pocket for more than a year. U.S. Fish and Wildlife Service records revealed that the band had come from a White Pelican banded in Gunnison Island on the Great Salt Lake in Utah on June 19, 1947.

FAMILY PHALACROCORACIDAE: CORMORANTS
Double-crested Cormorant: *Phalacrocorax auritus*
Rare in winter and spring.

The first park record of this large water bird was on April 18, 1984, at the entrance to Mariscal Canyon, by James Morlock and S. Jennings. Since then, it has been reported on a dozen occasions along the Rio Grande from December 27, 1990, at Sanderson Crossing in the Lower Canyons, by Marcos Paredes, Betty Moore, and George Simmons, to as late as May 9, 1994, at RGV, by Greg Oskay.

The number of park sightings, only since the mid-1980s, suggest that this bird has expanded its range in recent years. It is likely the result of an increasing population on Amistad Reservoir, at the eastern end of the Lower Canyons.

Neotropic Cormorant. *Phalacrocorax brasilianus*
Casual in spring.

This little cormorant has been reported along the Rio Grande from March 19 (a lone bird found at Hot Springs by E. Winter in 1994) to May 2 (one at RGV by Jeff Selleck and Karen Boucher in 1990). There also is an August 14, 1994, report at RGV by Robin Carter, and another one there by Stuart Dechke and C. L. Skulski on November 16, 1989. Except for two individuals observed by Thompson G. Marsh near SEC on March 23, 1960, all reports are of lone birds. Like the larger Double-crested Cormorant, park records have increased during the past ten years.

FAMILY ARDAEIDAE: BITTERNS AND HERONS
American Bittern. *Botaurus lentiginosus*
Uncommon spring and fall migrant; casual in winter.

Records extend from March 24 through May 30 in spring, and from October 3 through November 8 in fall. And there are two winter reports: Peter Lesica found one at RGV on December 10, 1978, and Bonnie McKinney found one at a lake on the Sombrero Ranch (just north of the park) on February 15, 1983. The majority of reports are from cattail ponds along the Rio Grande, especially at RGV.

Least Bittern. *Ixobrychus exilis*
Rare spring migrant; casual in fall and early winter.

Spring reports range from April 15 through June 21, and there are four fall and winter records, all at RGV: I observed one at the silt pond on September 9, 1967; E. G. and J. H. Strauss found one along the nature trail on October 24, 1977; John Duncan discovered one (probably the same individual) there on November 23, 1977; and another bird was recorded along the nature trail by James R. Stewart on December 2, 1985. Like the larger American Bittern, this species is most often reported from cattail ponds along the Rio Grande.

Great Blue Heron. *Ardea herodias*
Rare in summer; fairly common migrant and winter visitor.

This large bird is present along the Rio Grande year-round. There are no records of nesting, although George M. Sutton (1935) reported an adult and an immature bird near Boquillas on May 21, 1935. It is likely that this species once nested along the river and may do so again at the few scattered cottonwood and willow groves.

Sightings increase during mid-September and are most numerous from mid-October to early November in fall and from early March through the first week of May in spring. The majority of sightings are of one or two individuals, but James Morlock reported 15 at San Vicente on September 19, 1982, and Bruce Talbot found eight birds circling over Hot Springs on April 12, 1983. All park records are from the vicinity of the Rio Grande.

Great Egret. *Casmerodius albus*

Casual summer and winter visitor; uncommon spring migrant; rare fall migrant.

Records exist for every month but March and November. It is most numerous from April 8 through mid-May; there are a handful of summer sightings from June 10 to mid-August, probably post-nesting wanderers; and there are a few reports from mid-September through mid-October. Most of these sightings are of lone birds, but Bonnie McKinney found 82 individuals at the north end of Black Gap WMA on October 5, 1982, and 12 at Black Gap headquarters on October 12, 1982. There are three winter records only: at RGV on December 23, 1992 (Richard Boyden), at Ojo Caliente on January 21, 1987 (Laura Greffenius), and at RGV on February 8, 1992 (Alan Wormington and Bill Lamond).

Snowy Egret. *Egretta thula*

Uncommon spring migrant; casual in fall.

Spring records extend from a March 29, 1988, sighting at RGV (Jeff Selleck) to 12 individuals at upper Tornillo Creek bridge on May 13, 1975 (Tony Gallucci). Except for a flock of seven birds seen by Warren Dodson along the Old Ore Road on April 15, 1982, all spring sightings are from the vicinity of the Rio Grande. There are three fall reports: Vaughn Morrison found three at RGV on September 13, 1974; I recorded one there on September 14, 1969; and Frank Deckert reported "several on trees and on rooftops" at PJ on November 4, 1975.

Little Blue Heron. *Egretta caerulea*

Rare migrant; casual summer visitor.

Records are widely scattered from February 8 through August 25, and Bonnie McKinney found one with 12 Great Egrets at Black Gap WMA headquarters on October 12, 1982. Except for four individuals found by Paul Strong at Alamo Creek, below SEC, on July 28, 1980, all park records are of lone birds.

Tricolored Heron. *Egretta tricolor*
Uncommon migrant; casual summer visitor.

Records of this mid-sized heron have increased considerably since the mid-1980s. There are numerous sightings along the Rio Grande from April 5 to May 24, including birds "common all the way through" the Lower Canyons by Cynthia and Rich Simmons and Jim McChristal, April 22 to 26, 1988. Late summer and fall sightings extend from July 31 through September 11. Except for two "immatures" reported at RGV by Eunice Chynoweth on August 10, 1985, all sightings are of lone birds. I have found it to be surprisingly unafraid at times; more than once I have walked to within a few yards of a bird feeding along the shore of a pond at RGV.

Cattle Egret. *Bubulcus ibis*
Fairly common migrant.

The first park record of this African invader was reported at RGV by Roger Siglin and Gary Blythe on October 27, 1967. Since then it has been reported annually from along the Rio Grande, as well as the desert lowlands, from March 27 to May 29 in spring and from August 26 through November 21 in fall. Several records include rather large numbers: Sandra Naylor, Dave Dais, and Heraldo Ureste reported four flocks of 30 to 70 individuals near Boquillas on February 28, 1987; Bruce Talbot found 34 at upper Tornillo Creek bridge on March 24, 1983; Peter Scott and Frank Deckert reported 22 there on April 2, 1977; Paul Strong counted 24 at CC on April 9, 1981; and Bill and Sarah Bourbon observed "over 200" at Boquillas Crossing on April 17, 1989. All of the fall reports, however, are of ten or fewer individuals.

Green Heron. *Butorides virescens*
Rare summer resident; fairly common migrant; uncommon in winter.

This little heron, earlier known as "Green-backed Heron," has been reported every month but March. Although there is no positive nesting record in recent years, Josselyn Van Tyne and George M. Sutton (1937) reported a nest containing four eggs, 12 feet up in a mesquite near the Rio Grande at Castolon, on May 7, 1935. The breeding race was identified as the western form, *anthonyi*. Ralph Palmer (1962) reported that the eastern race is known to nest eastward to Pecos and Fort Stockton, Texas. It still may nest in cottonwood and willow groves along the Rio Grande, as there are numerous spring sightings, especially along the RGV nature trail. Kristin Larson reported "possible courtship" between a pair at RGV on May 10, 1983. It is most numerous along the Rio Grande and adjacent ponds from April 1 through May 19 in spring.

Post-nesting wanderers may appear by mid-July, and the fall migration generally extends through early November. Although most reports are of lone birds, five individuals reported by W. H. Fritz at RGV on May 26, 1982, may represent the peak of the spring migration. Winter records, all from RGV, extend from November through January 31.

Black-crowned Night-Heron. *Nycticorax nycticorax*

Rare spring migrant; casual in summer, fall, and winter.

This nocturnal heron has been reported in the park every month but November. It is most numerous along the Rio Grande in spring from April 12 to May 19. All reports are of lone birds except for three individuals reported at San Vicente Crossing on April 12, 1983, by George Wagner and H. P. Langridge; and two individuals at PJ by Betty Alex and Lorn Willingham on September 4, 1982. This latter record is the only one away from the immediate vicinity of the Rio Grande.

Yellow-crowned Night-Heron. *Nyctanassa violaceus*

Uncommon fall and rare spring migrant; casual in summer.

Fall records extend from early August to October 12, and a few spring records range from April 15 to May 23; many of the late summer and fall sightings are of juveniles. Except for a lone adult reported for PJ on July 4, 1971, by Dave Easterla and Jim Chambers, all park sightings are from the vicinity of the Rio Grande.

FAMILY THRESKIORNITHIDAE: IBISES AND SPOONBILLS
White Ibis. *Eudocimus albus*

Only two park records.

Mr. and Mrs. Joe Maxwell observed and photographed one along irrigation ditches at RGV on February 6 or 7, 1971. It apparently was killed by a predator, because Philip F. Allan reported a dead White Ibis there on February 8. The specimen was examined by Art Norton, who retained a number of feathers; I later obtained several characteristic primaries and deposited them in the BBNP study collection. A second record is a lone adult found by Jay and Debbie Liggett at Boquillas Crossing on April 4, 1984.

White-faced Ibis. *Plegadis chichi*
Rare migrant.

Records extend from March 24 through May 29 in spring from August 11 through September 24 in fall. Except for a lone bird found by Gary Smith at Dugout Wells on August 18, 1992, all reports are from the vicinity of the Rio Grande. And, except for 12 individuals at Hot Springs on May 27, 1979 (Robert DeVine) and two individuals at RGV on September 24, 1982 (David Muth), all the reports are of lone birds. There also is a single winter record of 20 birds found at "Boquillas, Coahuila, during a dust storm" on January 25, 1965 (NPS files).

Family Anatidae: Swans, Geese, and Ducks
Tundra Swan. *Cygnus columbianus*
Casual winter visitor.

Records range from November 24 through February 28. William Lay Thompson (1953) first recorded 12 individuals at a stock tank at Black Gap WMA in December 1951; all were reportedly killed by local ranchers. Since then it has been reported on nine occasions along the Rio Grande, from RGV, Hot Springs, and San Vicente, and an additional bird was found dead at Burro Tank on January 20, 1976, by Garrett Moynihan.

Greater White-fronted Goose. *Anser albifrons*
Casual in late winter and spring.

Ty and Julie Hotchkiss recorded it first along the Rio Grande at RGV on April 29, 1969, and they reported it to me the following day. After trying unsuccessfully to find it on May 1, I asked some of the Mexican boys at Boquillas Crossing if any of them had seen a *pato grande* (large duck). Siverio Athayde said that he had seen a large water bird the previous day. Without hesitation, he picked the White-fronted Goose out of a three-page series of ducks and geese in the field guide *Birds of North America*.

Since then, it has been reported along the Rio Grande five additional times between February 4 (at Castolon by Barbara Woods in 1991) and April 26 (at Burro Bluff in the Lower Canyons, by Cynthia and Rich Simmons and Jim McChristal in 1984). Except for a report by George Wagner and H. P. Langridge of two individuals at Talley on April 10, 1983, all of the sightings have been of lone birds.

Snow Goose. *Chen caerulescens*
Rare spring and casual fall migrant.

The majority of records are of lone birds along the Rio Grande from March 4 through March 31, but Rick LoBello observed 15 individuals flying over RGV in February, and Curt Fitrow reported 13 on March 18, 1979; and Hal Flanders found a late bird there on April 23, 1991. And Pat Grediagen reported a flock of 30 birds flying north over Dagger Flat on March 29, 1992.

Fall records are limited to one found by Carl Fleming on Terlingua Creek, October 31, 1994; I recorded one near the mouth of SEC on November 1, 1967; and Barbara McKinney observed an immature bird at a stock tank 10 miles south of Marathon on November 27 and 30, 1983. And there is a single winter record: Jeff Connor and Brooke Keeley found an immature bird near the mouth of Boquillas Canyon on January 10, 1976.

Ross' Goose. *Chen rossii*
There is a single record.

A lone bird was discovered by Manfred Noepel on the Rio Grande above RGV on March 27, 1991. Noepel found it again the following day at RGV, where it was seen by several other birders through June 7: Peter Scott and Anne Bellamy observed it on April 27; Sarah Bourbon found it near Boquillas on May 30; and Jim Hines found and photographed it near Hot Springs on June 6 and 7. The Hines' photographic documentation was made part of the NPS files.

Canada Goose. *Branta canadensis*
Casual in spring and winter.

Spring sightings include a flock of 65-plus individuals flying northwest over Boot Canyon on March 11, 1992 (Ian McCord), and lone birds near Boquillas Canyon on April 30, 1993 (D. B. and D. E. Burt) and at RGV on

May 4, 1988 (Bill Bourbon). Winter records include lone birds at RGV on November 30, 1967 (Wauer); in lower Mariscal Canyon on December 27, 1976 (Ken Branges); perhaps the same individual in Marsical Canyon on January 2, 1977 (Richie Bechimiddleton); and four individuals were recorded in the Lower Canyons on January 11, 1990 (Steve Swanke).

Wood Duck. *Aix sponsa*

Uncommon migrant; rare winter visitor.

It has been reported every month but September. Records range from August 18 (Dave Easterla) to May 6 (Milly McGuiness and P. Fieffer), and there also is a June 16, 1993 report (by William M. Shepherd) of a pair at Castolon. Except for a lone report of a pair of Wood Ducks at the sewage lagoons in the Chisos Basin on April 10, 1977 (Robert Morse), all the records are from the Rio Grande and adjacent ponds.

Green-winged Teal. *Anas crecca*

Common migrant; winter visitor.

This is Big Bend's most numerous waterfowl. Records extend from August 16 through May 18, mostly from the Rio Grande and adjacent ponds. It also is occasionally found at the sewage lagoons in the Chisos Basin: I discovered 37 individuals there on November 17, 1990, and five on April 29, 1970, and Betty and Tom Alex and Lorn Willingham reported 14 there on January 9, 1983.

Mallard. *Anas platyrhynchos*

The bird previously known as the Mexican Duck was lumped with the Mallard by the 1983 edition of the AOU Checklist. These two birds interbreed and distinct populations generally are rare. In the Big Bend Country, however, populations of both forms do occur with some regularity. Therefore, the two forms will be discussed separately.

The Mallard is an uncommon fall migrant and winter visitor, and a rare spring migrant. Records range from October 9 to March 13. One or two individuals usually spend December and January in the RGV area, but they cannot be expected regularly at any certain pond or stretch of the river. The largest number reported was 27 in a pool under the lower Tornillo Creek bridge on March 3, 1975, by "RKD."

The Mexican Duck is an uncommon permanent resident. This year-round resident can be expected anywhere along the Rio Grande and adjacent ponds and irrigation ditches. Most sightings are during spring, summer, and fall, but it can be found in winter as well. I discovered a hen with five very young chicks along the river's edge near CC on April 27, 1994, the first good evidence of nesting in the park. Most reports are of one or a pair of birds, but Thompson G. Marsh observed five at RGV on March 22, 1960, and Bill Mealy reported 30 individuals near Lajitas at the entrance of SEC on March 29, 1978.

Northern Pintail. *Anas acuta*

Uncommon migrant and winter visitor.

Pintails have been recorded along the Rio Grande from August 27 to March 22, and I recorded a flock of seven individuals flying over RGV on May 1, 1994, undoubtedly late migrants. The largest group reported was 43 birds flying in a V-formation over RGV on February 13, 1968 (Wauer). Early fall arrivals may linger at ponds for several weeks before moving on.

Blue-winged Teal. *Anas discors*

Common migrant; casual in summer and winter.

This little duck is most numerous along the Rio Grande and in adjacent ponds from early March to mid-May, but there are a few scattered reports to mid-June. There also are a few summer records, and sightings increase from late August through October. Winter records are limited to two reports in late November, perhaps only late migrants; none in December; and one each in January and February. There also is a single upland report: Ron Knaus found a pair on the sewage lagoons in the Chisos Basin on May 11, 1972. Most reports are of less than a dozen individuals, but I recorded 14 at RGV on April 13, 1990, Steve Kingswood found 26 at RGV on August 13 and 14, 1987, and Bonnie McKinney recorded 19 at RGV on September 21, 1983.

Cinnamon Teal. *Anas cyanoptera*

Common migrant; uncommon winter visitor.

Records extend from August 19 to May 28, and three June sightings probably represent late spring migrants: lone males at San Vicente on June 9, 1932 (Sutton 1935), at Glenn Spring on June 21, 1928 (Van Tyne and Sutton 1937), and at RGV on June 18, 1967 (Wauer). In the fall, Cinnamon Teal are most numerous along the Rio Grande from mid-August to October 19, but stragglers can be expected as late as November 1. Four flocks comprising 91 birds, a high count, were seen at RGV on October 8, 1970 (Wauer). There are no records from November 2 through December, but it becomes a regular visitor along the river during January, February, and the first half of March. Spring migrants pass through the area in numbers from mid-March through mid-April, and a few individuals can usually be found in mixed flocks of Green-wings and Blue-wings through May.

Northern Shoveler. *Anas clypeata*

Common spring migrant; uncommon fall migrant; casual winter visitor.

It is most numerous in spring from March until mid-May, there are scattered sightings to June 1, and I observed eight late migrants flying up and down the Rio Grande at RGV on June 14, 1968. Larger spring counts of 30 birds were reported at RGV on March 10, 1984 (Cynthia Simmons), and 33 birds were recorded at RGV on April 29, 1967 (Wauer). Fall records are scattered between September 5 and November 9. And there are a few reports in late November and December, none in January, and three in February.

Gadwall. *Anas strepera*

Fairly common migrant in spring; uncommon in fall and winter.

It is most numerous along the Rio Grande from late March through May, there are single August and September reports, and fall migrants appear between October 23 and November 5. Afterward, there is a scattering of wintertime reports between December 10 and late March. Although sightings of one to five individuals are most common, I recorded a flock of 20 at RGV on April 17, 1970.

American Wigeon. *Anas americana*
Fairly common migrant in spring; uncommon in fall and winter.

Spring migrants are most numerous from mid-March to May 16, and there are late sightings on May 28, 1968, and June 4, 1973 (Dave Easterla). There also is an August 12, 1967, sighting of a lone female at RGV (Wauer). Fall migrants do not reach BBNP until early October, and a few individuals can sometimes be found along the Rio Grande and at adjacent ponds throughout the rest of the fall and winter.

Canvasback. *Aythya valisineria*
Rare spring migrant; casual in fall and early winter.

It is most numerous along the Rio Grande from April 6 to 24, there is a single June 1 report (NPS files), and Cynthia and Rich Simmons and DeeRenee Ericks observed a lone bird at RGV on October 28 and 29, 1985. There also are a few late December reports: Lovie Mae Whitaker recorded the first park Canvasback at Hot Springs on December 25, 1939; it was not reported again until Roger Siglin found one at Castolon on December 21, 1967; and two were seen with Ring-necked Ducks at RGV on December 27, 1977 (Wauer).

Redhead. *Aythya americana*
Rare in early winter; two spring reports.

It is most numerous along the Rio Grande from early to late November, and Gene Henricks reported three drakes and four hens at the sewage lagoons in the Chisos Basin on November 7, 1991. Spring records include a lone male at RGV on March 11, 1976 (Phillip F. Allan), and two drakes and five hens at Hot Springs on March 15, 1994 (Ian McCord).

Ring-necked Duck. *Aythya collaris*
Rare migrant and winter visitor.

Records range from September 29 through May 1, all from the vicinity of the Rio Grande, except for two individuals found at the sewage lagoons in the Chisos Basin on November 7, 1986 (Anne Bellamy). The highest numbers recorded were 52 individuals at RGV on December 27, 1969 (Wauer), and Carol Edwards and I found 30 at RGV on March 25, 1995.

Lesser Scaup. *Aythya affinis*

Rare migrant and winter visitor.

It is most numerous in spring from early April through late May. It appears again in early October, and there are scattered sightings throughout the winter months. All park records are from the Rio Grande and adjacent ponds, and, except for three found in the Lower Canyons on November 11, 1989 (Marcos Paredes and Steve Swanke), all are of lone or paired birds.

Common Goldeneye. *Bucephala clangula*

Casual winter visitor.

It was first reported by Keith Olsen at RGV on December 27, 1969, and was seen by several other birders through January 9, 1970. A pair was next reported for the Gravel Pit by Jeff Connor and Brooke Keeley on January 16, 1976, and Robert DeVine observed a lone male at RGV on January 10, 1979.

Bufflehead. *Bucephala albeola*

Uncommon spring migrant; casual fall migrant; rare winter visitor.

This little duck is most numerous in spring from early March until May 3. Bill Bourbon reported a lone female at RGV on October 22, 1988, and there are several additional records from November 5 through January 3; there are no reports during January and February. Although most sightings are of lone birds along the Rio Grande, I found five near RGV on March 7, 1968, and five again on May 1, 1970; John C. Yrizany observed eight females at RGV on April 8, 1964; and Anne Bellamy reported two males and one female at the Chisos Basin sewage lagoons on November 14, 1982.

Hooded Merganser. *Lophodytes cucullatus*

Casual in fall and winter.

There are a scattering of park records from October 16 through March 22. Bill Bourbon, Jeff Selleck, and Jim Hines found two males at Panther Rapid in SEC on October 16, 1992; James Morlock and S. Kilpatrick observed a pair in the Lower Canyons on November 24, 1985; Richard D. Porter collected a specimen at RGV on December 1, 1958; a lone female was seen at RGV on December 16 (Linda Jarvis) and December 22 (Ian McCord and Robert DeVine), 1982; Henry Howe found a female at RGV on January 7, 1983; Anne Bellamy found a female (probably the same bird) there two days later; Peter and Ruth Isleib reported a lone bird at Hot Springs on February 4, 1956; A. L. Masley recorded 12 adults and 15 to 18 juveniles at CC on February 10, 1994; Don Dowde reported three pairs from Castolon on March 19, 1993; and Don Schaezler found a drake and two hens in Mariscal Canyon on March 22, 1989.

Common Merganser. *Mergus merganser*
Rare winter visitor.

Wintertime sightings extend from November 15 to March 16, and there is one later report: Kristin Larson found two individuals in SEC on May 4, 1983. It is a fairly common wintering bird at Lake Balmorhea, according to Greg Lasley.

Red-breasted Merganser. *Mergus serrator*
Two park records.

Sam Fried first reported a lone female at Hot Springs on May 1, 1977. And a second female was observed by numerous birders at RGV between November 11 and 15, 1985: Rich Simmons found it first; Anne Bellamy, Essie Kruse, Thomas Harvey, and Cynthia Simmons observed it on November 13; and Charles Callagan found it still present on November 15.

Ruddy Duck. *Oxyura jamaicensis*
Rare migrant.

The earliest record is a specimen collected on the Rio Grande near San Vicente by Richard D. Porter on October 26, 1957. It has since been reported between March 27 and May 7 in spring and from October 22 to November 26 in fall. All sightings have been of lone birds except for four reported with three Buffleheads, one Canvasback, and one Blue-winged Teal at RGV on April 6, 1977 (Mac Blair).

FAMILY CATHARTIDAE: AMERICAN VULTURES
Black Vulture. *Coragyps atratus*

Uncommon in summer and winter; fairly common migrant.

I have never seen a Black Vulture more than one mile from the Rio Grande. They can usually be found soaring over RGV, Boquillas, and Santa Elena Crossing at midday. The species can easily be identified in flight by its rapid wingbeats and broad wings, showing white patches near the tips; perched birds may be more difficult. The all-black to gray head and gray legs are good distinguishing marks most of the year, but these characteristics are less reliable during late summer when Black Vultures may be found perched alongside young Turkey Vultures that have not yet developed red heads.

Black Vultures presumedly nest in the park, although there are no actual records of nests. I did find two copulating birds at RGV on April 5, 1967, and a young bird at SEC on July 10, 1971. Most sightings are of two or three individuals, but George Simmons and Lee Daniel found 52 along the river at Lajitas on February 3, 1988; Leo Wesson reported "about 300" at Black Dike on February 15, 1978; and Paul Motts and Mark Kirtley found 34 soaring with two Turkey Vultures below La Linda Crossing on March 28, 1987. There also are two sightings some distance from the Rio Grande: Robert, Sean, and Timothy DeVine found a lone bird at K-Bar on August 26, 1978; and Bill Bourbon reported one in the Chisos Basin on September 6, 1988.

Turkey Vulture. *Cathartes aura*

Abundant summer resident and migrant; rare in December and January.

Regular spring arrivals begin to move into the lowlands the last week of February; Carol Edwards reported the earliest sighting in the Chisos Basin on March 1, 1995, and Ruth Jessen reported the earliest 1968 sighting in the Basin on March 2. Margaret Littlejohn found two early birds at PJ on January 24, 1978. Spring migrants can be expected anywhere, and often in large congregations: Robert DeVine found more than 30 individuals at the Lajitas Golfcourse on January 30, 1987; Mr. and Mrs. White reported 163 roosting at Desert Overlook near Castolon on March 12, 1987; and Bonnie McKinney observed approximately 400 birds at the mouth of Marvillas Canyon on March 17, 1983.

In summer, the Turkey Vulture is most numerous along the Rio Grande and in the Chisos Mountain foothills, but it also is present in smaller numbers in the higher Chisos. It undoubtedly nests throughout the park: I found a copulating pair at RGV on April 5, 1967; Murl Deusing discovered an adult incubating eggs under a small rocky overhang at Grapevine Hills on March 31, 1970; and immature birds have been seen in the Chisos Basin on a number of occasions during July and August.

By late September it becomes rare in the mountains. Only two were seen in Boot Canyon on September 28, 1969, and none were found in the Chisos Basin the following day (Wauer). David Wolf observed a flock of 150 birds moving southeast over the Basin at dusk on August 21, 1968. I watched 52 soaring over Casa Grande at dusk on September 12, 1967, and I found 85 birds roosting on cottonwoods at RGV on September 20, 1967. On October 20, 1967, there were 55 at the same location at RGV, but I could not find these birds early the next morning. Bill Bourbon had a similar experience at RGV; he found 20 birds "following a passage of a cold front" on October 28, 1988, but none were found the following day.

FAMILY ACCIPITRIDAE: KITES, EAGLES, HAWKS AND ALLIES

Osprey. *Pandion haliaetus*

Uncommon spring migrant; rare fall migrant; casual winter visitor.

It is most numerous from late March through April, and there are scattered reports to mid-May. Most sightings are from the vicinity of the Rio Grande, but it can be expected anywhere in the park; Dale and Marian Zimmerman reported one at K-Bar on April 10, 1971, and Robert Huggins and Jim Bellamy observed one in the Chisos Basin on May 19, 1984. Fall records range from one flying with a Zone-tailed Hawk in the Basin on August 30, 1979 (Alma Barrera), to a lone bird near Casa Grande on October 18, 1988 (Klause E. Gempel).

Winter records are limited to lone birds at RGV on December 24, 1981 (Susan and Richard Block), near Maverick on December 29, 1970 (Mrs. Cleve Bachman), at Hot Springs on January 22, 1980 (John Hunter), in the Lower Canyons on February 2, 1990 (Steve Swanke), and near SEC on February 11, 1983 (Devi Sharp).

American Swallow-tailed Kite. *Elanoides forficatus*
There are two park records.

On August 5, 1969, I discovered one of these large, graceful birds soaring over RGV and was able to take several photographs during its many passes over the four-square-mile area along the Rio Grande (Wauer 1970c). Cecil Garrett also saw it during the morning; Roger Siglin saw it at noon; and Dave Easterla found it still there in late afternoon. It could not be located the following morning. And on August 22, 1990, Kathleen Hambly reported two Swallow-tailed Kites "in company of 2 Turkey Vultures" soaring over Castolon.

White-tailed Kite. *Elanus leucurus*
Casual migrant and winter visitor.

Park records range from one found two miles west of PJ on December 27, 1990 (Phil Mastrengelo), widely scattered reports in winter and the spring months, to a late sighting at Study Butte on May 31, 1980 (NPS files). And there are two fall reports: Carol Edwards found one at Castolon on August 3, 1994, and Kat and Steve Perry and Barbara and John Perry reported one from SEC on September 3, 1994. It has been reported from all elevations, including from "the top of Crown Mt., 8000'. . . apparently migrating north" on March 31, 1994 (John Forsythe). This kite was known as "Black-shouldered Kite" for several years.

Mississippi Kite. *Ictinia mississippiensis*
Fairly common late spring migrant; sporadic summer resident; casual in fall and winter.

It is most numerous along the Rio Grande from very late April through mid-August, and some years birds linger all summer. Nesting is possible, but there is only circumstantial evidence: Jay and Debbie Liggett and Rich Simmons found an adult with an immature bird at RGV on May 25, 1984, and Peter Scott reported five adults and a subadult at RGV in late May and early June 1979. Birds at RGV and the Castolon area often perform fascinating acrobatics as they dash after cicadas, catch them in mid-air, and eat them in flight. These acts are not evidence of courtship.

There also are three late September reports: Bonnie McKinney observed a lone juvenile at PJ on September 24, 1986, and Fred and Geneva Barry reported it for the Chisos Basin and at Mariscal Canyon on September 29 and 30, 1975, respectively. There also are two winter reports by Bonnie McKinney: at Black Gap WMA on December 4, 1983, and near Persimmon Gap on January 6. 1983. This raptor has increased in numbers since DDT was banned in 1972; it now nests from El Paso to Balmorhea and eastward in Texas (Bolen and Flores 1993).

Bald Eagle. *Haliaeetus leucocephalus*

Casual spring migrant and early winter visitor.

This magnificent bird does not occur regularly, but there are scattered reports from March 2 through May, and again from October 1 through December. All sightings are of lone birds, and except for an adult seen flying over Boot Canyon on May 16, 1980 (James Stovall, Vidal Davila, and A. Robert), all reports are from the lowlands.

Northern Harrier. *Circus cyaneus*

Fairly common migrant; casual in summer; uncommon in winter.

It is most numerous in spring from mid-March through mid-May. A scattering of fall reports begin as early as late July, extend through August and September, increase during October, and fall off by the end of the month. There are increased sightings by mid-November, and a few birds linger all winter. Also, there are two summertime sightings, undoubtedly nonbreeding birds: one on Burro Mesa on June 7, 1955, and one at the South Rim on July 6, 1963 (Harold Brodrick). Harriers typically occur along the Rio Grande, but sightings within the Chisos Mountain foothills also can be expected.

Sharp-shinned Hawk. *Accipiter striatus*

Rare summer resident; fairly common migrant; uncommon in winter.

I found this little accipiter nesting near the top of an Arizona cypress in Boot Canyon during August 1966, on a Mexican pinyon along the north slope of Emory Peak in June 1969, and John Egbert consistently saw two birds believed to be nesting in Boot Canyon during May 1976. There are no recent nesting records.

Sharp-shins are most numerous in the spring from late March through mid-May, and also in the fall from mid-September through mid-November.

Records continue throughout the winter months, mostly from the lowlands, although this bird usually also can be found in the high Chisos Mountain canyons during pleasant weather when there is an adequate food supply.

Cooper's Hawk. *Accipiter cooperii*

Fairly common migrant; rare in summer; uncommon in winter.

There are at least three recent nesting records. In 1992, I discovered two active nests: one was photographed, along with the very defensive resident male, on a cottonwood behind the store at RGV on April 30 and again on May 2; and another at CC on May 2. Thirdly, Bill and Sarah Bourbon found a pair nest-building at CC on April 28, 1993.

Cooper's Hawks are most numerous in spring from early March through mid-April, and there are scattered reports to mid-May. The earliest fall migrants appear in early August, along with the first songbird migrants, reach a peak from late October to mid-November, and there are numerous records throughout the winter months. In winter, one or two birds usually can be found in a given day.

Northern Goshawk. *Accipiter gentilis*

Rare visitor year-round.

This large accipiter has been reported in the park for every month but October and November. Most records are from the Chisos Mountains, but Alan Wormington and Brian Wylie reported it at Santa Elena Crossing on February 22, 1977; an immature bird was found at RGV on September 10, 1985 (Cynthia Simmons and Anne Bellamy); and one was reported at RGV on December 29 and 30, 1982, by C. C. Wiedenfeld and Greg Lasley. Although there is no evidence of nesting in the park, the sightings of immature birds in May, June, and July suggests that these may be post-nesting wanderers from the higher and more extensively forested Maderas del Carmens, 50 miles to the southeast in Mexico. I found this species nesting there in 1972 (Wauer and Ligon 1977, Wauer 1992).

Common Black-Hawk. *Buteogallus anthracinus*

Sporadic summer resident; rare spring migrant; casual in fall and winter.

Although there are no positive nesting records, it more than likely does nest along the Rio Grande, at least some years: Robert DeVine reported an adult with two young one-half mile west of RGV on July 13, 1979; Glenn Ory observed a bird "carrying nesting materials" at about the midway point in Boquillas Canyon on April 12, 1988; and a lone bird was observed several times from April 6 to 20, 1994, near San Vicente Crossing, by Tom Alex, A. Gomez, J. Ivey, John Pearson, and (on April 17) by Bruce Talbot. It is most numerous from late March to mid-May, but there also are scattered sightings through October; there are no reports for November and December. Although the majority of records are from the vicinity of the Rio Grande, there also are a number of reports (in 1986, 1988, 1989, 1990, and 1992) for the Chisos Mountains. Because this species closely resembles the more common and somewhat similar Zone-tailed Hawk, care must be taken in identification.

Harris' Hawk. *Parabuteo unicinctus*
Rare summer and winter visitor and migrant.

This lovely hawk has been recorded in the park year-round, but nesting records are scarce. A nest containing two eggs was found in a mesquite near Nine Point Draw (ten miles south of Persimmon Gap) by Allen and Bruce O'Brian on August 10, 1964. It may have nested at RGV in 1985; it was present there all summer (Robert DeVine). However, it is most numerous during August and September, probably due to post-nesting visitors from north of the park; it nests on the Marathon and Alpine ranch lands. The majority of park records are from the vicinity of the Rio Grande. Exceptions include one at Dugout Wells on January 27 and December 29, 1971 (Wauer), PJ on April 5, 1979 (A. Palmes), Boot Canyon on May 28, 1968 (Wauer), Dugout on September 5, 1984 (Robert DeVine), and at the Basin Junction on September 18, 1984 (Marlene Zichlinsky).

Gray Hawk. *Buteo nitidus*
Uncommon summer resident; casual migrant and winter visitor.

This bird has nested in the park presumedly only since 1988. Since then it has been found nesting at RGV every year and at CC at least in 1989; Willem Maane discovered a "large stick nest" there on April 22. Summer records at RGV increased steadily during the 1980s, and Bill Bourbon discovered the first nest, "lined with fresh green leaves," on April 29, 1988. Numerous birders have observed nesting activities there every year since, except possibly in 1986. Doug Thompson reported two fledglings in

1990, and that the adults returned on March 12, 1991, and rebuilt the same nest. Also, Kelly Bryan, Tony Gallucci, Greg Lasley, and Chuck Sexton found two adults and two juveniles there on August 18 and 19, 1990. And on August 7, 1994, Lasley found a "full-grown, recently fledged" Gray Hawk in a nest along the River Road at the Johnson Ranch.

Sightings elsewhere in the park are few and far between. One was reported for the Chisos Basin on January 7, 1994 (David Goodson); at lower Oak Creek (below the Window) on April 23, 1993 (Peg Abbott and Lynn Tennefoss); at the mouth of Marvillas Canyon on October 28, 1983, and November 5, 1982 (Bonnie McKinney); and in the Chisos Basin on November 21, 1988 (Barbara and Sam House).

In addition, a nest discovered by Lee Daniel near Santa Elena Crossing in "late" April was being tended by a mixed pair of Gray and Red-shoul-

Gray Hawk, *Buteo nitidus*

dered hawks. The following description was taken from a report written by Greg Lasley and Chuck Sexton that appeared in *American Birds* (Lasley and Sexton 1989):

> Undoubtedly the event of the season was the nesting of a male Gray Hawk with a female Red-shouldered Hawk near Castolon in Big Bend. Various observers watched either a Gray Hawk or a Red-shouldered Hawk (which was often misidentified as an imm. Gray) at a nest there through April and there was a good deal of lively discussion and confusion among the birders about which species was nesting where. In early May, various observers saw the Red-shouldered incubating and the Gray flying overhead calling (JA [John Arvin], GL [Greg Lasley], ph. [photographed], LA [Lynne Aldrich], PG [Peter Gottschling]). Finally, suspicions of a mixed pair were confirmed May 18, when [R. Dan] Purrington and [David] Muth observed the Gray Hawk deliver a lizard to the nest where it was accepted by the Red-shouldered. One downy chick was clearly visible peeking over the edge of the nest. On May 22 & 24 [John] Gee watched this odd couple standing shoulder to shoulder at the edge of the nest in what he felt was an attempt to shade the eggs or young from the sun. By the last few days of May it was apparent that the pair had deserted the nest (fide BBo [Bill Bourbon]) and that the young bird(s) had not survived. This hybridization is almost certainly unprecedented.

Red-shouldered Hawk. *Buteo lineatus*

Casual spring and fall migrant.

Spring records extend from a February 17, 1988, sighting at RGV by Alan Wormington, to the May co-nesting records listed with the Gray Hawk. Fall records range from a sighting at CC on August 26, 1985, by Willie Sekula and Steve Hawkins, to a November 21, 1973, report at RGV by Albertine Bauguess.

Broad-winged Hawk. *Buteo platypterus*
Rare migrant.

Springtime records range from March 27 to early May, and there are two late reports: from Castolon on May 18, 1969 (Wauer), and RGV on June 4, 1970 (Charles Bender). Fall reports extend from August 19, 1970, at RGV (Wauer), to October 15, 1987, at RGV (Rob Pearson). Except for a sighting on Pulliam Ridge by Jim Liles on July 5, 1981, and one in the Chisos Basin by Jon Dunn on April 15, 1993, all reports are from the lowlands.

Swainson's Hawk. *Buteo swainsoni*
Fairly common migrant; uncommon summer visitor.

Records extend from March 8 to December 12. As far as I can determine, this species does not nest in the park. It does nest on mesquite and yucca north of the park and in northern Coahuila and Chihuahua, Mexico, where it is the common breeding Buteo of the mesquite-yucca flats. Post-nesting birds visit the park during June and July, and are most numerous along the river, near Persimmon Gap, and near the South Rim. Most records are of five or fewer individuals, but John Gee reported a "small kettle of 12–14 birds (all adults) over Castolon Store and nearby Rio Grande cliffs being harassed by a Peregrine," on July 21, 1990.

White-tailed Hawk. *Buteo albicaudatus*
Casual in late winter and spring.

There are scattered records from February 3 (in 1985 near Mule Ears by Kathie Smith) to June 4 (in 1956 in Green Gulch by Adele Harding). Additional records include one along Terlingua Creek on February 17, 1991 (Bill and Sarah Bourbon); at Sombrero Peak Ranch on March 30, 1983 (Bonnie McKinney); at SEC on March 31, 1978 (Bill Mealy and Dave Mobley); Jim Court and I watched one as it flew over the Rio Grande from Santa Elena, Chihuahua, to CC and upriver on April 15, 1967; at Persimmon Gap on April 22, 1994 (Jean Dow); and near Dugout Wells on May 19, 1985 (H. Paish).

Zone-tailed Hawk. *Buteo albonotatus*
Uncommon summer resident and migrant.

Park records range from January 18 (at RGV by Martha Michener in 1993) to October 6 (Mariscal Canyon by Steve Harris in 1990). Zone-tails nest in canyons throughout the park: a pair usually frequents RGV area, and it often can be found soaring along the limestone ridge just west of the cottonwood grove and silt pond. It has nested in the canyon below Hot Springs; members of the Texas Ornithological Society observed nest-building on a cliff on the U.S. side of the river there on April 29, 1972. Juveniles often can be seen at RGV during July and August. During the summers of 1968, 1969, and 1970, I monitored a pair nesting in an Emory oak near Pinnacles Pass, east of the Emory Peak Trail; I photographed the nest containing two young on June 10, 1969. Another nest, discovered on Crown Mountain by Don Davis on May 7, 1969, contained one egg. And Jim Liles and Gil Lusk found a nest with young at Alto Relex on May 6, 1981.

Zone-tailed Hawk, *Buteo albonotatus*

Park records are most numerous in spring from mid-March through mid-May, and in fall from early August to mid-September. Migrants and post-nesting wanderers can be expected anywhere. But some of the better places to find this Southwestern raptor include RGV and SEC in spring, and above Boulder Meadow along the Pinnacles Trail during summer. Zone-tails often soar along the cliffs with Turkey Vultures and may be difficult to identify because of their similar appearance. However, a Zone-tail's banded tail and feathered head distinguish it from the darker and bicolor-winged Turkey Vulture. And from April to early July, a Zone-tailed Hawk can often be located by its high-pitched calls.

Red-tailed Hawk. *Buteo jamaicensis*

Fairly common year-round.

Breeding birds are permanent residents and usually can be distinguished from northern winter residents. Resident Red-tails are members of the Fuertes race that possess very light-colored underparts. It was originally described in 1935 by George M. Sutton and Josselyn Van Tyne; the Fuertes race breeds in Texas only from Brewster County east to Corpus Christi and south to Coahuila and Chihuahua, Mexico. I found a nest containing one youngster near the top of an Arizona cypress in lower Boot Canyon on May 25, 1967; Mr. and Mrs. Murl Deusing located a nest on a high cliff at Grapevine Hills on March 27, 1970; Forest Koefe reported a nest containing one young and one egg on a cliff just south of the Fossil Bone Exhibit on April 14, 1983; Bruce Talbot found a nest at mile 813.5, on the Mexican side of the Lower Canyon, on February 8, 1984; and Mary Doll found a family with three juveniles circling over Blue Creek Canyon on September 3, 1984.

There is no noticeable increase of northern birds until early November, when darker northern Red-tails reach the area and mingle with resident birds. Also, very dark Harlan's Hawks, one of the northern races of the Red-tailed Hawk, have been reported on two occasions: at RGV on December 11, 1978 (Tim Lehman, D. Holcomb, J. Doherty, and J. Carter), and at Hot Springs on April 16, 1984 (Bruce Talbot). Many of the nonbreeders remain all winter. Northbound birds begin to pass through the Big Bend by mid-March, and this movement continues until early May.

Ferruginous Hawk. *Buteo regalis*
Rare migrant and winter visitor.

This light-colored hawk has been recorded every month but June and July; records extend from August 9 (a 1982 sighting at PJ by Jim Liles) to May 25 (a 1989 report near Boquillas Canyon by Janette Parks and Bill Snebold). It may be somewhat sporadic in occurrence, present in fair numbers some winters and rare others. I found it on a number of occasions during the 1967–68 winter; on November 15, 1967, eight individuals were perched on utility poles along the highway between Marathon and Alpine. The majority of park sightings are from the lowlands between Tornillo Flat and Maverick, but it also has been seen in the high Chisos: I found lone birds soaring over Boot Canyon on November 3, 1968, and January 27 and March 22, 1968; and Iris Wiedenfeld observed one "harassing a Golden Eagle" over Pulliam Peak on December 28, 1976.

Rough-legged Hawk. *Buteo lagopus*
Casual and sporadic winter visitor.

This northern raptor is absent most winters but present in small numbers in others. It was first recorded near Maverick on December 19, 1967 (Wauer). Bonnie McKinney found one in the Chisos Basin on November 7, 1981; Andy Weaks observed one near San Vicente Canyon on October 15, 1983; McKinney found one on the Harte Ranch on November 28, 1983; and Charles Callagan reported one in the Grapevine Hills on August 12, 1988.

Golden Eagle. *Aquila chrysaetos*
Uncommon summer resident; fairly common migrant and winter visitor.

At least five pairs of these magnificent birds appear to summer in the park. There are numerous records that verify breeding status: Peter Koch first reported a nest high on the north face of Pulliam Ridge that was "used by Golden Eagles for many years." During February and March 1967, I found a pair in this area on a number of occasions, and a recently fledged bird was seen nearby on August 24, 1970 (Wauer and Guy Anderson). I believe that a pair also nested near the South Rim in 1968; I observed an immature bird there on June 8. Rick LoBello and D. Sawyer found an immature bird along the Rim on October 1, 1977; Robert Mayer reported one young bird there on May 26, 1979; and Victor Emanuel observed two adults and an immature bird along the Rim on July 30, 1983. Another pair of Golden Eagles has been seen on a number of occasions near SEC, and it undoubtedly nests somewhere along this long, dissected canyon: D. R. Mullins reported seeing three immature birds over Fern Canyon on April 4, 1985. Also, John Peterson reported an adult carrying nesting materials in San Vicente Canyon on March 20, 1979; Jim Liles found a nest on upper Tornillo Creek on April 5, 1983; and Bonnie McKinney reported a pair circling over the Dead Horse Mountains on May 28, 1985.

Golden Eagles are most numerous in migration during February and March and in August and early September. These large predators hunt their food on the open flats. Burro Mesa and the open desert to the west and north are excellent locations to find migrant and wintering birds, although it can be expected almost anywhere in the park. Its preferred food is rabbit, but Golden Eagles will feed on everything from road-killed deer to insects. On November 6, 1961, Lloyd Whitt saw a Golden Eagle with what appeared to be a cottontail in its beak. As the bird circled to gain altitude, a Red-tailed Hawk overtook it and harassed it in the air until the eagle dropped its prey. The hawk caught the falling rabbit in midair and glided to earth with it. The eagle flew off to find dinner elsewhere. Also, Ray Skiles watched an adult Golden Eagle feeding on a jackrabbit along the roadway near the Chimneys Trailhead on December 31, 1983.

Van Tyne and Sutton (1937) reported that "local ranchers kill these splendid birds at every opportunity and hang the carcasses from the roadside fences as 'scarecrows' or evidence of their own prowess." Considerable "varmint control" still occurs throughout the Big Bend Country, but, since this species has been given federal protection, dead birds are seldom displayed along the main highways. In spite of continued illegal persecution, the Golden Eagle apparently has not been appreciably reduced within the park.

FAMILY FALCONIDAE: CARACARAS AND FALCONS
Crested Caracara. *Caracara plancus*
Casual visitor in spring and late summer.

Josselyn Van Tyne and George M. Sutton (1937) reported that Setzer found a broken humerus of this species in a cave on the south peak of Mule Ears. Stan Fulcher told me that he and his brother found a nesting pair of these birds in a cottonwood along Terlingua Creek ten miles north of Terlingua in 1922. Van Tyne and Sutton (1937) reported that a pair was "infrequently seen along the Rio Grande in the vicinity of the mouth of Tornillo Creek." More recent sightings are few and far between. Susan and Richard Block observed one near Terlingua in June 1968; I found one soaring with several Turkey Vultures along the cliffs in Boquillas Canyon on March 22, 1969; Ted Weems reported one near SEC on August 12, 1978; James and Dorothy Forenof found one at Hot Springs on April 22, 1980; David Fuller reported one five miles east of Castolon on February 6, 1983; and David Elkowitz and Sharon Weiss saw one at Dugout Wells on July 10, 1991.

American Kestrel. *Falco sparverius*

Uncommon summer resident; common migrant and winter resident.

This little falcon is surprisingly hard to find in summer because it nests in inaccessible locations. It annually nests along the cliffs east of the South Rim; I found a nest on Crown Mountain in upper Pine Canyon on May 7, 1967; and an adult with two juveniles were seen along the ridge just west of RGV on July 26, 1969.

By late July, with the dispersal of young and adults, Kestrels become easier to find, but there is no evidence of migration until early September. A peak is reached in late October, and stragglers can be found during most of November. Wintering birds can be numerous in the lowlands but also can be found along the high ridges and cliffs of the Chisos Mountains on mild days; they move into the adjacent lowlands during stormy periods. Northbound migrants begin to pass through the Big Bend Country as early as mid-March, and this movement continues until early May. It is not uncommon to find eight to ten birds perched on ocotillos and other tall desert shrubs along the roadways during migration.

Merlin. *Falco columbarius*
Rare migrant and winter visitor.

This is a northern bird that is probably sporadic in occurrence in the Big Bend Country, present some winters and totally absent others. The earliest park record is September 26 (in 1966 at RGV by Wauer) and the latest spring sighting is March 28 (in 1994 at Ernst Tinaja by Jan and Will Risser).

Aplomado Falcon. *Falco femoralis*
There are no verifiable sightings in recent years.

Although a few widely scattered reports have been received, there are no verified records; photographic documentation is necessary for this species. It once nested in the yucca grasslands of the Big Bend Country; Van Tyne and Sutton (1937) reported one from "along the Rio Grande on the Johnson Ranch," and Karl Haller and Pete Koch observed one near Mariscal Mine in February 1952. More recently, numerous birders observed and photographed a lone Aplomado Falcon west of the park in the vicinity of Valentine, Texas, that was present at least from January 2 through May 26, 1992 (Lasley and Sexton 1992a, 1992b). This bird more than likely was a wanderer from a known Mexican population that exists in Chihuahua approximately 50 miles south of the border and east of Chihuahua City.

The Aplomado Falcon is a tropical species that barely reaches the United States in summer. It preys on insects, lizards, and ground-nesting birds. Its apparent decline was undoubtedly due to the abuse of the grasslands throughout its U.S. range in the late 1800s and early 1900s. Although grazing within the park grasslands is officially over, considerable trespass by Mexican stock persists, especially near the Rio Grande. As the park's grasslands continue to recover, in conjunction with restoration efforts, it is likely that this long-tailed falcon will again appear.

Peregrine Falcon. *Falco peregrinus*
Uncommon summer resident and spring migrant; rare in fall and winter.

Records of this dynamic bird exist every month, but it is reported most often between February and mid-July, when nesting birds are most active and while northbound migrants are passing through the area. Nesting occurs as early as February, and young of the year can be found by April and May. Sightings can be expected anywhere in the park, but the majority of the reports are from Santa Elena, Mariscal, Boquillas, and the Lower Canyons, and also from the high Chisos Mountains: near Casa Grande, the Basin, and the South and East Rims. Fall migrants are less numerous; many apparently pass east of the Dead Horse Mountains.

Because of its endangered status, Big Bend's Peregrines received considerable study in recent years, and monitoring by the NPS continues. Current information suggests that BBNP and adjacent wildlands in Mexico support one of the largest populations of Peregrines south of Alaska. This does not mean that the Big Bend population is free from the effects of DDT and other deadly chemicals that threaten the species elsewhere. Although the use of DDT is no longer permitted in the United States, it continues to be manufactured in the U.S. and is used on agricultural lands in Mexico. There, northbound migrants that overwinter or pass through

Peregrine Falcon, *Falco peregrinus*

these areas, especially waterfowl and shorebirds that provide an important food base for Peregrines, ingest pesticides from insects and pass it on to their predators.

Prairie Falcon. *Falco mexicanus*

Rare summer and winter resident; rare fall and uncommon spring migrant.

Although the Prairie Falcon has been reported year-round, and it can be expected anywhere in the park, it is never easy to locate. Nesting birds seem to prefer isolated cliffs away from regular traffic. I watched a pair courting over Mouse Canyon, near PJ, on March 4, 1967; I found another courting pair within Mariscal Canyon on April 26, 1969; Richard and Wendy Wallace watched a pair in Boquillas Canyon, that "went into a hole" on the cliff, on April 29, 1982; an active aerie with two birds was reported from the south slope of Vernon Bailey Peak on May 20 and 21, 1982, by Vidal Davila, Brete Griffen, Bob Huggins, Jim Liles, and Lee Sterrenburg; Hal Flanders reported a courting pair north of SEC on March 4, 1988; and Carol Edwards found a pair nesting at Mule Ears in 1995.

Prairie Falcons are most numerous as a spring migrant from early March through mid-May. Most of the southbound migrants apparently pass east of the Dead Horse Mountains.

FAMILY PHASIANIDAE: PARTRIDGES, GROUSE, TURKEYS AND QUAIL
Wild Turkey. *Meleagris gallopavo*

Rare visitor year-round.

This large, well-known bird apparently is on the increase throughout the Big Bend Country. There were no park records for the first edition of this book (1973); there were "numerous reports from the park and Lower Canyons since 1974" in the 1985 revision; and there have been many more sightings since then. Records now exist in the park for every month and range from the Rio Grande to about 4,000 feet elevation; there are several sightings at PJ: Frank Deckert found a lone bird there on May 4, 1976; Glenn Britt reported three on December 22, 1991; Rick LoBello observed seven hens on April 30, 1992; and James and Sheri Durden reported seven Turkeys on October 5, 1993.

There is no good evidence of nesting, although from the numerous birds seen along the Rio Grande, especially in the Lower Canyons, it is likely. The largest flock reported included 15 individuals in the Lower Canyons at mile 658, on January 27, 1988 (James Morlock and Eric Morey).

The appearance of Wild Turkeys in places where they had not previously occurred suggests introductions by the state or private interests, but none have been undertaken by the Texas Parks and Wildlife Department and none are acknowledged by private ranchers. It appears that this bird has moved into the park area without human help. It has increased its range throughout West Texas in recent years. A significant natural population is present in the Burro Mountains, east of the Sierra del Carmens in northern Coahuila, according to David Riskind and Bonnie McKinney. Whether or not a viable population will persist within the park can only be answered with time.

Montezuma Quail. *Cyrtonyx montezumae*

Current status is uncertain.

This Southwestern quail has had an interesting history in BBNP. Van Tyne and Sutton (1937) reported that as early as 1933 it seemed to be on the decline: "Local hunters and ranchers testified unanimously to the great decrease in the numbers of this quail in recent years in even remote areas. No adequate explanation of this decrease was offered but surely overgrazing, which now prevails in nearly every part of the country, must be an important contributing factor." Extensive overgrazing in the 1930s and early 1940s, plus the severe drought that hit the Big Bend area during the 1940s and 1950s, probably resulted in the extirpation of this species. Except for a report in the Chisos Basin by Adele Harding on May 19, 1962, and a pair reported near Laguna Meadow by Ben Feltner in May 1964, there have been no records of this bird since the early 1940s.

In January 1973, with the valuable assistance of David Brown, Arizona Fish and Game Department, Gil Valenzuela and I netted 26 Montezuma Quail near Nogales, Arizona, transported them to BBNP, and released them in Pine Canyon. In early May 1973, David Riskind and I found five individuals in the same vicinity (two of the males were singing); and I later flushed two birds in upper Boot Canyon, fairly close to the South Rim. Since then, despite the abundance of birders in those areas, there have been only two acceptable reports: Mike Warren observed a lone male in upper Boot Canyon on June 23, 1980, and Terry Schmidt reported "4 or 5 near the Rim" on May 13, 1983.

Montezuma Quail do occur in the Del Norte, Glass, and Davis mountains to the north of the park, and also to the south and southeast in the Maderas del Carmen (Wauer 1992) and Burro Mountains (Bonnie McKinney). The most likely place in the Big Bend Country to find this lovely bird—also known as Fool, Mearn's, or Harlequin quail—is in the Davis Mountains, at Davis Mountain State Park or along the road to the McDonald Observatory.

Scaled Quail. *Callipepla squamata*

Common permanent resident.

This is the only often-seen quail of the Big Bend Country, although it is subject to natural cycles. Coveys of 10 to 40 birds usually can be found along the park's roadways at dawn and dusk from November through March. They begin to pair in March, singing of territorial males is commonplace throughout the desert lowlands, and tiny, precocial young can be seen as early as late May. A high count of 16 young was seen at PJ on June 7, 1971, but only six of this clutch were present by July 2 (Wauer). I believe that during the very wet spring of 1968, pairs near PJ produced four broods. Small chicks were seen as late as mid-October.

Scaled Quail are widespread below approximately 5,000 feet elevation, but rarely are seen at higher elevations. Texans call this bird the "Blue Quail," an appropriate name because of its overall blue-gray color. It also is called "Cottontop" because of the white tuft of feathers on its head.

Gambel's Quail. *Callipepla gambelii*

Rare resident year-round.

This is the only Texas quail with a black, teardrop-shaped plume. It is the common desert quail of the western deserts, but the Big Bend Country is at the eastern edge of its range and it is seldom seen. It occasionally occurs in coveys with the more common Scaled Quail. Recent sightings have been reported for Fresno Creek, along the Maverick Road, the Old Ranch, and Buttrill Spring.

Scaled Quail, *Callipepla squamata*

Family Rallidae: Rails, Gallinules and Coots
Yellow Rail. *Coturnicops noveboracensis*

There is a single record.

An injured bird was found at RGV on January 31, 1976, by Norris Follett, who gave it to Park Ranger Harry Steed. Steed cared for it for two days before it died. The specimen is now in the study collection at BBNP.

This record is most unusual because the Yellow Rail was previously known in winter only from the eastern half of Texas (Oberholser 1974).

King Rail. *Rallus elegans*
Casual migrant.

The earliest park records include three birds at the RGV silt ponds on August 24, 1969 (Wauer), and Bert Schaughency photographed one there on April 22, 1970. It was not reported again until 1986: Rose Ann Rowlett and Susanne Winkler found one at the same location on May 14; Rich and Cynthia Simmons found and photographed one there on May 18 and 19; and one was seen there on August 18 by Anne and Jim Bellamy, Thomas Harvey, Cynthia Simmons, and Jim and Joann Unruh; it also was reported separately the same day by Ted and Chris Koundakscan. Since then, Rich and Nanette Armstrong reported one from the same RGV site on May 9, 1991, and Donn Mattsson reported one from the RGV nature trail on March 27, 1994.

Virginia Rail. *Rallus limicola*
Rare spring migrant; casual in fall and winter.

There are scattered records that extend from a juvenile observed at RGV on August 20 (in 1970 by Dave Easterla and Jim Tucker), throughout the winter months, to May 11 (at RGV by Wauer in 1969). It is most often reported during April and early May. Except for three individuals that responded to a taped call played by Bruce Talbot and Cynthia Simmons at RGV on January 20, 1983, and two found by Bonnie McKinney at the lake on the Sombrero Peak Ranch, north of the park, on October 8, 1983, all records are of lone birds.

Sora. *Porzana carolina*
Casual in summer; fairly common migrant; uncommon in winter.

At least one pair was seen or heard calling at the RGV silt pond throughout June and July 1967 (Wauer); I believe that they nested, but I did not see young birds.

It is most numerous as a migrant in spring from mid-March to late May, and in fall from August 20 to early November, when it is seen easily at ponds and at weedy patches along the Rio Grande. On May 1, 1969, I found six individuals feeding along the runways at the beaver pond on the RGV nature trail; on September 13, 1967, I watched seven Soras "grazing" along the bank of the silt pond; and on September 18, 1969, I found a total of eight individuals at RGV. A few remain all winter; they usually can be seen or detected by their loud "eek" call at the silt pond or the beaver pond with a little squeaking or a loud clap.

Purple Gallinule. *Porphyrula martinica*
Casual in spring and early summer.

There are only a handful of records between April 20 and July 8. I first found one foraging along the runways at the RGV beaver pond on April 20, 1967, and called it to the attention of Hanlon, McCarroll, Meyer, Kuehn, and Rowe, who were birding in the area. I found what I assumed to be the same bird on April 25 and May 1 at the same location. A second record is one seen at the RGV group campground pond on June 30, 1970. It was found first by Lauri Miller and Bill Jensen, and later the same morning by Dave Easterla and Ty and Julie Hotchkiss, who photographed the bird. It remained at this pond until July 3. Since then it has been recorded a few additional times, all at RGV, except for one that was killed by a house cat at Black Gap WMA on June 6, 1983 (Bonnie McKinney).

Common Moorhen. *Gallinule chloropus*
Casual migrant and winter visitor.

Spring records range from April 20 to May 29, and fall records extend only from September 30 to October 15. There also are two winter sightings: Tim and Susan Wallis reported one at RGV on December 28, 1989, and Eunice Holm found one along the RGV nature trail daily from February 19 to 22, 1984. Except for two birds reported by David and Roy Brown at RGV on April 27, 1966, all records are of lone birds.

American Coot. *Fulica americana*
Rare summer resident; fairly common migrant; uncommon in winter.

It nested at the RGV silt pond during the summers of 1967, 1970, and 1971, but I did not find it in 1968 and 1969. The pond was dredged to deepen the channel in 1967 and 1970, but not in the intervening years, which suggests that the ecological requirements for the American Coot, as well as for the Sora and the Pied-billed Grebe, include an open pond with nearby concealment.

Coots are most numerous during spring migration from early March through May, and in fall from early October to mid-November. Migrants often occur in small flocks; on October 27, 1966, I found a high of 14 individuals at RGV. Wintering birds usually occur at ponds, but they also are rare along the Rio Grande itself.

FAMILY GRUIDAE: CRANES

Sandhill Crane. *Grus canadensis*

Uncommon migrant; rare in winter.

This long-legged bird has been recorded in the park from mid-September to mid-March; Charles Callahan found 10 birds at RGV on September 15, 1988, and R. H. Dean and Angie Price reported 50 birds flying northeast of SEC on March 10, 1987. Fall migrants apparently peak from mid-October to mid-November, and northbound birds are most numerous from early February to very early March. The majority of sightings are of flocks flying overhead; the largest of these was 72 birds reported at Talley on February 19, 1990 (Charles Callagan). Although most of the records are from the vicinity of the Rio Grande, Tim Brush reported 25 birds in flight over Mule Ears on February 3, 1976; Virginia Brown reported 25 birds flying north over Ernst Tinaja on March 3, 1976; and Bruce Talbot found 35 flying in a V-pattern north of Devil's Den on February 22, 1983.

FAMILY CHARADRIIDAE: PLOVERS AND LAPWINGS

Killdeer. *Charadrius vociferus*

Uncommon summer resident; fairly common migrant and winter visitor.

The majority of sightings are from the vicinity of the Rio Grande, especially at RGV and near Castolon. I found three fledged young at the RGV sewage lagoons on May 24, 1969, and again on May 2, 1972. In migration, it can be expected anywhere in the lowlands, including the open desert.

FAMILY RECURVIROSTRIDAE: STILTS AND AVOCETS
Black-necked Stilt. *Himantopus mexicanus*
Rare spring migrant and casual in fall.

It is most numerous from March 23 through May 24, and there are three fall reports: at RGV on August 18, 1978 (Brad Stilwell), October 3, 1969 (Wauer), and three birds at Black Gap WMA on September 11, 1983 (Bonnie McKinney). There also is a single winter report by Robert DeVine at RGV on January 25, 1979.

American Avocet. *Recurvirostra americana*
Uncommon spring migrant; rare fall migrant; casual in summer.

This lovely shorebird is most numerous in spring. The earliest record is six birds at the SEC Put-in site on March 14, 1988 (Patricia Baron); there are numerous reports in April, and scattered sightings extend to June 1. Afterward, reports are few and far between, including four individuals reported at Hot Springs on June 28, 1983 (Bill Graber); one at Hot Springs on July 28, 1981 (Robert DeVine); one three miles west of the Basin Junction on July 30, 1990 (Roberto Dean); eight birds at the western tip of the park on August 10, 1988 (Bill Bourbon); four at RGV on August 11, 1983 (Cynthia Simmons); 15 along the Rio Grande between SEC and Castolon on October 6, 1970; and one at RGV on October 6, 1970 (Wauer). Except for a lone sighting by Bruce Talbot of five birds at the Chisos Basin sewage lagoons on April 22, 1983, all of the park records are from the vicinity of the Rio Grande.

The breeding range of this wader extends as far south as southern New Mexico and San Luis Potosi, Mexico (AOU 1983), and east from near Midland, Texas, to the central and southern Gulf Coast (Oberholser 1974). Nesting within the Big Bend at suitable ponds is possible.

FAMILY SCOLOPACIDAE: SANDPIPERS, PHALAROPES, AND ALLIES
Greater Yellowlegs. *Tringa melanoleuca*
Fairly common migrant; casual winter visitor.

Spring records range from March 17 through April 14, and I found a very late bird at RGV on May 20, 1968; fall records extend from July 14 through October 15, all from the vicinity of the Rio Grande. There are two winter reports as well, both from the Lower Canyons: James Morlock and Eric Morey found one on January 25, 1988, and Marcos Paredes and Steve Swanke observed one at mile 896 on January 26, 1990.

Lesser Yellowlegs. *Tringa flavipes*

Uncommon spring migrant; casual in fall, winter, and summer.

It is most numerous in spring from April 1 to mid-May, and there are scattered records in mid-summer, in the fall, and in February. I found lone birds at PJ and RGV on July 17, 1968, and July 23, 1969, respectively; I discovered five individuals at RGV on September 16, 1970, one at RGV on October 26, 1969, and one at RGV on November 3, 1970. There are two February reports from RGV: Pete and Ruth Isleib found one on February 3 and 5, 1965, and Louis and Eric Winston observed one there on February 24, 1990.

Solitary Sandpiper. *Tringa solitaria*

Fairly common migrant.

Records range from March 23 through May 10 in spring, and July 15 through mid-October in fall; there also is a November 9, 1989 sighting at RGV (Wauer). Most sightings are of lone birds, but I found four at RGV on April 26, 1990, and a flock of seven there on August 5, 1969.

Willet. *Catoptrophorus semipalmatus*

Rare spring migrant; casual fall migrant.

Springs records extend from March 10 to May 20, including one by Alexander Sprunt, Jr., in the Chisos Basin on March 15, 1950. There are two early fall sightings: I found 16 birds bathing in the Rio Grande at RGV on August 15, 1969, and John MacDonald and Tom Meyer reported one there on August 19, 1970.

Spotted Sandpiper. *Actitis macularia*

Common migrant and winter resident.

It is most numerous in the spring from mid-March through mid-May and in the fall from late July through October, but late spring birds can occur until June 12. Fall migrants may appear as early as July 17. It is unreported for the park between those two dates. It is somewhat less abundant in winter, but several can usually be found along the river on any given day; on February 1, 1968, I recorded more than 30 individuals while rafting through Mariscal Canyon. Although most records are from the river area, there also are a handful of reports from desert springs and the Chisos Basin sewage lagoons.

Spotted Sandpiper, *Actitis macularia*

Upland Sandpiper. *Bartramia longicauda*

Rare migrant.

Spring reports range from April 3 (Bert Schaughency) to May 15 (Bill Bourbon), all at RGV; fall records extend from a July 31, 1974, sighting at RGV (Scott Lanier) to 12 birds found at an irrigated field at RGV by Dave Easterla and Jim Tucker on August 30, 1970. Although most records are from the vicinity of the Rio Grande, Carol Edwards reported two birds at upper Tornillo Creek bridge on August 1, 1994; Greg Lasley and Peter Scott found two in the Grapevine Hills on August 22, 1986; and Judge Charlie Shannon and I observed a lone bird at PJ on August 28, 1970.

Whimbrel. *Numenius phaeopus*

Casual spring migrant.

There are five records: Harold Brodrick found one first near PJ on April 27, 1957, and Robert M. Lavall reported one along Tornillo Creek at Hot Springs on April 26, 1969. He reported it to me, and I found it still present two days later. It was collected and represents the first specimen of this species for West Texas. Since then it has been recorded on three other occasions: I found four birds at RGV on May 2, 1972; Alan See and Janet Goodland reported one along the Rio Grande one mile below Lajitas on May 4, 1990; and Byron Stone, Clark Terrell, Dave Cornman, and Max and Mary Rodell found three along the river near CC on May 5, 1995.

Long-billed Curlew. *Numenius americanus*

Uncommon spring migrant; casual in fall.

It is most numerous in spring from March 16 through mid-April, and there are scattered reports to late May. Fall records range from August 16 to September 12. Although the majority of the sightings are from the vicinity of the Rio Grande, it may occur anywhere in the lowlands: Bruce Talbot found one north of upper Tornillo Creek bridge on April 7, 1983; Mr. and Mrs. G. W. Ethridge reported two near Nine Point Draw; and R. D. Leopold found two along the Dagger Flat Road on August 16, 1980. Except for sightings by Rich Simmons of 14 birds at RGV on April 4, 1984, and six near Talley on March 24, 1993 (J. Howard and Ruth Frederick), all reports are limited to one or two birds.

Western Sandpiper. *Calidris mauri*

Casual spring migrant; rare in fall and early winter.

Josselyn Van Tyne and George M. Sutton (1937) were first to report three birds feeding along the river at Lajitas on May 10, 1935. The only other spring sighting is four birds reported by Steve Swanke and George Simmons at mile 782 in the Lower Canyon on April 22, 1990. Fall records range from August 20, 1989 (Rothe family), to four at RGV on September 10, 1966 (Wauer). Winter sightings are limited to lone birds at RGV on December 8 and 27, 1969 (Wauer), and one at Black Gap WMA on November 12, 1981 (Bonnie McKinney).

Least Sandpiper. *Calidris minutilla*
Uncommon migrant and winter visitor.

This is the most abundant of Big Bend's "peeps"; it has been recorded every month but May and June. Spring sightings range from mid-March to April 30; high counts include 12 birds near Boquillas Crossing on April 5, 1970 (Wauer), and Bonnie McKinney counted more than 20 birds on sandbars along the Rio Grande between RGV and La Linda on April 21 to 23, 1980. The majority of winter reports range from late November through January.

Baird's Sandpiper. *Calidris bairdii*
Rare spring migrant; casual in fall.

It is most numerous in spring from April 15 to May 11; Van Tyne and Sutton (1937) first recorded it in April and May 1935, collecting a specimen at Lajitas on May 10. I found two along the Rio Grande at RGV on April 16, 1971, and Jim Tucker reported two birds at the sewage lagoons in the Chisos Basin on May 10, 1969. Tom and Helen Nelson also found five birds at the Basin lagoons on May 11, 1988; one was found (also photographed by Steve Kerr) there on May 3, 1990, by Kerr, Jim Hayes, Tom Boyle, and Ward Dorsey; and Greg Lasley saw three at Hot Springs on May 3, 1989. Fall records extend from July 26 to November 8: Warren Pulich found six birds at Green Valley Ranch, north of the park, on July 26, 1961; I collected a bird at RGV on September 2, 1967, and saw lone birds there on September 29, 1967, and November 8, 1969. There are two winter records: one at Hot Springs in January 1963 (Joseph Woolfenden) and 12 there on January 1, 1965 (Dingus).

Long-billed Dowitcher. *Limnodromus scolopaceus*
Casual migrant and winter visitor.

There are scattered records from early February to early May, none in June, a few from July 21 to October 17, none in November, and a few again in late December. All of the dowitcher records are assumedly Long-bills. Except for a lone sighting at the sewage lagoons in the Chisos Basin by Bruce Talbot on March 4, 1984, all reports are from along the Rio Grande and of one or two individuals.

Common Snipe. *Gallinago gallinago*
Uncommon migrant and winter visitor.

Reports of this plump water bird range from August 31 through May 11, but it is most numerous from October 15 to early November. A few can usually be found at pond edges and irrigation ditches at RGV and CC all winter. There is a slight increase in numbers toward the end of March as spring migrants pass through the area. This northbound movement, which is not as extensive as it is in the fall, subsides by mid-April, but stragglers continue to be seen until May 11. Most records are of lone birds, but I found 12 together at RGV on September 29, 1970.

Wilson's Phalarope. *Phalaropus tricolor*
Rare spring migrant; casual in fall.

It is most numerous in spring from April 15 to May 6; all records are from RGV except for two pairs that Bonnie McKinney found at a stock tank on the Black Gap WMA, from April 24 to 28, 1982. The largest numbers reported in spring were ten and eight birds at RGV, found by Bruce Talbot on April 15 and 22, 1983, respectively. Fall sightings range from 13 birds found by Cynthia Simmons at RGV on August 11, 1983, to a lone bird at RGV on September 20, 1966 (Wauer).

FAMILY LARIDAE: SKUAS, GULLS, TERNS AND SKIMMERS
Laughing Gull. *Larus atricilla*
There are five reports.

The first record was of a dead bird found at an earthen tank at Black Gap WMA in June 1951 (Thompson 1953). Dave Easterla next observed an adult near Terlingua Abaja on June 4, 1973; Paul Strong and Betty Alex found one at PJ on October 19, 1983; Jim and Deva Burns reported one approximately five miles southeast of PJ on June 5, 1987; and Bill Bourbon found five gulls with a lone Forster's Tern at Lajitas on December 9, 1991.

Franklin's Gull. *Larus pipixcan*

Casual spring and fall migrant.

Spring sightings extend from April 5 through June 10, and fall reports range from October 19 to November 13. Two of the records are rather interesting. On the very windy morning of April 14, 1971, I observed 29 black-and-white gulls flying together up Tornillo Creek, near the lower bridge, at about 7 a.m. At 10:30 the same morning, Dick Brownstein, Ed Seeker, Paul Benham, and Joe Grzybowski saw 29 Franklin's Gulls flying north about 20 miles south of Marathon. If both sightings were of the same 29 gulls, they traveled 55 miles in three and a half hours.

On October 19, 1983, Bonnie McKinney observed and photographed nine immature gulls at Black Gap WMA headquarters. The photographs were later sent to Dr. Keith Arnold of Texas A&M University, who identified the birds as this species.

Ring-billed Gull. *Larus delawarensis*

Rare spring migrant; casual summer, fall, and winter visitor.

It is most numerous in spring from early March to late April, and there is one sighting in May; Ray Hertman reported three birds at RGV on May 19, 1980. A high number of 23 birds was seen flying at "the west end" of the park by Peter Vennema on March 20, 1989. Mark Hoffman found one at RGV on July 5, 1977. Other scattered records are: October 12, 1983, at Boquillas by A. Weeks; two on December 3, 1984, at SEC by Kathleen Hambly and Garrett Moynihan; one on the Rio Grande at CC on January 5, 1995, by Tom Plant.

In reviewing the records of this gull, it appears to have increased considerably in recent years, probably due to a growing population at Amistad Reservoir. Only two records were listed in the original version of this book (1973); five records were included in the 1985 revision; and 15 records were available for the current (through mid-March 1995) revision.

Forster's Tern. *Sterna forsteri*

Casual spring migrant.

This bird was first reported by Charles Gill at RGV on May 1, 1976. One bird was found at RGV by Ken Soltesz on May 9, 1978, and Mimi Wolf

observed it the next day. Bonnie McKinney reported one at Black Gap
WMA on March 20, 1982. Also, there is a lone winter record at Lajitas: Bill
Bourbon found one with five Laughing Gulls on December 9, 1991.

Black Tern. *Childonias niger*

There are two park records.

Robin Boughton and Mark Crotteau reported (separately) one at RGV
on May 16, 1984, and Charles Howell found and photographed one at
CC on September 5, 1993. There also are a few earlier reports in the Big
Bend area: Jody Miller found lone birds on her ranch near Valentine on
August 23, 1956, May 20, 1957, and August 30, 1965; I observed one just
west of Marathon on August 21, 1970; and Jim Scudday collected one of
several seen at Lake Balmorhea on September 16, 1970.

FAMILY COLUMBIDAE: PIGEONS AND DOVES
Rock Dove. *Columba livia*

Casual summer visitor.

This is the domestic pigeon of American cities. There are only a handful of park records, extending from June 10 through August 16, all from PJ
and the RGV-Boquillas area. The most interesting of these sightings
occurred at RGV on June 24, 1970, when Dave Easterla watched a Peregrine Falcon capture one of two Rock Doves.

Band-tailed Pigeon. *Columba fasciata*

Fairly common summer resident; sporadic in winter.

It may first be detected by its owl-like "oo-whoo" call, which can be
rather ventriloquistic within the narrow mountain canyons. Band-tails
usually can be found in Boot and Pine canyons year-round, and they visit
lower canyons during periods of good acorn crops. Seventy birds, a high
count, were found in Boot Canyon on August 8, 1969 (Wauer). In July and
August of 1969 and 1970, this bird was found in numbers in the oak
groves along the lower Window Trail. Walter Rooney, who lived at Oak
Creek (just below The Window) from 1916 to 1923, told Doug Evans that
"millions of pigeons" came into Oak Creek, scattered over a mile "like the

Band-tailed Pigeon, *Columba fasciata*

wind blowing," when the acorns were on the trees (Rooney 1966). One pigeon that was killed had 28 acorns in its gut.

Although Band-tails undoubtedly nest at preferred sites, such as lower Boot and Pine canyons, there are only three records of nests: Pete Peterson reported one with two eggs in Boot Canyon on July 24, 1981; Brete Griffen found a nest 25 feet high on an Arizona pine in Pine Canyon on August 6, 1982, and John Gee reported one at Laguna Meadow on July 17, 1990.

An occasional bird may move out of the mountains altogether in fall: Charles Bander saw one at Dugout Wells on August 21, 1966, and Bill

Bourbon found three at Tuff Canyon on August 28, 1988. And in winter this species appears to be common at times but very difficult to find at other times. On December 23, 1968, CBC participants Roger Siglin and Dick Nelson tallied 58 in Boot Canyon. I found it common there on January 27 and February 22, 1968, and again on March 9, 1969, but I did not find a single bird there on January 28 and 29, 1967 (Christmas count dates).

White-winged Dove. *Zenaida asiatica*

Common year-round resident.

The majority, if not all, of the park's White-wings are permanent residents; one banded at PJ on April 23, 1968, was recaptured there on February 3 and June 6, 1969. The species is commonly found at mesquite

White-winged Dove, *Zenaida asiatica*

thickets along the Rio Grande, in adjacent washes, at springs below approximately 5,000 feet, and locally within the lower canyons of the Chisos Mountains.

Lowland birds begin to pair early in February, and the earliest "who-cooks-for-whoo" call was heard on February 14. I found and photographed a nest five feet high on a willow at the Old Ranch on May 1, 1993; another on a branch of an Emory oak along the Window Trail on May 11, 1968; one 45 feet high on a huge cottonwood at Boquillas Crossing on May 21, 1968; I accidentally frightened two juveniles from a nest in lower Blue Creek Canyon on June 18, 1970; and I found a pair nest-building at RGV on July 18, 1970.

In winter, Big Bend's White-wings flock at preferred areas, such as RGV (I found 70 there on January 22, 1970), Dugout Wells, PJ (I found 22 there on November 10, 1967), and along the lower portion of the Window Trail. On ten (1985–94) CBCs at RGV, participants tallied an average of 41 individuals, none in 1987, and a high of 104 in 1988. The park's White-wings are considered to be of the "Mexican Highland" race of central Mexico and the lower Big Bend Country, according to Clarence Cottam and James Trefethen's excellent book, *Whitewings: The Life History, Status, and Management of the White-winged Dove* (1968).

Mourning Dove. *Zenaida macroura*

Common summer resident and migrant; fairly common winter resident.

Some birds are year-round residents. Birds banded at PJ include one banded on April 6, 1967, and recaptured on April 13 and December 8, 1969; another banded on January 22, 1968, was recaptured on May 25, 1968, and January 30, 1969; and one banded on March 26, 1968, was recaptured on December 2, 1968.

Nesting occurs from March through June most years, but much later during wet years. During the fall of 1966, I found a nest with one egg on a cottonwood at RGV as late as September 17; Felix Hernandez III reported finding a nest on the ground under a creosote bush at Castolon on July 8, 1981; and John Egbert found a pair of birds in Boot Canyon, on June 2, 1976, that he believed was nesting.

Winter birds are most numerous in the lowlands, and usually occur in small flocks of 10 to 20 individuals. CBC participants at RGV tally 20 to 50 Mourning Doves annually.

Inca Dove. *Columbina inca*

Fairly common summer resident and migrant; uncommon in winter.

This little dove favors areas of human habitation; it is most often seen at RGV, but also can be found at Castolon and in the adjacent Mexican villages. Tarleton Smith (1936) reported it feeding with chickens at Boquillas during June and July 1936.

Nesting apparently occurs most of the year: W. Leavens and C. Davis reported courting birds at RGV on February 10, 1983; I found a copulating pair at RGV on May 7, 1971; and Darryl Rathbun observed two at a nest on a cottonwood tree at RGV on August 3, 1982. Except for lone birds reported at PJ on June 25, 1972 (Dave Easterla), and at Dugout Wells on April 5, 1979 (A. Palmes), all park records are in the vicinity of the Rio Grande.

Common Ground-Dove. *Columbina passerina*

Rare summer resident; uncommon migrant; sporadic in winter.

This tiny dove nests in mesquite thickets along the Rio Grande and on adjacent flats, such as those at RGV, where it was found nest-building on June 23, 1969, and incubating two eggs on September 7, 1968 (Wauer). It is most numerous in migration from mid-March through May and from mid-August through October. Sightings away from the Rio Grande are few and far between: a lone bird was seen at PJ on April 6, 1967, and I banded one there on September 1, 1969. James Stovall and A. Robert found one at PJ on September 17 and 23, 1979, and Cathy Blumig reported one from K-Bar on September 9, 1991.

In winter, it is usually present in small numbers on open weedy and mesquite flats along the Rio Grande (12 were recorded on the December 12, 1968 CBC at RGV, and I found seven near Castolon on January 25, 1969), but apparently it is sporadic in occurrence. I could not find a single bird during the cool, dry winter of 1969–70. More recent (1985–94) CBC participants at RGV found this species only once in ten years, 14 in 1990.

Ruddy Ground-Dove. *Columbina talpacoti*
Casual winter resident.

There are at least four records, two of which were validated with photographs. A lone male, discovered by Florence and Roy Mazzagatt at RGV on December 5, 1987, remained until early May, 1988. Numerous birders observed this tropical dove, including Alan Wormington, who photographed it on February 17; the Wormington photograph later appeared in *American Birds* (Williams 1988; Lasley and Sexton 1988). A second male Ruddy Ground-Dove was found feeding with Inca Doves near the Lajitas Golfcourse on February 20, 1990 (Jim Hines); it was last seen and photographed by Mark Lockwood on March 22 (Lasley and Sexton 1990a). On December 24, 1991, Wolf Kappes reported a third bird at CC that remained at least until May 5, 1992. Finally, Wesley Cureton reported one at RGV on May 13, 1994.

FAMILY CUCULIDAE: CUCKOOS AND ALLIES
Black-billed Cuckoo. *Coccyzus erythropthalmus*
Casual migrant.

There are four records only: I first discovered a bird in Boot Canyon on June 16, 1976; Gordon Kennedy found an immature bird there on October 11, 1979; Steve Munden photographed one in Boot Canyon on May 10, 1984 (NPS files); and Karen Bricher and Sonja Paspal found one at Buttrill Spring on May 24, 1991.

Yellow-billed Cuckoo. *Coccyzus americanus*
Fairly common summer resident.

This secretive bird is the last of the summer residents to arrive on its breeding grounds. The earliest record is one at CC on April 15, 1990 (Wauer); it was the only one I found during an eight-day stay in the park. The latest sighting is one near SEC on September 24, 1968 (Wauer), although it becomes quite scarce by early September.

This cuckoo is commonly found at cottonwood groves along the Rio Grande, such as those at RGV and CC, and less commonly at riparian areas up to 5,500 feet. On June 30, 1971, I heard one calling in lower Boot Canyon. Nesting records (all at RGV) include two nests found on cottonwoods on June 8, 1969, and another containing one egg on a mesquite on July 23, 1968, and I found an adult feeding a cicada to a nestling on July 31. On September 8, 1969, I observed a Greater Roadrunner with a recently captured young Yellow-billed Cuckoo.

Greater Roadrunner. *Geococcyx californianus*

Common resident year-round.

I know of no better place to find this ground cuckoo than at RGV, where it is numerous. Courting begins in February; I heard the first "bark" of the season at RGV on February 15, 1968, and nest-building was taking place in mid-March; I found one egg on a nest there on March 20. In addition, the park staff at RGV reported that on March 25, 1982, they watched a roadrunner "trying to reach a roadrunner's nest that was on display behind an outside window. After numerous attempts to gain access to the nest, the roadrunner laid an egg on the 1-inch window sill and flew off." Other nesting records include one nest with three eggs at RGV on March

Greater Roadrunner, *Geococcyx californianus*

31, 1970 (Murl Deusing); E. Smith and Hilka Ahlers reported birds copulating at RGV on April 20, 1988; a nest with three eggs near the Chisos Basin sewage lagoons on May 25, 1969; one with three eggs and three young at RGV on June 19, 1968 (Wauer); and another one there with two young ready to leave the nest on August 5, 1969.

Several other interesting reports have been recorded. There are three high elevation records: S. Chamberlain found a Roadrunner at the South Rim on November 27, 1981, and Ruth Young and David Elkowitz separately reported birds along the higher portions of the Lost Mine Trail on April 19 and 20, 1988. And there are some interesting predation records: I discovered a Roadrunner with a recently captured young Yellow-billed Cuckoo on September 8, 1969; Robert DeVine watched one eating a fresh road-killed rabbit near Dugout Wells on December 22, 1982; and Alan Van Valkenburg found a Roadrunner eating a Chipping Sparrow at the Chisos Basin ranger station on April 19, 1988.

In addition, Martha Whitson lived in BBNP while studying Roadrunners for her dissertation: "Field and Laboratory Investigations of the Ethology of Courtship and Copulation in the Greater Roadrunner" (1971).

Groove-billed Ani. *Crotophaga sulcirostris*

Sporadic summer visitor and migrant.

The first record for the Trans-Pecos was one collected north of the park at the Black Gap WMA by W. Frank Blair in June 1951 (Thompson 1953). Roger Siglin next saw one at RGV and watched it for several minutes before it flew across the Rio Grande on August 4, 1967. And on May 21, 1968, one of two birds seen at RGV was collected (Wauer 1968).

Since these first records, the Groove-billed Ani has been reported sporadically in late spring and summer at RGV and the adjacent floodplain, arriving in June and remaining until October; the latest report is from RGV on October 19, 1974, by Gene Blacklock and Bruce Fall. There is a lone report for CC, by John Martin on September 28, 1992, as well. Some years it builds nests, although there are no records of a successful nesting. For example, a pair built a nest along the RGV nature trail on July 26, 1969; they deserted this nest within a few days but constructed two more in a cottonwood at the pond next to the campground on August 5 and 12. These nests were deserted as well.

FAMILY TYTONIDAE: BARN OWLS
Barn Owl. *Tyto alba*

Rare migrant.

There are scattered records from March 1 to May 24 in spring and from July 24 through September 13 in fall. Except for one reported in the lower Chisos Basin by Bill Bourbon on September 13, 1988, and a heard bird in lower Pine Canyon on April 24, 1994 (Wauer), all reports are from the desert lowlands. Also, all of the records are of lone birds, except for two found at RGV by Betty and Bull Trumbauer on April 30, 1986. Although there are no actual nesting records, it is likely; Barbara Peterman and Alan See independently reported a "roost site with lots of pellets" at Muskhog Spring on May 4, 1991 and April 24, 1994, respectively.

FAMILY STRIGIDAE: TYPICAL OWLS
Flammulated Owl. *Otus flammeolus*

Uncommon summer resident.

This little owl with all-brown eyes has been found most often in Boot Canyon, where I saw a juvenile with a captured monarch butterfly on June 8, 1968. Records range from March 30 to mid-June, and there is a scattering of reports until September 24.

During May and June, it usually can be called up right after dark with a few hoots that need only partially resemble the deep "boot" call of this bird. One must stay overnight at Boot Spring, however, for the best chance of finding this shy bird. It begins its nightly activities about one hour after sunset (10:00 to 10:15 p.m.), and can usually be found in the main canyon just below the cabin. On several occasions I have sat quietly on a rock in the drainage, beneath open tree branches, until I have heard their first song. It is then a matter of calling one into the open branches outlined against the sky. Once a bird flies in and perches, it can be studied by flashlight.

Flammulated Owls also have been reported in Pine Canyon (on April 27, 1995, by Fred Wong) and on the north slope of Casa Grande on two occasions: N. C. Hazard photographed one there on April 19, 1965, and Dave and Ginger Harwood found two birds there on April 20, 1970.

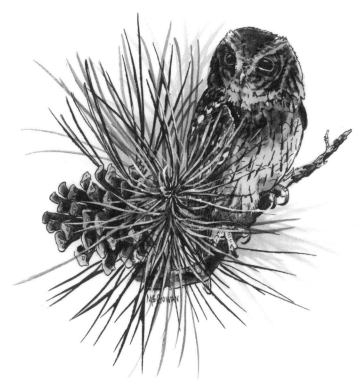

Flammulated Owl, *Otus flammeolus*

Eastern Screech-Owl. *Otus asio*

Rare permanent resident.

Eastern and Western Screech-Owls are impossible to separate in the field except by voice. The Eastern Screech-Owl sings a characteristic quavering whistle, while the Western Screech-Owl has a "bouncing-ball" song. Both species are present along the Rio Grande floodplain, at riparian areas at desert springs, as well as in the Chisos Mountain woodlands. And they interbreed. Joe Marshall (1967) discovered that the Texas Big Bend area represents one of the few areas in North American area where the two birds overlap. He found a mixed pair with a grown young at Boquillas in July 1962. But in spite of this, the Screech-Owl was split into two species by the AOU in 1983.

Western Screech-Owl. *Otus kennicottii*
Uncommon permanent resident.

The Western Screech-Owl is somewhat more abundant than the Eastern, although both can be found in the proper habitat throughout the park. Nesting has been recorded at all elevations: Bruce Talbot reported a nest at RGV on March 12, 1983; I found an adult carrying food to a hole in a large willow tree at Boquillas on June 8, 1978; Carl and Ann Erickson observed two adults and three juveniles at Dugout Wells on June 13, 1992; Harold Brodrick found a pair with three youngsters at the K-Bar on June 29, 1960; and Dave Easterla observed two adults feeding young at Boot Spring on July 9, 1968.

Great Horned Owl. *Bubo virginianus*
Fairly common year-round resident.

This large owl occurs in all habitats below approximately 5,500 feet elevation. It is likely that most Great Horned Owls are permanent residents, but there is a distinct increase in sightings from mid-March to mid-May and from early September through late November. It is one of the park's most important nighttime predators, taking mammals, birds, and a wide variety of smaller creatures whenever possible. George Howarth and Margaret Littlejohn found one with a dead ring-tailed cat at Panther Pass on January 19, 1978.

Northern Pygmy-Owl. *Glaucidium gnoma*
Casual migrant and summer visitor.

Park records range from April 17 to May 9 in spring and from August 7 to September 28 in fall. The early August record represents the first accepted record for Texas (TBRC); Kenneth Nanney heard one at Boot Spring on August 7, and Greg Lasley observed one there on August 12. The only other accepted Texas record is one reported by Jan and Will Risser from Boot Spring on April 25, 1993. There also is a report for Boot Canyon on June 29, 1984 (Jane Burns). And, although it has been reported for the lowlands, those records are questionable.

This bird is extremely rare in Texas; further reports must be well documented; see the example form toward the back of the book. It is likely that many of Big Bend's fall Pygmy-Owl records represent post-nesting visitors from Mexico's Maderas del Carmen, the forested mountains 50 miles southeast of the Chisos Mountains (Wauer and Ligon 1977).

Elf Owl. *Micrathene whitneyi*

Fairly common spring migrant and summer resident.

Park records extend from one at RGV on February 24, 1994 (Steve LaForest), to one at PJ on October 11, 1985 (Robert DeVine). This tiny owl is most obvious from early March to late April, when they are calling from "posts" along the edges of their breeding territories. By mid- to late April, however, when their territories have been defined and nesting has begun, they become silent and more difficult to find. Three or four pairs nest in the RGV area; they usually also nest at Dugout Wells; and several pairs nest along the Window Trail and near the Chisos Basin Amphitheater. I found family groups of adults with three youngsters on two occasions at Dugout: on July 4, 1968, and August 17, 1968. By late June, Elf Owls sometimes can be found at night hunting moths around lights at RGV and in the Chisos Basin.

Burrowing Owl. *Athene cunicularia*

Rare spring migrant; casual in summer, fall, and winter.

It has been recorded for the park every month but February. There are two reports of nesting: I found a pair at a burrow near the Loop Camp turnoff on the River Road on April 17, 1969, and Roger McNeil discovered a family of six birds 13 miles south of Persimmon Gap on July 3, 1991. Migrants most often are reported from early March through April, and the majority of these sightings are from Tornillo Flat (especially in the vicinity of the Fossil Bone Exhibit), along the Maverick Road, and along the western half of the River Road.

Long-eared Owl. *Asio otus*

Casual migrant.

Spring records extend from a March 8, 1975, sighting along the Old Ore Road, by Jim and Teresa Weedin, to three later records: Doug and Doris Evans photographed one (NPS files) at Oak Spring on April 30, 1988, and I heard calling birds at Boot Spring on June 11, 1967 and June 7, 1970. There are fewer fall sightings ranging from one near Study Butte on September 16, 1977 (J. W. Duffield), to November 19, 1981, from Fresno Creek (Rod Hesselbert).

Elf Owl, *Micrathene whitneyi*

Short-eared Owl. *Asio flammeus*
Casual in winter and spring.

There are only six reports that extend from January 4 to May 6 and a pair of sightings by James Morlock of two birds along the Rio Grande near Pantera on July 18 and 19, 1981. The highest number reported was four birds in an arroyo two miles west of Grapevine Hills Road on February 10, 1981 (R. D. Leopold).

Northern Saw-whet Owl. *Aegolius acadicus*
Casual in late winter, spring, and fall

I first heard one calling near Boot Spring after dark on November 3, 1967, but could not call it close enough for a good look. Then, on February 3, 1968, one was taken from a mist net and photographed at Boot Spring (Wauer 1969b). On March 7 and 9, 1976, Philip F. Allan reported hearing two birds calling at RGV; he observed one by flashlight for five minutes. Robert DeVine next heard one calling at RGV on April 16, 1983; Bonnie McKinney found one just above the Chisos Basin campground on April 29 and 30, 1985; and Greg Keiran reported that one responded to a taped call at Boot Spring on September 4, 1993. The fall and winter birds probably are visitors from Mexico's Maderas del Carmen, where it is known to nest (Wauer and Ligon 1977).

FAMILY CAPRIMULGIDAE: GOATSUCKERS
Lesser Nighthawk. *Chordeiles acutipennis*
Common summer resident and migrant.

It occurs almost everywhere below 4,000 feet in summer, but it is most numerous along the Rio Grande floodplain and in adjacent open washes, where its hoarse "purring" songs can be heard as a low roar at dawn. Lesser Nighthawks do not reach the Big Bend area until early April, and they become most numerous from mid-April to the end of May. On May 25, 1957, I found two eggs beneath a small creosote bush near San Vicente. Summering birds depart by late August, but southbound birds can usually be found along the river until October 18. Although the vast majority of sightings are from the lowlands, migrants have been recorded at Boot Spring and the South Rim. The largest number reported was a flock of 51 individuals north of Persimmon Gap on August 17, 1963 (C. Phillip Allen).

Lesser Nighthawk, *Chordeiles acutipennis*

Common Nighthawk. *Chordeiles minor*

Uncommon spring migrant; rare in summer and fall.

There is no indication that this bird nests within the park, but it is resident in summer north of the park in the Del Norte, Davis, and Glass mountains. It is most numerous in the park from April 22 to mid-May, and there are scattered records through September. All summer sightings are probably post-nesting birds. Fall migrants are scarce; the majority of the southbound birds apparently pass to the east of the Dead Horse Mountains.

Common Poorwill. *Phalaenoptilus nuttallii*

Fairly common summer resident; common migrant; rare in winter.

There are records of this small goatsucker for every month. By the middle of March it usually can be found along all the park roads below 4,500 feet. In summer it is most numerous on open desert flats below the pinyon-juniper-oak woodlands, but a few frequent the high, open slopes and ridges; I heard Poorwills calling from about 7,000 feet on the southern side of Emory Peak ridge on June 8 and 11, 1968. Fall migrants are most numerous from early September until late October. During migration, it often can be found on all the park roads soon after dark and again before dawn; their red eye-shine may be visible in vehicle lights for a hundred feet or more. The road between RGV and Boquillas Canyon has consistently provided sightings during the evening hours in spring. But winter records

Common Poorwill, *Phalaenoptilus nuttallii*

are few and far between, probably depending on temperatures. Estivating Poorwills have not been found in Big Bend as they have in the Mohave Desert; it is more likely that the majority of Big Bend's breeding birds migrate south for the winter. There is, however, minimal winter activity some years; Anne Bellamy reported Poorwills "catching insects attracted to house lights" at PJ on December 29, 1988, and January 3, 1986.

Whip-poor-will. *Caprimulgus vociferus*

Fairly common summer resident.

Records extend from April 2 through September 23. The majority of these are from Boot and Pine canyons, but birds also can be heard along the Lost Mine Trail and at Juniper Flat and Laguna Meadow. And Chuck Sexton found one at the Chisos Basin Amphitheater "at first light" on May 1, 1982. Nesting birds are extremely vociferous in May; I found an adult and two juveniles in lower Boot Canyon on June 17, 1971, and Steve Van Pelt discovered a nest with one spotted youngster on a steep oak-covered slope at 5,300 feet on the east side of Ward Mountain on July 19, 1970. Although Whip-poor-wills are easily detected before nesting by their loud songs, they are quiet while nesting, and by late July may be almost entirely silent except for dusk and dawn songs.

FAMILY APODIDAE: SWIFTS
Chimney Swift. *Chaetura pelagica*

Casual spring migrant.

I observed and heard two individuals over Hot Springs on April 27, 1968; one over RGV on April 28, 1969; and another lone bird, flying with several Violet-green Swallows, over the Chisos Basin campground on May 3, 1991. And in 1995, Harold Hedges reported one flying over RGV on March 10. Apparently this species has increased its former range; since at least 1988, it has been a summer resident at Alpine, Texas (Mark Lockwood).

White-throated Swift. *Aeronautes saxatalis*

Common summer resident and migrant; uncommon in winter.

In summer, it can be found almost anywhere high cliffs exist, from the lower canyons of the Rio Grande to the top of Emory Peak in the Chisos

White-throated Swift, *Aeronautes saxatalis*

Mountains. It also spends considerable time foraging over the open desert flats. Spring migrants move through the area from late March through May, but fall migrants are less conspicuous, although I observed a flock of 60 to 75 birds at PJ on July 27, 1968. Wintering birds can best be found in the river canyons on mild days. I counted 75 birds at SEC on December 22, 1967, and 45 near Boquillas Canyon on December 30, 1969. Also, Chris Weeks reported 10 to 15 birds at Persimmon Gap on January 2, 1984; and John Burkhart found eight to ten at Sotol Vista on December 3, 1979. This swift also utilizes a wintertime roost in a cave under the South Rim, and birds appear on mild days.

FAMILY TROCHILIDAE: HUMMINGBIRDS

Broad-billed Hummingbird. *Cynanthus latirostris*

Casual summer resident, and spring and fall visitor.

This gorgeous little hummingbird, with obvious white undertail coverts and a red bill, was first found in the park by Roy Quillin (1935), who discovered a nest containing eggs at the Johnson Ranch on May 17, 1934. It was not reported again until October 20, 1966, when Mr. and Mrs. Leon Bishop found one feeding on mountain sage along the Lost Mine Trail. I observed a lone male at Boot Canyon on August 7, 1969, and Terry Maxwell reported a female "feeding on [tree] tobacco on the river" at the Johnson Ranch on April 20, 1970. Although there were no additional reports during the 1970s, it was reported on five occasions during the 1980s: Bill Bouton, Dave Powell, and Vic Reister found a nest containing two young in a side wash off lower Blue Creek Canyon on May 26, 1981; Bonnie McKinney reported a male at Hot Springs on April 12, 1984; Jeff Selleck and Karen Boucher observed a female at the Old Ranch on May 7, 1986; Steve Matherly reported a male at RGV on March 30, 1988; and J. Beard discovered a male in the Basin at Window View on June 13, 1988. There also are two reports in 1991. Mark Lockwood found one in the Chisos Basin on May 18; this sighting was submitted and accepted by the TBRC. And Sue Wiedenfeld reported one feeding on tree tobacco along the Rio Grande at CC on November 13.

White-eared Hummingbird. *Hylocharis leucotis*
Rare summer visitor.

A female collected by Tarleton Smith in the Chisos Mountains on July 7, 1937, represents the first Texas record of this species. It has since been reported in the mountains on numerous occasions between April 27 and September 1; there are no indications of nesting. Records more than likely are spring wanderers and post-nesting vagrants. Most sightings are in July and early August at mountain sage blooming on the high slopes; there also are a few reports in and about the Chisos Basin campground: Ben Feltner reported one on August 4, 1974; Joe Kuban and John Lowley found a female there on June 7, 1980; and L. E. Sellers reported one on July 17, 1992.

Blue-throated Hummingbird. *Lampornis clemenciae*
Fairly common summer resident; casual spring migrant.

It can be surprisingly common in Boot Canyon in summer; I counted five pairs along a one-mile stretch on May 9, 1969, and 12 individuals there on August 9, 1969. It is less numerous during dry years. Birds do not arrive on their nesting grounds until early to mid-April, and they usually depart by mid-September; I found only three individuals in Boot Canyon on September 19, 1970, and there is a specimen at Texas A&M University taken at Boot Spring on September 26, 1955.

This large hummingbird nests high on Arizona cypress trees along the canyon, and Jody Palmer reported a female on a nest at the Old Ranch on June 13, 1981; she found young on July 16. Other rather dependable locations for seeing this bird in summer include Cattail Falls and Pine Canyon. While on its breeding territory, Blue-throats utter loud "seep" notes from a perch and constant "seep, seep, seep" notes in flight; these calls can be heard for a considerable distance. The sharp "chip" of the Magnificent Hummingbird is heard far less often.

Spring migrants are few and far between and can be found almost anywhere: Roy Hudson reported one at Lajitas on May 22, 1964; I observed a lone male at Boquillas Crossing on April 11, 1969; Barbara Pettit found a male at her feeder at PJ on May 19, 1978; Anne and Jim Bellamy observed one at CC on March 12, 1986; and Bonnie McKinney reported one feeding on the flowers of a tree tobacco at SEC on March 18, 1986.

Blue-throated Hummingbird, *Lampornis clemenciae*

Magnificent Hummingbird. *Eugenes fulgens*

Uncommon summer resident; casual migrant.

It is rarely seen below 6,000 feet, but Peter Koch observed one at Cattail Falls on April 28, 1967, and Barbara Pettit and George Howarth reported one at a feeder at PJ on May 25, 1978. This and the Blue-throat are the two largest of North America's hummingbirds. The male Magnificent, unlike the Blue-throat, has no white in the tail. Magnificent Hummers prefer the somewhat higher and drier pinyon-juniper-oak woodlands, whereas Blue-throats are more numerous in the moist canyons. However, Magnificent Hummers often frequent wet areas, especially waterfalls, such as Cattail Falls and the pour-off in Pine Canyon.

Although there is no proof of nesting, Magnificent Hummingbirds have been found in the park from April 1 to August 23 and are considered a nesting species. They have been reported for the Chisos Mountains regularly since 1955, when Keith Dixon first found one at Boot Spring on July 21 and 26 (Dixon and Wallmo 1956).

Lucifer Hummingbird. *Calothorax lucifer*

Fairly common spring, summer, and fall resident.

This little hummingbird with a decurved bill arrives in the park as early as March 8 and has been recorded as late as November 10; a May 7, 1901, report for the Chisos Basin by the U. S. Biological Survey was the first ever in the United States (Bailey 1905). During May, except on the Rio Grande floodplain, where Black-chins are more plentiful, it may be the hummer most commonly seen from the desert lowlands to the highest slopes of the Chisos Mountains. And when century plants are in bloom, usually from May through September, Lucifers can be found with patience, at just about any plant. Joe Kuban's study of hummingbirds in the Chisos Mountains (1977) suggested that Lucifers do better during dry years, when Black-chin numbers are reduced.

Nesting occurs almost anywhere above the low desert and below the forest and woodland habitats in the higher mountains. A nest discovered on a lechuguilla stalk by Warren Pulich and son (1963) near Terlingua on July 13, 1962, represented the first nesting record of this species for the United States. Since then, several nests have been found; during May and June 1982, Peter Scott located 24 nests between PJ and the Chisos Basin. Post-nesting birds frequent the mountain canyons; I counted eight males and seven females in Boot Canyon on August 9, 1969. By late August, highland birds begin to move into the lowlands, and they usually can be found in the lower mountain canyons until the second week of September, when there is a noticeable decline in sightings. From early October to November, they most often are seen in the lower parts of the desert and along the Rio Grande, where they frequent areas with flowering tree tobacco plants.

Lucifer Hummingbird, *Calothorax lucifer*

Ruby-throated Hummingbird. *Archilochus colubris*

Casual in spring; rare in fall.

There are only a handful of spring reports, ranging from one by Anne Bellamy at PJ on April 18, 1986, to a male reported for the RGV nature trail by Jim Cameron on May 11, 1968. There are no reports for June, but fall records extend from July 15 through October 19, apparently reflecting the arrival of post-nesting vagrants and migrants. Although most reports are from the lowlands, Greg Lasley found an adult male in Boot Canyon on August 18, 1990.

Black-chinned Hummingbird. *Archilochus alexandri*

Common summer resident and migrant; casual in winter.

Black-chins arrive the second week of March and immediately begin courtship and nesting on cottonwoods and mesquites along the Rio Grande. Two eggs already had hatched in a nest found at Boquillas Crossing on April 18, 1970; the young were ready to leave the nest on May 4 and were fledged by May 6 (Wauer). Nesting apparently continues through-

Black-chinned Hummingbird, *Archilochus alexandri*

out the summer; I found a nest with two eggs at RGV on June 12, 1970, and a young bird still in a nest in Panther Canyon (4,200 feet in elevation) on August 12, 1967.

Males begin to move into the Chisos foothills in late March, and by early July Black-chins can be found in the higher portions of the park. I counted 23 individuals along the Window Trail on July 19, 1969. Their numbers decline after mid-September, but they can usually be found along the Rio Grande during December and January. A February 13, 1987, report of two birds in SEC, by Bonnie McKinney, may be of wintering birds or very early spring arrivals. Like the Lucifer Hummingbird, finding Black-chins in winter is most likely to be located, sometimes with patience, at flowering tree tobacco plants.

Anna's Hummingbird. *Calypte anna*

Rare fall visitor; casual in winter.

Adrey Borell (1938) first collected one in the Chisos Basin on October 23, 1936, and Lena McBee and Lovie Mae Whitaker found one at Boot Spring on July 24, 1940. There were no other reports until 1967, when Kent Rylander and I collected an immature male near SEC on November 5 (Wauer and Rylander 1968), after which birds were seen several additional times in the SEC area during December, including one on the December 21 CBC. Since then, it has been seen along the Rio Grande on numerous occasions, and it apparently overwinters in the area some years; Betty Alex reported an immature male at PJ from early November to December 28, 1994. This normally western hummingbird has expanded its range eastward in recent years (Zimmerman 1973); it has been found throughout West Texas since the 1970s.

Costa's Hummingbird. *Calypte costae*

Sporadic visitor in spring, fall, and winter.

This tiny hummingbird of the western deserts has been reported only for March, May, August, and December. The first two records included a lone male at 7,000 feet on the Lost Mine Trail on August 7, 1966 (Wauer), and Dick Russell and I found one perched on an ocotillo at RGV on December 17, 1966. It was not reported again until 1983, when there were three sightings at RGV: Anne Bellamy found a male there on April 12, Debbie Liggett observed one on May 2, and Ben Feltner reported one on May 3.

Calliope Hummingbird. *Stellula calliope*
Rare fall migrant.

All of the park records occur in August, except for a pair of reports on September 17. This tiny Rocky Mountain species was first observed feeding on mountain sage in upper Boot Canyon on August 7, 1969 (Wauer). Wesley Cureton next reported one on the Emory Peak Trail, August 20, 1975. Rick LoBello and Marlene Igo found one at a feeder in the Chisos Basin on August 20, 1976; Elton Stilwell reported "three or four females" near the Pinnacles on August 22, 1978; and Barbara and John Ribble found a male at Boot Spring on August 6, 1982; probably the same bird also was observed by Greg Lasley on August 12 and Wendy Watson on August 15. Additional August reports include a male near the Chisos

Calliope Hummingbird, *Stellula calliope*

Basin Lodge on August 4 and 5, 1986 (John Arvin), and a male on the Lost Mine Trail on August 15, 1990 (Derek Muschalek, Willie Sekula, and Chuck Sexton), and one on the Pinnacles Trail on August 17, 1990 (Greg Lasley). There also are two September 17 reports, including one in Campground Canyon in 1986 (David Sibley) and a female on the Pinnacles Trail in 1989 (Bill and Sarah Bourbon).

Broad-tailed Hummingbird. *Selasphorus platycercus*

Common summer resident; fairly common migrant; casual in winter.

The Broad-tailed Hummingbird has been recorded every month, and in summer it may be the most numerous hummingbird in the mountain woodlands. I have found it along the Rio Grande as early as February 3, but it does not reach its nesting grounds until late March. I watched an adult defending a territory at Boot Spring on March 20, 1967, and Julie Hotchkiss, Becky Wauer, and I found an adult female feeding two fledged young at Laguna Meadow on May 17, 1969. There is some post-nesting movement to the lower slopes of the mountains when century plants begin to bloom in May, but mountain sage blossoms become dominant food sources for all the Chisos hummers by July. A high count of 26 Broad-tails was recorded in the vicinity of these red-flowering shrubs in Boot Canyon on August 9, 1969 (Wauer).

Hummingbird numbers in the mountains drop off dramatically by mid-September, when there is a general exodus throughout the park, except on the Rio Grande floodplain, where there is a slight increase. For the most part, hummingbird sightings through November and December are restricted to stands of flowering tree tobacco plants along the river.

Rufous Hummingbird. *Selasphorus rufus*

Common in late summer and fall; casual in winter and spring.

This is the first of the fall migrants to arrive in the mountains; males may appear as early as late June and are numerous at flower-covered slopes by late July. Charles Bender counted more than 50 Rufous Hummingbirds along the South Rim Trail on August 19, 1966, and Roger Muskat reported "at least 200" on a hike to Boot Canyon on August 26, 1984. Like other post-nesting hummers, Rufous prefer mountain sage to century plants. Its numbers decline considerably by mid-September, but a

Rufous Hummingbird, *Selasphorus rufus*

few individuals can usually be found at late flowering mountain sages until October; I discovered a male at a mountain sage half-way up the Lost Mine Trail on November 19, 1994. An occasional bird remains along the Rio Grande through December, January, and February, and the first of the northbound bird can be expected in early March.

FAMILY TROGONIDAE: TROGONS
Elegant Trogon. *Trogon elegans*
Casual winter and spring visitor.

There are only two acceptable reports of this tropical fruit-eater for the park. A female was present in the Chisos Basin from early January to mid-April in 1980. It was first reported along the Window Trail on January 8 by Ron Tibball and party; Norman Scott and Hope Spear also found it that day. The next day, Jerry and Nancy Strickling and Jim Shiflett saw it in the same vicinity. K. H. Husmann next reported it on February 10 near the Chisos Mountains Lodge, and C. L. Sackett, Jr., reported it near the stone cottages on March 9 and 16. It was last seen by Patricia Collins and Stephanie Frederick near Boulder Meadow on April 15. A second report of a male Elegant Trogon, along the Pinnacles Trail in lower Boot Canyon on April 29, 1993 by Beverly Van Dyke, was submitted to and accepted by the TBRC (Greg Lasley 1994).

Elegant Trogons have been reported for the park on a number of other occasions, but all of these are questionable because they are poorly documented and/or in very unlikely locations. These reports include one near the Chisos Basin sewage lagoons on May 9, 1969; a female at Boot Spring on August 29, 1972; a male on the Window Trail on February 21, 1988; and a male above the Old Ranch on November 24, 1989, and at nearby Burro Mesa Pour-off four days later.

FAMILY ALCEDINIDAE: KINGFISHERS
Belted Kingfisher. *Ceryle alcyon*

Fairly common migrant; rare winter visitor.

It has been recorded every month but June; records are absent only from May 14 to July 9. The earliest southbound birds may appear along the Rio Grande by July 10, but it becomes more numerous by early September to mid-October; a few individuals remain at ponds and appropriate stretches of the Rio Grande for several weeks. Spring migrants are most numerous from late March through April, with scattered reports to mid-May. The majority of the migrants and winter visitors occur along the river, but I found a lone bird at PJ on April 6, 1969, and one at 6,600 feet in Boot Canyon on September 28, 1969, and Suzanne St. Onge reported one in the Chisos Basin on September 8, 1979. Most sightings are of one or two birds, but I recorded six at RGV on October 3, 1968.

Green Kingfisher. *Chloroceryle americana*

Casual visitor year-round.

Although there were no park records prior to 1966, it has now been reported every month. However, most records are probably post-nesting wanderers along the Rio Grande, especially from mid-June through October. The majority of reports are from RGV, although it is likely to appear at any water area in the lowlands at any time of the year.

FAMILY PICIDAE: WOODPECKERS AND ALLIES
Lewis' Woodpecker. *Melanerpes lewis*
Casual fall and late winter visitor.

The earliest record is a bird collected at Boot Spring on May 1, 1935, by George M. Sutton (1935). It was next reported by Joseph and Harriet Woolfenden at RGV in January 1963; I found one flying over Boot Canyon on October 22, 1968; James Stovall and Doug Evans observed one at PJ on October 30, 1982; C. McIlroy reported one in Pine Canyon on February 22, 1985; Bonnie McKinney found one in the pinyons in Green Gulch on February 10, 1986; and the Rothe family observed one in the Chisos Basin campground on November 21, 1987.

Red-headed Woodpecker. *Melanerpes erythrocephalus*
Casual spring and summer visitor.

Records extend from April 3 (a 1974 report in Maple Canyon by J. Adkins) to May 7 (a 1991 report along the Window Trail by Arch C. Griffith, Jr.), and a July 27, 1936, observation in the Chisos Basin by Tarleton Smith. There also are three reports from RGV: on June 15, 1979 by Marge Eaton, Ann Ayers, and Gloria Hunter; in May 1981 by James Stovall; and on May 10, 1979 by Peter Scott and Bob Fieney.

Acorn Woodpecker. *Melanerpes formicivorus*
Common permanent resident.

This colorful bird is most numerous in the upper Chisos Mountain canyons but also frequents oak groves at the lower edge of the woodlands in late summer and fall. And there also are several records at a considerable distance from the mountain woodlands: Bonnie McKinney banded a male at Black Gap WMA on August 6, 1983; G. V. Oliver and J. M. Fitzgerald found one at Dugout Wells on August 18, 1975; Esequiel Richard found one at PJ on July 11, 1977; Bill Bourbon observed one at Terlingua on September 6, 1989; Elton and Brad Stilwell reported one at RGV on August 19, 1978; and I found one among the mesquites at Solis on November 11, 1967.

Acorn Woodpecker, *Melanerpes formicivorus*

There are several nesting records, all in live oak or pinyon trees from early May through July. There also are some interesting reports. A banded bird, found at Boot Spring by Mike Kelly, Maryann Santos, Kirk Anderson, and Dixie Douglas on March 16, 1977, was undoubtedly one of eight Acorn Woodpeckers that I had banded there in 1968, 1969, or 1970. And Paul Gerrish found a dead Acorn Woodpecker on the Boot Canyon Trail on October 10, 1969, shortly after an extremely heavy, 15-minute hailstorm had passed through the area.

Golden-fronted Woodpecker. *Melanerpes aurifrons*

Common year-round resident.

The status of this bird has changed dramatically since the first edition of this book. In 1973, it was consider a "rare migrant," based on less than a dozen park sightings; the 1985 edition listed it as a "rare spring migrant; rare nesting bird along the river;" but by the mid-1980s it had become a

Golden-fronted Woodpecker, *Melanerpes aurifrons*

common year-round resident at RGV, CC, and PJ. Now it is the dominant woodpecker wherever cottonwood groves occur along the Rio Grande.

Yellow-bellied Sapsucker. *Sphyrapicus varius*
Uncommon migrant; fairly common winter resident.

This and the following species were lumped under "Yellow-bellied" Sapsucker until the AOU split it into three species in 1983; two occur in BBNP. Records of Yellow-bellied Sapsuckers range from September 23 to March 29, and there is a late sighting of a lone bird at RGV, following a period of stormy weather, on May 3, 1969 (Wauer). It occurs throughout the wooded areas of the park in winter but is most easily found at cotton-wood groves in the lowlands, such as at RGV and CC. Migrants usually occur singly, but I found 20 or more birds at RGV on October 25, 1967.

Red-naped Sapsucker. *Sphyrapicus nuchalis*
Uncommon migrant and winter resident.

Although early park records of these sapsuckers are unclear, it appears that both winter in the park at about the same time, although the Red-naped birds, of western affinity, are somewhat less numerous than Yellow-bellied Sapsuckers, of eastern affinity. It also is of interest that Van Tyne and Sutton (1937) reported only Red-naped Sapsuckers (racial identity) taken in the Big Bend Country (two in the Chisos Mountains and three near Alpine) between 1914 and 1936.

Williamson's Sapsucker. *Sphyrapicus thryoideus*
Sporadic migrant and winter resident.

It was first reported by Richard D. Porter, who collected one in Pine canyon on October 18, 1957. There were no further reports until the 1967–68 winter, when it was seen on a number of occasions from October 28 through February 23. I did not see it at all during my six years' residency as chief park naturalist (1966–72), although Maurice Mackey reported one on the Lost Mine Trail on November 26, 1970, and Jim Tucker found one at Laguna Meadow on December 29 the same year. It was reported again during the winters of 1979–80 and 1980–81; during early spring in 1986, 1988, 1990, and 1995; and in the fall of 1983, 1984, and 1988. The majority of records are from the

Chisos Mountain woodlands, but Tom and Betty Alex found a female at PJ on February 4 and 5, 1995, and Mark Flippo reported a male there on February 12, 1995.

Ladder-backed Woodpecker. *Picoides scalaris*
Common permanent resident.

This is the common woodpecker of the Chihuahuan Desert, and it also occurs throughout the Chisos Mountain woodlands. I have found it nesting in cottonwoods, willows, oaks, pinyon pines, century plant stalks, utility poles, and wooden sign posts. Van Tyne and Sutton (1937) referred to this species as "Cactus Woodpecker," former name, and reported it to be an early nester from late April through June. Totals of 15 to 34 birds are normally recorded on CBCs at RGV.

Northern Flicker. *Colaptes auratus*
Uncommon year-round resident; common migrant and winter resident.

Big Bend's breeding flicker is of special interest because it represents the northern breeding population of the Mexican race (*nanus*) of the red-shafted form, which is resident in the United States only in the Chisos Mountains. Adult birds were discovered feeding young at a nest 12 feet high in a dead Arizona pine snag near Boot Spring on May 8, 1968 (Wauer). By early July, post-nesting birds disperse into lower elevations and can be found in the Chisos Basin and Green Gulch.

Flickers are most numerous in migration from late February to mid-April in spring, and mid-September through November in fall. Migrants and wintering birds can be expected anywhere, although they are most numerous below 5,600 feet elevation.

All of this information applies to red-shafted birds, although yellow-shafted (eastern) birds are rare in migration and sporadic in winter. Records of yellow-shafted flickers range from mid-October to late March, and the vast majority of sightings are from the lowlands near the Rio Grande; higher elevations reports are extremely rare.

FAMILY TYRANNIDAE: TYRANT FLYCATCHERS AND ALLIES
Tufted Flycatcher. *Mitrephanes phaeocercus*

One record.

The series of observations of this little tropical flycatcher at RGV represents the first time this bird has been recorded in the United States. It was initially discovered by Barbara Duplisea on the very cool morning of November 3, 1991; it was located and identified the following day by Duplisea and Jack and Gail Askew; and over the next several weeks, at least through January 17, 1992, it was observed, videotaped and tape

Tufted Flycatcher, *Mitrephanes phaeocercus*

recorded, and photographed by several hundred birders. Barry Zimmer and Kelly Bryan later prepared an article summarizing its presence that was published in the spring 1993 issue of *American Birds*. That article contained the following:

> The Tufted Flycatcher is resident from northwestern Mexico to the Andes of Western Ecuador (A.O.U., 1983). Within Mexico it occurs in the Sierra Madre Occidental from northern Sonora and western Chihuahua south to Chiapas. It is more localized in the Sierra Madre Oriental of eastern Mexico, but is regular at least as far north as the vicinity of Ciudad Victoria in southern Tamaulpias. Tufted Flycatchers are typically upper-elevation birds of montane pine-oak woodlands and cloud forests. Movement to the lowlands in winter, however, is of annual occurrence in varying numbers throughout most of the northern portion of its range. Small numbers of birds invade riparian habitat along the Rio Sabinas in southern Tamaulipas (elevation 300 feet) each winter. . . . Hence, the occurrence of the Tufted Flycatcher at Rio Grande Village (elevation 1874 feet), which at first seems odd for a montane species, fits into a normal pattern.

Olive-sided Flycatcher. *Contopus borealis*

Fairly common migrant.

Records extend from April 4 to June 8 in spring and from July 31 through October 4 in fall. Peaks seem to occur during the first two weeks in May and from late August to mid-September; I counted a high of 19 individuals in the Chisos Mountains May 12 to 15, 1967. Although most of the park records are from the mountains, there also are a few reports from the lowlands. And except for six individuals recorded by Bonnie McKinney at the RGV silt pond on September 12, 1983, all the reports are of one to three birds.

Greater Pewee. *Contopus pertinax*

Casual spring and fall visitor; two winter records.

Spring reports, all from the high Chisos Mountains, extend from an April 26, 1984 sighting at Boot Canyon by Anne and Jim Bellamy, to a

June 8, 1968, observation of a singing bird on Emory Peak above Laguna Meadow (Wauer). Fall reports range from mid-August to mid-September; four of these are from RGV: Morgan Jones and Steve Hawkins reported one on September 3, 1978; Bonnie McKinney found one there on September 12, 1983; and Charles and Louise Gambill recorded it on September 15, 1988. The two winter records, both from CC, include one by Jerry and Nancy Strickling on December 21, 1974, and William and Alice Roe reported one, perhaps the same bird, there on January 6, 1975.

Western Wood-Pewee. *Contopus sordidulus*
Abundant migrant.

Spring records begin with two very early sightings at RGV on March 3, 1967 (Russ and Marian Wilson), and near Persimmon Gap on March 15, 1971 (Wauer), followed by a lapse in reports until mid-April when greater numbers of northbound migrants reach the Big Bend area. The spring movement continues until June 12, reaching a peak between April 25 and May 18, when this bird can be found almost everywhere from the Rio Grande floodplain to the highest portions of the Chisos Mountains. Although there are no nesting records, I found a lone Western Wood-Pewee vigorously singing and defending a territory within the RGV campground on June 12 and 27 and July 13, 1971. It does nest in the Davis Mountains, 100 miles north of BBNP (Wauer and Ligon 1977, and Peterson, et. al. 1991). Post-nesting birds may reach the park as early as mid-July, and fall migrants are most numerous from August 6 to late September, after which there are a scattering of records to October 30.

Eastern Wood-Pewee. *Contopus virens*
Casual spring migrant.

Harry Oberholser (1974) reported that a specimen was taken in spring in the Big Bend area. There are only two additional records: I found lone birds at RGV and Boquillas Crossing on May 17, 1970. Since this Eastern Wood-Pewee is difficult to separate from the Western, it may be more common than these few reports suggest.

Yellow-bellied Flycatcher. *Empidonax flaviventris*
Casual migrant.

I collected specimens in lower Pine Canyon on September 3, 1968, and at RGV on September 1, 1969, and there are two spring reports: Bonnie McKinney found one in the Chisos Basin on May 7, 1983, and Richard Schneider reported one near Boot Spring on May 9, 1990. Because this bird is silent in migration and may be easily overlooked, it may be more common than the few records indicate.

Willow Flycatcher. *Empidonax traillii*
Rare migrant.

Several specimens have been taken within the park area: two males from Glenn Springs on August 6, 1928; one male from near Hot Springs on May 12, 1933; a male and a female from Boquillas on May 18 and 21, 1935; a male from San Vicente on May 20, 1935 (all by Van Tyne and Sutton 1937); another from Glenn Spring on June 17, 1932 (J. E. Jacot); one from Grapevine Spring on July 21, 1956 (Texas A&M University); one from a stock tank near PJ on June 14, 1968 (Dave Easterla); and one at RGV on August 25, 1967 (Wauer). Spring records range from May 9 through June 17, and fall records extend from a July 16, 1980, sighting at Castolon by Vernon and Anne Waters, to September 24. The great majority of fall records are from the lowlands. Although this flycatcher has nested near Alpine (Oberholser 1974), there are no actual nesting records in the park. The summer reports probably all represent late or early migrants or post-nesting vagrants. However, nesting is possible, and any territorial bird found in spring should be carefully monitored for that possibility.

Least Flycatcher. *Empidonax minimus*
Rare spring and uncommon fall migrant.

It has been recorded at all elevations but is most numerous in the lowlands. Spring records range from April 1 to May 28, and fall records extend from July 21 through October 10; southbound birds peak during the second week of September. Several specimens have been collected in the park. There are six at Texas A&M University: two taken at Grapevine

Spring on July 21 and 24, 1956; three from Oak Creek—one on May 27 and two on August 28, 1955; and one from Ash Spring on August 17, 1955. I collected four specimens in September at various elevations, and one in the Chisos Basin on May 3, 1967.

Hammond's Flycatcher. *Empidonax hammondii*
Fairly common spring and casual fall migrant.

This western flycatcher has been recorded at all elevations but is most numerous in the mountains. Spring records extend from March 24 to May 17, and fall records are limited to three reports: I found one along the Window Trail on August 24, 1971, Richard D. Porter collected one at RGV on September 6, 1968, and I observed another at Boot Spring on September 19, 1968. Additional specimens were taken from the Chisos Basin on March 24, 1935, from Laguna Meadow on May 3, 1935, from Boot Canyon on May 6 and 7, 1932 (Van Tyne and Sutton 1937), and from Boquillas Crossing on April 12, 1967 (Wauer).

Dusky Flycatcher. *Empidonax oberholseri*
Fairly common spring migrant; two fall records; sporadic in winter.

During the first week of May, this little flycatcher may be numerous within the Chisos Mountain woodlands and rare along the Rio Grande. The latest spring record is one on the Lost Mine Trail on May 24, 1995 (Dan and Barbara Williams). There are two fall records: Greg Lasley and Bret Whitney found and photographed two individuals within the burned area at Laguna Meadow on August 30, 1980, and I found one at Castolon on September 15, 1969. It is sporadic in winter; there were several records along the Rio Grande floodplain during the winters of 1968–69 and 1970–71, but I did not find it there during the winters of 1966–67 and 1969–70. I collected one bird from five observed near SEC on December 30, 1968; at least one remained through February 8, 1969.

Several additional specimens exist: E. C. Jacot took one at Boot Spring on May 5, 1932; M. M. Peet collected birds at Boot Spring on May 7, 9, and 15, 1932; and additional birds were taken in Pine Canyon by George M. Sutton on May 11, 1933, and by A. C. Lloyd on May 13, 1933 (Oberholser 1974). Other specimens were collected from Maple Canyon on

May 2, 1967, from Laguna Meadow on May 4, 1967, from Boot Spring on May 9, 1969, and from Green Gulch on May 16, 1968 (Wauer).

Gray Flycatcher. *Empidonax wrightii*
Uncommon spring migrant; rare in fall and winter.

It is most numerous in spring from early April to mid-May, and there are scattered records to June 6. Post-nesting birds appear as early as August 3 (John Gee in 1994), fall migrants are most numerous during early September, and winter records occur from November 10 to mid-February; curiously, there are no reports for October. Although spring sightings are primarily from the highlands and the fall reports are primarily from the lowlands, it usually can be found anywhere in migration. All of the winter reports, however, are from along the Rio Grande, mostly from RGV and CC. Although there are no indications of nesting within BBNP, it does nest in the pinyon-oak-juniper woodlands in the Davis Mountains (Jim Peterson, et. al. 1991).

There are numerous specimens from the park. Van Tyne and Sutton (1937) reported one from the Chisos Mountains on June 6, 1901, three males and seven females from the Chisos Mountains between May 5–23, 1932, a female from Pine Canyon on May 1, 1933, a male and two females from Pine Canyon on May 11–13, 1933, and a male and female from the Chisos Basin on April 26 and April 27, 1935. I took no specimens during my tenure; compared with most of the *Empidonax* species, this bird can be more easily identified in the field.

Cordilleran Flycatcher. *Empidonax occidentalis*
Rare summer resident; uncommon migrant.

Records range from April 1 through October 5. Breeding birds arrive in mid-April and remain through August. Nests are built on cliffs and overhangs along rocky canyons with a protecting canopy of trees. I found nest-building at Boot Spring on June 10, 1969, and fledged birds on July 19; David Wolf reported an adult feeding young there on August 22, 1968; and Anne Bellamy found a nest there on May 29, 1983. Fall migrants occur throughout the mountains and there are a few reports in the lowlands: lone birds were found at Dugout Wells on September 11, 1967, and September 11, 1968 (Wauer), and Bill and Sarah Bourbon reported one from Buttrill Spring on September 4, 1989. It has been found only once along the Rio Grande; I observed one at RGV on April 1, 1969.

Although Boot Canyon is the surest place in the park to find this yellowish flycatcher, it also nests in Pine Canyon. Van Tyne and Sutton (1937) reported a total of 13 specimens taken in Boot and Pine canyons between May 1 and July 21, from 1901 to 1935. This bird was earlier known as "Western Flycatcher," but was split from the western birds, now known as "Pacific-slope Flycatcher," by the AOU in 1983. It appears, from my examination of numerous reports, that the status of this bird in BBNP has declined since the first edition of this book (1973). BBNP is at the eastern edge of its range.

Black Phoebe. *Sayornis nigricans*

Common year-round resident; rare migrant.

Resident birds occur only along the Rio Grande and at a few scattered ponds; for instance, John Gee reported adults "feeding recently fledged young" at the Chisos Basin sewage lagoon on July 22, 1990. During a February 18, 1995 float-trip from RGV to about five miles into Boquillas Canyon, Carol Edwards found about 200 individuals. On March 26, 1969, nest-building was found inside the motel ruins at Hot Springs; a Say's Phoebe was building a nest not more than 50 feet away (Wauer). And Julie Hotchkiss observed fledglings being fed at SEC on May 20, 1969. Although this black-and-white flycatcher usually can be found easily before nesting, one must often search for it during the nesting period. Soon after mid-July, however, adults and young appear everywhere along the river and at adjacent ponds.

Migrants are few and far between but pass through the area from mid-March to mid-April and from early August through September. Sightings are all from the vicinity of the Rio Grande, except for a lone bird at the Old Ranch on September 9, 1966 (Wauer), Boot Springs on August 10, 1970 (Walter Boles, Jim Shields, and John St. Julien), PJ on September 2, 1977 (Danny Covos), Chisos Basin on March 14, 1981 (Rick LoBello), and Buttrill Spring on September 3, 1989 (Bill and Sarah Bourbon).

Black Phoebe, *Sayornis nigricans*

Eastern Phoebe. *Sayornis phoebe*

Fairly common winter resident; rare migrant.

Records extend from mid-October through mid-March, and there are a few reports of early and late migrants: Bonnie McKinney found four birds at RGV on September 12, 1983, and I recorded lone birds at RGV on March 29 and April 1, 1968. There are no reports away from the vicinity of the Rio Grande. It seems to have an affinity for human settings.

Say's Phoebe. *Sayornis saya*

Fairly common summer resident; common migrant and winter resident.

Some birds are permanent residents; I have banded and recaptured birds at PJ year-round. Breeding birds begin to nest in mid-March; I found nest-building underway at RGV on March 21, 1967. In 1968, a pair nested in the deserted Daniels House at RGV in April and again in July, and fledged birds were seen on May 10 and August 6; young birds left a nest at PJ on July 7, 1970; and a pair was nesting on a cliff 60 feet high along Campground Canyon on May 31, 1971 (Wauer). There is some post-nesting movement into the highlands, where birds can be seen on the highest ridges.

Migrants pass through the park from mid-March through mid-May and during September and October. Although the majority of the migrating Say's Phoebes are found in the lowlands, they occasionally are reported in Boot Canyon, along the Lost Mine Trail, and at other highland areas. From November through April, however, there are no reports above 5,500 feet.

Vermilion Flycatcher. *Pyrocephalus rubinus*

Common summer resident and migrant; fairly common in winter.

In adjacent Mexico, this gorgeous little bird is known as la *brasita de fuego*, or "little coal of fire." At RGV and CC, where it can be numerous at times, it is the park's most attractive resident. Nest-building begins in early March on cottonwood and mesquite branches five to 35 feet above the ground, usually in full view. I observed an adult male feeding a fledged youngster as late as August 1, 1967. There apparently is some post-nesting movement along the river and into the lowlands; the RGV population declines somewhat during mid-July, and Dick Rasp found one at Oak Spring on July 12, 1964. However, most of the breeding birds remain on their nesting grounds until late September.

The Vermilion Flycatcher is most numerous during the spring migration from March 7 through mid-April, when it may occur up to 4,500 feet; on March 25, 1995, Carol Edwards and I found at least 45 individuals at RGV; Margaret Littlejohn found birds at the Chisos Basin Ranger Station on March 29 and April 6, 1978. There are numerous spring reports from the desert lowlands, and it regularly visits PJ from March 7 to March 25,

Vermilion Flycatcher, *Pyrocephalus rubinus*

probably the peak of the northbound movement. Fall migrants are most numerous in September; there seems to be a hiatus during early October, with another wave of migrants during the third week of October, increasing the lowland populations. A few remain all winter at RGV and CC. CBCs at RGV annually tally two to six birds.

Dusky-capped Flycatcher. *Myiarchuis tuberculifer*

Casual spring migrant; sporadic summer and fall visitor.

A specimen reported by Van Tyne and Sutton (1937), taken by Edouard C. Jacot nine miles southeast of Glenn Spring on June 17, 1932, represents the first for Texas. It has since been reported a number of times in spring; records range from a very early sighting at Grapevine Hills on March 4, 1979 (Margie and Bob Sakol); Chuck Sexton photographed and tape recorded one in Pine Canyon on May 6, 1991; to a May 24, 1972 report at

Laguna Meadow by Margery Williams. And there are other scattered reports, one for each month: I found one along the upper Pinnacles Trail on July 7, 1969; Joe Marshall reported three in the Chisos Basin on July 8, 1962; Randy Pinkston, Willie Sekula, and Charles Bender found one near the Basin sewage lagoons on August 22, 1986; John Gee and Rich and Nanette Armstrong reported one from Pine Canyon on September 6, 1991; I recorded one at RGV on October 23, 1966; and the latest report is one seen and heard at RGV on December 19, 1977 (David Pashley). There is no evidence of nesting, although I found three singing birds in Boot Canyon on May 8 and 9, 1970, and Brete Griffen reported one near the K-Bar on May 7, 1982.

Ash-throated Flycatcher. *Myiarchus cinerascens*

Common summer resident and spring migrant; uncommon fall migrant; sporadic in winter.

From mid-March until late July, this is one of the park's most numerous birds. It nests along the Rio Grande floodplain, at desert springs and in arroyos, and upward into the highest parts of the pinyon-juniper woodlands. I recorded adults feeding young in a cavity in a cottonwood at Dugout Wells on May 16, 1968, feeding young at Juniper Flat on May 25, 1967, and nesting in a snag at Boot Spring on June 11, 1967. By the last of July, when summer birds leave their breeding grounds, it becomes uncommon; most reports are then from along the Rio Grande and in the desert washes. Although in other parts of the Southwest these birds gather in family groups after nesting, the majority of the late summer birds, as well as fall migrants that pass through the Big Bend until late September, are alone.

Wintering Ash-throats occur rather sporadically. Two or three individuals sometimes can be found at cottonwood and mesquite groves in the lowlands. I found it at RGV and near Castolon regularly during the winters of 1966–67, 1967–68, and 1968–69, but only twice during December, January, and February, 1969–70. During ten years (1985–1994) of CBCs at RGV, participants recorded it every year but 1989, with a high of eight birds in 1990.

Great Crested Flycatcher. *Myiarchus crinitus*

Casual fall migrant; two spring reports.

There were no records of this eastern *Myiarchus* for the park prior to 1968, but after that I found it regularly. All three specimens (collected at

Ash-throated Flycatcher, *Myiarchus cinerascens*

Castolon on September 15, 1969, and at RGV on September 16, 1970, and September 28, 1968) were juveniles. There are only two spring reports: Bill Bourbon found one at RGV on April 21, 1988, and Bill and Sarah Bourbon watched one "defending a water faucet" at CC on June 1, 1990.

Brown-crested Flycatcher. *Myiarchus tyrannulus*

Sporadic summer resident; rare migrant.

Records range from March 8 through September 13, and it is most numerous from May 6 to 27; I found six individuals at CC on May 26, 1968. It apparently nests some years; John Gee found two pairs of adults and a recently fledged youngster at CC on July 24, 1991. Post-nesting birds can be expected by late July; Anne Bellamy reported it at RGV from July 22 through October 9, 1986. Except for two records for the Chisos Mountains—one in the Chisos Basin on March 10 (NPS files), and Joe and Barbara Hirt reported two at the Basin campground on May 12, 1978—all reports are from the lowlands.

Sulphur-bellied Flycatcher. *Myiodynastes luteiventris*

Casual spring migrant; two fall reports.

On May 11, 1969, Jim Tucker, Doug Eddleman, and I discovered a lone bird at RGV; it represented the first known record for Texas. Since then, Glenn Lowe, Jr., reported one at Boulder Meadow on August 5, 1973; Ruth Snyder found one just below Laguna Meadow on May 9, 1976; and there are two separate reports for the mouth of Boquillas Canyon in 1980: A. R. Winshall discovered one on April 18, and Albin Zeitler found it there two days later. The latest report is one found at CC on a rainy November 13, 1991, by Sue Wiedenfeld.

Couch's Kingbird. *Tyrannus couchii*

Casual summer resident and migrant.

Records extend from an early sighting at Boquillas on April 27, 1966, by David T. and Roy Brown, through the summer and fall months, to an October 9, 1971 sighting at RGV (Wauer). During the summer of 1971, I found a lone bird defending a territory and building a nest on a cottonwood at RGV; it remained in the area near the pond behind the store from June 22 through August 4. As far as I could determine, it remained alone but continued to vigorously defend a territory. In the fall, I have recorded Couch's Kingbird on a number of occasions; one of three birds seen at CC on September 2, 1968, was collected, and the specimen was later identified as *couchii* by Allan Phillips.

Cassin's Kingbird. *Tyrannus vociferans*

Uncommon spring migrant; casual summer resident; casual in fall and winter.

Some years it nests at RGV and/or CC: I discovered a nest high on a cottonwood at CC on May 18, 1969, and a fledged bird was found there June 7; Barbara Pettit reported a pair with a nest on a cottonwood at RGV on May 17, 1977; and Keith Erickson and John Humphrey reported nest-building at RGV on May 30, 1979.

This kingbird is more common north of the park, along Calamity and Limpia creeks and in the Davis Mountains. Early spring migrants reach the Big Bend area as early as March 10, peak from late April to mid-May, and there are a scattering of records to May 31. Fall migrants trickle through the area from late September to the last of October; I found three at PJ on the evening of September 29, 1970. There also are three winter reports: RGV on January 11, 1978 (George Griffen), Hot Springs on February 22, 1984 (Virginia Simmons), and along the Window Trail on February 23, 1992 (Don Burt).

Thick-billed Kingbird. *Tyrannus crassirostris*

Sporadic summer resident; casual migrant and winter visitor.

The first park record, a lone bird found and photographed at the Chisos Basin sewage lagoons by Michael and O. R. Henderson on June 21, 1967, represents the first Texas record (Wauer 1967e). The next report was of a lone bird on the mesquite flats near Boquillas Canyon on December 23, 1970 (Wauer); it remained in this vicinity throughout the winter. Mrs. James Owen observed it in late February 1971; Captain and Mrs. E. B. Hurlbert, Becky Wauer, and I found it there on March 20; and Dave Easterla and Dave Snyder saw it on April 5. On May 25, 1971, I discovered a lone (perhaps the same) bird on the floodplain near San Vicente Crossing. Al Crockett reported one next at RGV on December 28, 1973; and Bonnie

Thick-billed Kingbird, *Tyrannus crassirostris*

McKinney found one near La Linda on April 1, 1982, and another at Persimmon Gap Ranger Station on September 30, 1983.

This tropical flycatcher was next reported for Boquillas Canyon on March 27, 1985, by Peggy Baker and Marilyn Troxel. Richard B. Henderson found one at RGV on July 30, 1985, and this bird apparently remained in the vicinity at least until September 24; it was observed by numerous birders. In 1986, it was reported at RGV on May 29 by L. and T. Army. Charles Easley found it there on June 2; John Arvin and Peter Scott observed it on August 6 and 7; Willie Sekula and Charles Bender reported it near the silt ponds on August 20; and it apparently remained at least to September 2 (Bonnie McKinney).

There were no 1987 reports, but in 1988, a Thick-billed Kingbird was discovered at CC on August 5; Greg Lasley's photograph represented only the fourth accepted state record (Lasley and Sexton 1989); it remained at least through September 18. It was next reported at CC on April 1, 1989 (Roxanne Gunter); Charles Callagan found it the next day; it nested in May and was verified by numerous birders; Bill Bourbon last found a pair of birds feeding a chick on June 30. Also in 1989, a pair of Thick-billed Kingbirds also nested at RGV: they were reported first by Ken and Betty Christopher on April 11; Charles Callagan found them there on April 13; Bill Bourbon found an adult feeding a chick on June 30; and Bill and Sarah Bourbon found them on and off through September 18.

Nesting pairs were reported at CC again in 1990 and 1991 by numerous birders, and there was a single 1990 report at RGV; Marguerite Gross, Tim Jenkins, and Robin Leong found one there on April 27. But there were no sightings reported anywhere in the park in 1992, 1993, and 1994.

Western Kingbird. *Tyrannus verticalis*

Rare summer resident; fairly common spring migrant; uncommon in fall.

Western Kingbirds nested on cottonwoods at PJ during June and July 1968 and 1969, on a willow next to the Rio Grande at RGV in June 1970, and on a tall cottonwood at RGV in the summer of 1971; nest-building was found on June 22, adults were feeding young on July 13, and a fledged youngster was seen there on August 4 (Wauer). There are also a number of nesting reports from CC in 1989 and 1992 (Bill Bourbon).

Spring migration begins as early as March 19 (1986 report by Bonnie McKinney), reaches a peak from April 28 to May 21, and there are scattered reports to early June. Most sightings are from the vicinity of the Rio Grande, but it has been seen almost everywhere below the Chisos woodlands. Fall migrants are few and far between and have been recorded as late as October 12 (Wauer). Most sightings are of lone birds, but family groups of three to five birds are also occasionally reported.

Eastern Kingbird. *Tyrannus tyrannus*
Rare migrant.

There are a scattering of spring reports from April 9 to June 11, and a very late migrant at Boquillas on June 28 and 29, 1978 (Tony Gallucci). Fall reports range from August 24 to September 18 (Anne Bellamy), and there is a late fall sighting at Lajitas on October 21, 1991 (Bill Bourbon). In addition, Josephine Potter reported one at RGV on February 18, 1977. Except for the April 9, 1988, report (at Boot Canyon by Harold Hedges), and a May 13, 1968, sighting at Dugout Wells (Wauer), all records are from the vicinity of the Rio Grande.

Scissor-tailed Flycatcher. *Tyrannus forficatus*
Uncommon migrant.

Spring records extend from an early bird found at the entrance to the Dagger Flat Road by L. Henley on March 20, 1986, many more to May 16, and there are scattered reports to June 28 (Wauer). Fall sightings range from an August 12, 1983 report, at RGV by Cynthia Simmons, through mid-October. The latest report is one by Rich Simmons and DeeRenee Ericks at RGV on October 20, 1985. Although there are no nesting records in the park, this graceful bird does nest on utility poles in and around Marathon.

Rose-throated Becard. *Pachyramphus aglaiae*
Casual in late winter, spring, and fall.

Reports of this tropical flycatcher are widely scattered from early February to October 22, but none are verified by a specimen or photograph. The earliest report is from the SEC picnic site, where Richard B. Starr found three males and two females on September 24, 1965. Craig Booth next reported one at Santa Elena Crossing on April 26, 1975. Jim and Natalie Baines observed one male and two females near the Chisos Basin campground on February 26, 1976; Ira Taylor reported one male near the Basin sewage lagoons on October 22, 1979; and M. F. Marchase observed a lone female there on February 7, 1982. In 1985, W. R. Furley reported one from CC, on May 4. Jay and Alfred Viola recorded it halfway down the Window Trail on February 7, 1992. And John Crim reported one at RGV on June 6, 1994.

FAMILY ALAUDIDAE: LARKS
Horned Lark. *Eremophila alpestris*

Uncommon migrant; rare winter visitor.

It has been reported for the park every month but July, August, and September, but it does not occur regularly anywhere. Most reports are of small flocks of three to four birds along the River Road, on Tornillo Flat, or in the Chisos Basin. It is more numerous on the sparse grasslands north of the park, and Van Tyne and Sutton (1973) found the remains of one "clinging to the spiked leaves of a low-growing yucca, where the carcass evidently had been impaled by a shrike."

FAMILY HIRUNDINIDAE: SWALLOWS
Purple Martin. *Progne subis*

Casual migrant.

There are scattered spring reports, ranging from one at Hot Springs on April 22, 1971 (Bert and Millie Schaughency), to June 11, 1936, north of the park, by Tarleton Smith. A male was collected at San Vicente on May 20, 1935 (Van Tyne and Sutton 1937). There are three fall reports: Alexander Sprunt, Jr., and John H. Dick found one at Hot Springs on July 24, 1951; Dave Easterla reported a female at RGV on August 17, 1972, and Anne Bellamy and Cynthia Simmons observed one at PJ on August 26, 1986. Except for two pairs reported by Ben Archer at RGV on May 7, 1985, all sightings are of lone birds.

Tree Swallow. *Tachycineta bicolor*

Uncommon migrant and casual winter visitor.

It is most numerous from early March to May 1 (Wauer) in spring, and from July 31 to September 9 in fall. And there are a few scattered reports in winter, including a flock of 13 birds at Rooney's on December 29, 1977 (David and Karl Wiedenfeld and Ed Gildenwater). All sightings are from the vicinity of the Rio Grande.

Violet-green Swallow. *Tachycineta thalassina*

Fairly common summer resident and spring migrant; rare fall migrant.

This species begins to move along the Rio Grande as early as February 18 (the Rothe family reported 10 at Hot Springs in 1990); it becomes more numerous from February 24 to April 11, and afterward is seen in the lowlands in spring only during stormy weather. Breeding birds reach their nesting sites in the mountains by mid- to late March, utilizing cliffs above 5,500 feet in Green Gulch, the Chisos Basin, upper Juniper and Pine canyons, and on Emory Peak. By the second week of July, nesting apparently completed, the majority of birds move elsewhere; there are only a few records for the park from July 7 through most of August. Southbound migrants begin to appear along the Rio Grande by the last few days of August. The fall migration is sparse but extends through October. There also is a single winter report: Raymond Fleetwood found two birds at RGV on December 28, 1965.

Northern Rough-winged Swallow. *Stelgidopteryx serripennis*

Fairly common summer resident; common spring migrant; uncommon fall migrant and winter resident.

It is most numerous from mid-February through May, when northbound migrants are passing through the area and summer residents are nesting; two pairs were seen carrying nesting materials into holes in a mud bank at Solis on February 21, 1969 (Wauer). Sightings continue throughout the summer at localized areas along the river, such as RGV, Hot Springs, Solis, and Castolon. There is a slight increase in numbers in late September as fall migrants move along the waterways. Wintering birds usually can be found in small flocks of three to a dozen along the Rio Grande. Recent (1985–1994) CBCs at RGV tally three to 22 individuals annually. Except for a small flock of birds seen at Dugout Wells on October 8, 1969 (Wauer), all park reports are from the vicinity of the Rio Grande.

Bank Swallow. *Riparia riparia*

Uncommon migrant in spring; rare in fall.

Although never found in numbers, and always with other migrating swallows along the Rio Grande, it is most numerous from February 24 through May 28. There are a few reports in fall, from August 17 to September 1, and there is a lone winter record: I found a lone bird at RGV on December 8, 1967.

Cliff Swallow. *Hirundo pyrrhonota*

Common summer resident along the Rio Grande and less numerous in the desert; fairly common spring and rare fall migrant.

The earliest spring reports are those by R. A. Wolinski at RGV in 1983: one with Violet-green and Rough-winged swallows on March 7, five more on March 12, and two on March 14. By mid-March it becomes numerous and nesting begins immediately at select sites adjacent to the river; sever-

Cliff Swallow, *Hirundo pyrrhonota*

al were seen nest-building in Boquillas Canyon on March 22, 1969 (Wauer). Early birds also reach bridges and cliffs a considerable distance from the river during normal nondrought years; I found 12 birds at nests on the upper Tornillo Creek bridge on March 25, 1969. And in wet years it nests on cliffs in rather inhospitable places, such as on Tornillo Flat. C. Phillip Allen searched for Cliff Swallow nests in 1963 and reported 53 at the upper Tornillo Creek bridge, 55 at Hot Springs, eight at the Alamo Creek bridge west of Castolon, and 21 at Devil's Den.

The bulk of the nesting birds leave their initial breeding sites by mid-July, but there apparently is a second nesting some years. I found occupied nests under the bridges at Nine Point Draw and upper Tornillo Creek during August 1970. Lone birds or small flocks of migrants can be expected along the Rio Grande until mid-October, and seven were found at Hot Springs on October 20, 1967 (Wauer).

Cave Swallow. *Hirundo fulva*

Rare summer resident and migrant.

Don Davis first found unoccupied nests in the twilight part of a cave along the eastern slope of Mariscal Mountain in January 1969. On May 27, he and I visited this area and found a total of 13 Cave Swallows using two caves; there were three active nests; and Cliff Swallows were nesting near the entrance of one of the caves (Wauer and Davis 1972). On July 17, Dave Easterla found 20 to 25 birds at these same caves and three more active nests. They were found nesting there again in May and July 1970. Also, on June 1, 1988, Jeff Selleck and Robert Rothe found a pair nesting under the roof overhang of the PJ public school. And Bob Reid reported Cave Swallows at the Cliff Swallow colony on Tornillo Bridge on May 29, 1992.

Migrants are few and far between, and sightings along the Rio Grande are difficult to separate from nesting birds. In total, it has been reported as early as March 29 (by Will Risser at Solis in 1994) to October 5, 1969, at RGV (Wauer). Surely, one found by Mike Austin at PJ on April 28, 1990, three found by Willie Sekula near Santa Elena Crossing on August 21, 1988, and 25 to 30 individuals found at RGV on September 14, 1968 (Wauer), are migrants.

Barn Swallow. *Hirundo rustica*

Common summer resident and migrant.

The earliest arrival date at PJ is March 2, 1983 (John Pearson). Nesting occurs on buildings at RGV, Castolon, PJ, and the Chisos Basin. The first young are usually fledged by late June; young left the nest at the RGV store on June 26, 1968 (Wauer). A second clutch is often produced in late summer; I banded nestlings at PJ on September 11, 1966, and September 2, 1968. It is most numerous in migration, and flocks of 15 to 50 birds can be found regularly along the river at least to October 24; there also is a late sighting at RGV on November 5 (Wauer). Migrants occur from the desert lowlands to the Chisos Mountains highlands.

FAMILY CORVIDAE: JAYS, MAGPIES AND CROWS
Steller's Jay. *Cyanocitta stelleri*

Sporadic winter and spring visitor.

There are two series of records for this crested jay. In 1972, it was found first on November 13 near Boulder Meadow by Mr. and Mrs. Don Troyer; Don Troyer found one in upper Juniper Canyon on December 12; it was recorded on numerous occasions in Boot Canyon from December 30 to April 5, 1973 (William King reported 6 to 8 birds); and K. C. Cummings and Gerald Brown reported 15 to 20 individuals on April 17. A second series of reports began on November 17, 1989, when Rick Fredrick, Robert Rothe, and Bryant Woods found one at PJ. One was next seen near the Chisos Basin Trailhead by Bernard Fay on January 3, 1990; one at the Pinnacles Trail Junction by Marjory Beaty on April 29; and John Forsythe reported it again at PJ on May 20, 1990.

There also are a number of isolated reports. The earliest was a lone bird seen by Mrs. Campbell Steketee at the South Rim on March 16, 1970; Zeke and Teresa Waters and Danny Kovos found one at PJ on June 20 and 21, 1977; William Hechroell reported one on Emory Peak on February 19, 1978; Judith Rose found four near the cottages in the Chisos Basin on April 14, 1991; and Earl Likes observed one in the Pinnacles area on July 29, 1992.

The nearest breeding population of this Western jay to BBNP is in the Davis Mountains, 100 miles to the north (Wauer and Ligon 1977).

Blue Jay. *Cyanocitta cristata*

Casual fall, winter, and spring visitor.

It was first reported for the park by Harold Brodrick, who found one at PJ on November 2, 1956. One stayed at Castolon from December 30, 1967 to February 6, 1968 (Jim Court and Wauer). It was next found again at Castolon, from February 3 (two by Gerald Maisel) to April 21 (Doris and Julian Darden) in 1976. And Bert and Millie Schaughency and Dean Amadon found one at RGV on April 29, 1977. It was recorded on numerous occasions in the 1980s, ranging from October 24, 1982, at Black Gap WMA (Bonnie McKinney) to May 26 and 27, 1984, in the Chisos Basin (Chuck Sexton). Records range from various elevations, from along the Rio Grande (at RGV on November 30, 1987, by Glenn and Penny Cureton) to approximately 6,000 feet on the Lost Mine Trail on November 9, 1985 (Diane Foster).

Scrub Jay. *Aphelocoma coerulescens*

Sporadic fall, winter, and spring visitor.

This jay was first recorded in the park in Green Gulch on December 28, 1967 (Wauer). It was next reported in 1976, between February 4 (four to six birds in the Chisos Basin by Gerald Maisel) through May 18 ("some below the Basin campground" by Randy Koroter), then at Laguna Meadow on November 7 (Rick LoBello), and Peter Scott found a pair in the Basin Campground on December 15. It was not reported again until 1979: Robert Harms found several along the Window Trail on January 4; LoBello heard and saw one in Blue Creek Canyon on March 20; and David Wolf and Rose Ann Rowlett reported three at the start of the Laguna Meadow Trail in the Basin on April 20. During the 1980s, it was reported on numerous occasions: from November 1, 1983 to June 5, 1984 (Panther Canyon by Anne Bellamy; Basin Campground by Jan and Will Risser; Emory Pass by Daryl and Margaret Giblin); Green Gulch on April 8 and 9, 1988 (LoBello); Buttrill Spring on September 4, 1989 (Bill Bourbon); and several times from November 10 (Green Gulch in 1989 by Wauer) to January 4 (Old Ranch in 1990 by Charles Callagan); and again at the Old Ranch on May 2, 1991 (Wauer). Finally, Carol Edwards found one at PJ on February 23 and April 23, 1995. With only a few exceptions, Scrub Jays appear to stay below the forested slopes where the dominant Mexican Jay is so numerous.

Mexican Jay. *Aphelocoma ultramarina*
Common permanent resident.

This jay was known as "Gray-breasted Jay" for several years until its earlier name was restored by the AOU (according to Van Remsen). It is one of the most conspicuous birds of the Chisos Mountains, where flocks of five to 18 individuals are commonplace. CBC participants tallied 25 in 1966, 222 in 1967, 180 in 1968, 18 in 1969, and 106 in 1970. Nesting occurs during April, May, and June; I found nests on a Grave's oak near Laguna Meadow on May 8, 1970, and on an Emory oak near the Window on May 11, 1968. Anne Bellamy found a nest she referred to as a "large arrangement of disarranged small sticks," at Boot Springs on May 29, 1983; and C. Phillip Allen reported fledged birds at Boot Spring on June 1, 1963. There apparently is some movement to lower elevations during some winters. I found one in upper Big Brushy Canyon, in the northern part of the Dead Horse Mountains, on October 13, 1969, and another at RGV on December 13, 1969.

Mexican Jay, *Aphelocoma ultramarina*

Clark's Nutcracker. *Nucifraga columbiana*

Casual winter visitor.

John Galley (1951) was the first to find one, on the Lost Mine Trail on October 16, 1950. Mr. and Mrs. Forrest Rowlands reported five there on October 30, 1966. Paul and Carol Krausman and John and Mary Bissonette watched one feeding in their yard at PJ on November 9, 1972. E. Kendall and L. Feazel next reported one in upper Juniper Canyon on February 28, 1979. And Elton Stilwell found one at the stone cabins in the Chisos Basin on January 1, 1993.

Chihuahuan Raven. *Corvus cryptoleucus*

Rare spring migrant; casual during the remainder of the year.

Although there are park records every month but January, it can be expected in the park only from mid-March into early May. Afterward there are scattered reports through early June, again during the first two weeks of July, and then only one per month during the remainder of the year. North of the park in the Marathon and Alpine areas it is a reasonably common nesting bird, constructing loose, stick nests on utility poles and isolated yuccas and mesquites. The status of this raven in the park has apparently changed since pre-park years when much of the area was heavily grazed. It was more numerous then; Van Tyne and Sutton (1937) reported that it was common and nesting in the lowlands all around the Chisos Mountains.

Common Raven. *Corvus corax*

Common permanent resident.

This is the raven common throughout the park; the smaller Chihuahuan Raven is only occasionally reported, and only in the lowlands. Common Ravens nest in early spring. Bruce Talbot reported a nest in Hot Springs Canyon on April 12, 1983; young were fledged from a nest on Tornillo Flat in mid-April 1968; I found adults feeding nestlings in lower Hot Springs Canyon on May 4, 1970; Ansel Atkins reported a nest on Vernon Bailey Peak, visible from the Chisos Basin campground, on May 3, 1985; and Tom and Betty Alex found two adults and two fledglings at Hot Springs on June 12, 1983.

Post-nesting birds residing near the mountains roost in the highlands and move into the desert to feed each morning; they often are found

Common Raven, *Corvus corax*

patrolling the roadways early each morning to feed on any roadkills not already claimed by the nighttime scavengers. They often can be found soaring over the mountain ridges and peaks in the afternoons: I found 43 birds over the South Rim on May 10, 1969, and 32 circling over Boot Canyon on October 22, 1967. Bill Bourbon found more than 95 ravens soaring over Toll Mountain on October 13, 1988; Betty and Tom Alex counted more than 200 birds along the Maverick Road on October 17, 1984; and Frank Deckert reported a flock of 65 Common Ravens flying northward over PJ on October 26, 1979. In winter, more than 40 individuals commonly use a deep cut in a cliff near the Boot Canyon Pouroff as a nightly roost.

FAMILY PARIDAE: TITMICE

Tufted Titmouse. *Parus bicolor*

Common permanent resident.

This black-crested tit of the mountains nests during April, May, and June; nest-building was found at Juniper Spring on May 1, 1932 (Van Tyne and Sutton 1937), I found a nest at Juniper Flat on May 20, 1967, and adults were feeding young at Boot Spring on June 11, 1967. It occasionally wanders into the lowlands. There are several reports at RGV: I found birds there from November 11 to December 12, 1969; David Wolf reported an immature bird on September 7, 1973; J. Speer found one on January 6, 1983; Cynthia Simmons found one on February 18, 1984; and C. L. Skulski reported one on November 19, 1989. This bird was once known as "Black-crested Titmouse," but it was lumped with the Tufted Titmouse of the Eastern U.S. by the AOU in 1983.

FAMILY REMIZIDAE: VERDINS

Verdin. *Auriparus flaviceps*

Fairly common permanent resident.

This little bird can be difficult to find, but a search along the desert washes and at mesquite thickets along the river is sure to produce one or more. It usually can be detected first by its distinct high-pitched call note. Nesting is most common in April, May, and June, but late summer nesting is not unexpected. There is some post-nesting wandering; I found one at Laguna Meadow on October 18, 1969. Wintertime nest-construction does not signify nesting; the species maintains nests that also are utilized for roosting year-round.

Tufted Titmouse, *Parus bicolor*

FAMILY AEGITHALIDAE: BUSHTIT
Bushtit. *Psaltriparus minimus*

Common permanent resident.

During most of the year, Bushtits occur in flocks ranging in size from small family groups of eight to ten birds to much larger groups of 45 and 55 individuals. They usually are easy to locate because they constantly call to one

Verdin, *Auriparus flaviceps*

another as they move through the woodlands, feeding on insects gleaned from the foliage. Their calls may be heard from as far away as 200 feet. During the nesting season, they may be more difficult to find because they usually are quiet when incubating or feeding young. Nests have been found from mid-March to early June, usually with difficulty, because they are placed in the dense foliage of junipers and pinyons. I discovered a nest among mistletoe on a drooping juniper in Boot Canyon on May 8, 1969, and a nest found in 1901, by F. M. Bailey in the Chisos Mountains, was described as follows: "12 to 15 feet from the ground in a nut tree, a greenish bag 6 to 8 inches long, made of lichens, oak flowers, and catkins, woven with cocoon silk" (Van Tyne and Sutton 1937).

Bushtits come in two phases, black-eared and plain. The two phases were once considered two separate species, but studies in Arizona, New Mexico, BBNP, and Mexico proved that most of the black-eared birds were merely juvenile males (Raitt 1967). Some breeding males also may possess the black ears; I found a black-eared bird copulating with a "plain" bird near the Window on March 19, 1967. It also is possible to see black-eared birds feeding plain birds and vice versa. Adults have been found to lay a second clutch of eggs before the first young have left the family; black-eared fledged birds actually help feed their younger siblings. Additional information about these birds can be obtained by reading *The Birds of Arizona,* by Allan Phillips, Joe Marshall, and Gale Monson (1964:111–113).

FAMILY SITTADAE: NUTHATCHES
Red-breasted Nuthatch. *Sitta canadensis*
Sporadic migrant and winter visitor.

This bird is reasonably common some years but completely absent others. Records extend from September 16 (one reported by Vicki Glen from the East Rim in 1982) through the winter to one at the Old Ranch from May 10 to 12, 1988 (Brad Vaughn and Bruce Hallett). Although the vast majority of the reports are from the Chisos Mountains, it also has been reported a few times from RGV and CC. And except for two individuals at Boot Spring on May 3, 1979 (Walter Ellison and Rick Prum), two in Juniper Canyon on April 22, 1986 (Charlie Callagan), and two at Boot Spring on May 2, 1992 (Wauer), all reports are of lone birds.

White-breasted Nuthatch. *Sitta carolinensis*
Uncommon permanent resident

In summer it can best be found at Laguna Meadow and Boot and Pine canyons among the tall pines and cypress. There is some wandering into the lowlands in the fall: one was reported in the Chisos Basin on September 1, 1950, and I found two at RGV September 9 through 12, 1969. The

Chisos Mountain population of White-breasted Nuthatches represent the Mexican race *mexicana* that extends south to Central America; the Davis and Guadalupe mountain populations are *nelsoni,* the Rocky Mountain race (AOU 1957).

Pygmy Nuthatch. *Sitta pygmaea*
Sporadic winter visitor.

Records range from November 27 (in 1981 at Boot Spring by C. Strum) to a series of winter and spring sightings in Boot Canyon from January 28 to April 15, 1967 (Wauer and Russ Wilson). The largest number of birds—five individuals—was reported by Ted Eubanks for Pine Canyon on November 28, 1987. This species nests to the north in the Davis Mountains and about 50 miles to the southeast in Mexico's Maderas del Carmen.

FAMILY CERTHIIDAE: CREEPERS
Brown Creeper. *Certhia americana*
Sporadic migrant and winter visitor.

Records extend from October 20 (lone birds found in the Chisos Basin and at Boot Spring in 1968 by Wauer) through May 19 (one at the Old Ranch in 1975 by Stephen Churchill). The Brown Creeper was quite common at RGV and less numerous in the Chisos woodlands during the 1967–68 winter. I did not find it during the following two winters, but it was present again in the winter of 1970–71, and there were reports in 1975 and 1979, as well. And I found two individuals at RGV on November 17, 1990.

FAMILY TROGLODYTIDAE: WRENS
Cactus Wren. *Campylorhynchus brunneicapillus*
Common permanent resident.

This large desert wren can hardly be missed because of its loud and raucous songs and conspicuous, football-shaped nests. Nest-building occurs year-round, and almost every kind of tree, shrub, and man-made structure has been used. Bill Degenhardt found a nest in a pair of shorts hanging on a line, and my wife discovered a nest in the fold of a sheet one time and in the pocket of my field pants another. There are two interest-

Cactus Wren, *Campylorhynchus brunneicapillus*

ing records of behavior: I found one eating several chilipitins (ornamental peppers) at PJ on November 27, 1978, and Robert DeVine watched one tear apart an active Barn Swallow nest, tossing the nestlings out, at PJ on June 30, 1980.

Rock Wren. *Salpinctes obsoletus*

Uncommon summer resident; common migrant; fairly common winter resident.

Summertime birds may be found from the cliffs along the Rio Grande to the top of Emory Peak. Rock Wrens almost always can be found at Hot Springs, along the RGV nature trail, and along the lower end of the Window Trail. Van Tyne and Sutton (1937) reported a nest with five eggs at Lajitas on May 10, 1935; Henry Howe found it nesting at Grapevine Hills on July 23, 1966; and I found three fledged young on the rocky slope below Laguna Meadow on July 20, 1969.

About the first week of September there is a brief spurt of migrants through the area. Some years this movement increases dramatically from mid-October until early November, when birds are numerous below 5,500 feet. Many apparently remain as winter residents, but wintering birds may be somewhat sporadic: Chisos Mountains CBC participants recorded 15 in 1966, 14 in 1967, 129 in 1968, 14 in 1969, and 47 in 1970. Another increase in birds is evident in mid-March, and northbound migrants continue to pass through the area until the second week of April.

Canyon Wren. *Catherpes mexicanus*

Common permanent resident.

This is the bird with the wonderful clear, descending and decelerating whistle song. Although it prefers rocky cliffs and canyons for nesting and singing, it also spends considerable time foraging for food in the mesquite thickets along the Rio Grande and in lowland washes, and also in the pinyon-juniper-oak woodlands. Nest-building was found just above the Wilson Ranch house in Blue Creek Canyon on April 5, 1969, and adults were seen feeding young at Boquillas on May 24, 1969 (Wauer). Also, during the very dry spring of 1995, on March 24, I discovered a pair of Canyon Wrens within the RGV campground carrying nesting materials into the open hitch of a fifth-wheeler.

Carolina Wren. *Thryomanes ludovicianus*

Casual summer and winter visitor; rare migrant.

Although there are no records of nesting, it probably is only a matter of time. On March 25, 1995, I heard three separate singing birds from along

Canyon Wren, *Catherpes mexicanus*

the RGV nature trail. This eastern wren has been reported every month
but October. It is most numerous from mid-March to mid-April and from
mid-August to mid-September. Although most records are for the lowlands, especially Boquillas and RGV, it also has been recorded in the highlands: C. Phillip Allen found one at Laguna Meadow on May 28, 1963;
Rose Ann Rowlett reported one from Boot Spring on June 4, 1965; David

Simmon found one in the Chisos Basin on August 31, 1967; and Greg Lasley heard one singing at Boot Spring on August 17, 1990.

Bewick's Wren. *Thryomanes bewickii*

Abundant summer resident; fairly common migrant and winter resident.

This is the most numerous summering bird in the park's pinyon-juniper-oak woodlands and only slightly less numerous at thickets down to about 4,000 feet. Singing birds are commonplace throughout the park woodlands, and their vast repertoire of songs can be very confusing. Migrant Bewick's Wrens move through the area from early March to early April in spring, and from late August through October in fall. Migrants and wintering birds can be expected anywhere, but from April 10 to August 27, it occurs only above approximately 4,500 feet.

House Wren. *Troglodytes aedon*

Fairly common migrant; uncommon winter resident.

Migrants are most numerous from early April to May 12 in spring and from early September to early November in fall. They may be found from the Rio Grande floodplain to the high Chisos canyons. Some years there appears to be a second fall movement from mid-November to early December. Wintering bird populations are rather stable and usually can be found at Boquillas Crossing, along the RGV nature trail, near Santa Elena Crossing, and along the Window Trail.

There also are six records of the southern brown-throated form of House Wren, known prior to the 1983 AOU reclassification as "Brown-throated Wren": I found one in the Chisos Basin on December 3, 1966; T. Paul Bonney reported one at Laguna Meadow on May 19, 1973; Gail Hodge, Georgia Porter, and Rose Marie Stortz found one in the Basin on May 3, 1975; Chuck Sexton and Greg Lasley reported a well-documented sighting at RGV on May 15, 1979; Frank Oatman found one below Laguna Meadow on January 16, 1989; and Michael C. Williams reported one in the Basin on July 22, 1989. The Brown-throated Wren is a common nesting bird in Mexico's Maderas del Carmen, 50 miles southeast of the park (Wauer and Ligon 1977).

Winter Wren. *Troglodytes troglodytes*

Rare migrant; early winter visitor.

Records extend from November 10 through May 20. Northbound birds usually can be detected by their very distinct song, which they sing over and over again during the early morning. Spring migrants are most numerous between mid-March and mid-April. Fall migrants are most numerous from November 20 to 24. Except for a sighting at Laguna Meadow on November 15, 1966 (Wauer), one at the Chisos Basin sewage lagoons on May 20, 1978 (Roy Welch), and one at Neville Spring on March 24, 1984 (Will and Jan Risser), all records of this tiny wren are from the vicinity of the Rio Grande.

Sedge Wren. *Cistothorus platensis*

Casual winter visitor and spring migrant.

There are scattered reports from December 18 through May 14, all from along the Rio Grande. I first found one near Boquillas Crossing on February 14, 1967. Mark and Jeanne Leckert next reported one at the Gravel Pit on December 13, 1971. Victor Emanuel found one at the Boquillas Canyon Overlook on February 14, 1976; J. R. Bider reported one at RGV on March 8, 1977; Robert Harms reported it at Boquillas on January 2 and 5, 1979; Bruce Talbot found one at Terlingua Creek Junction on April 18, 1984; and L. E. Ramsey reported two near SEC on February 10, 1986.

Marsh Wren. *Cistothorus palustris*

Fairly common spring migrant; uncommon fall migrant and winter resident.

There is a report of a bird carrying nesting materials at RGV on March 27, 1979 (R. Rogers), but there is no further evidence of nesting. It is entirely absent from the park from mid-May to early September. The bulk of the spring migrants pass through the area from mid-March to early May, but a few stragglers have been reported as late as May 20 (Wauer). During the peak of the northbound movement, during the last week of March and the first week of April, this wren is occasionally found a considerable distance from the river. I found one at Oak Creek on March 26 and another at PJ on March 30, 1968.

Fall migrants are not as numerous as those in spring, with the bulk of the southbound migrants passing through the park from mid-October to mid-November. Wintering birds occur at cattail areas along the river, such as the silt pond and beaver pond at RGV, where they usually are detected first by their rapid, jumbled songs. CBC participants at RGV tally three to nine birds annually.

FAMILY CINCLIDAE: DIPPERS
American Dipper. *Cinclus mexicanus*
Casual winter resident.

There are only five or six records for the Big Bend area. Steve Zachary and Jim Walker first reported one on upper Fresno Creek, February 25, 1975, that "flew from under a waterfall—landed on a rock—bobbed up and down." Bonnie McKinney next reported one at a creek just east of the Agua Fria Ranch headquarters, 65 miles south of Alpine, on November 12, 1980. Next, there was a series of reports at The Window in 1985 and 1986: Harold and Myrtle Hill discovered it first on December 10; Paul Motts found it there on December 15; Paul and Billie Demant reported it on December 20; Alan Van Valkenburg on December 31; and Bonnie Neathery found it there on March 16. Also, Bill Pulliam found it (assumedly the same individual) at nearby Cattail Falls on March 12, 1986. In addition, James Morlock found one in the Lower Canyons on January 16, 1988, and Gary Emerson reported one at Hot Springs on March 19, 1988.

FAMILY MUSCICAPIDAE: KINGLETS, GNATCATCHERS, AND THRUSHES
Golden-crowned Kinglet. *Regulus satrapa*
Sporadic migrant and winter visitor.

Records range from October 20 to March 4, and there is a late sighting at Boot Spring on March 31, 1968 (Wauer). A few Golden-crowned Kinglets usually can be found within the Rio Grande floodplain vegetation below SEC almost any winter, but the species' occurrence elsewhere is very irregular. During the winters of 1966–67 and 1967–68, I found it regularly in the high Chisos woodlands but could not find it in 1968–69 or 1970–71. High counts included 20 birds along the trail from Boot Spring to the South Rim on January 28, 1967, and more than 25 individuals, along with a "wave" of Brown Creepers and Ruby-crowned Kinglets at RGV on October 27, 1967 (Wauer).

Ruby-crowned Kinglet. *Regulus calendula*

Abundant migrant and winter resident.

This bird can be the most numerous species on the Rio Grande floodplain and in the higher parts of the mountains from early October through the first week of May. Records extend from as early as August 17 to as late as May 20, and there also is a much later report at Boot Spring on June 15, 1987 (David Narins). Winter residents may be somewhat sporadic; CBC tallies ranged from a low of eight to a high of 336 individuals on ten (1985–1994) counts at RGV.

Blue-gray Gnatcatcher. *Polioptila caerulea*

Common summer resident; fairly common migrant; sporadic winter resident.

Breeding Blue-gray Gnatcatchers are restricted to the mountain woodlands where nesting is well under way by late March. I found three nests under construction in Boot Canyon on March 30, 1967. Summer birds remain on their breeding grounds until late August, when they begin to move out of the area. Southbound birds reach the park at about the same time, and the fall migration continues to about October 20. Wintering birds are somewhat sporadic in occurrence: three to five individuals were located on each of six (1966–1971) Chisos Mountains CBCs, except in 1969, when none were found. Most years it also is recorded on the RGV CBC; a high count of 19 was tallied in 1986. Spring migrants are most numerous from mid-March to mid-April.

During migration, when two species of gnatcatchers may be found together in the lowlands, they can be difficult to tell apart. Black-tails do not always possess a tail with solid black underparts, and Blue-grays often show considerable darkness in their tail underparts. However, their calls are very distinctive, and squeaking and "spishing" will usually solicit vocalizations: Black-tail calls are sharp and buzzing, while those of Blue-grays are wheezy or plaintive.

Black-tailed Gnatcatcher. *Polioptila melanura*

Common permanent resident.

This desert gnatcatcher nests from March through June. Mr. and Mrs. Murl Deusing found a nest with one egg on an allthorn at Dugout Wells on May 17, 1967; James Swartz reported a nest near the PJ visitor center on May 18, 1982; and I found a nest containing two gnatcatcher eggs and a single Brown-headed Cowbird egg on a mesquite at Nine Point Draw on June 6, 1969. Before nesting, Black-tails are vociferous, but they become quiet and sometimes difficult to find while nesting. As soon as the young are fledged, however, they again can be detected by their constant, loud buzzing calls. There is some post-nesting dispersal into higher elevations: Greg Lasley, Chuck Sexton, Derek Muschalek, and Willie Sekula reported one at 5,750 feet on the Lost Mine Trail on August 15, 1990, and Lasley found "several on the upper Window Trail" in August 1994. Although it is considered to be a year-round resident, there is an obvious decline in numbers during November and an increase in numbers in mid-February. A search among the open mesquite flats along the Rio Grande from Boquillas to SEC and along the lower desert washes always will disclose at least a few of these little desert birds.

Eastern Bluebird. *Sialia sialis*

Uncommon and somewhat sporadic winter and spring visitor.

There is one record of nesting: on April 15, 18, and 23 and May 2, 1972, I observed an adult male feeding four spotted youngsters at RGV. The fledglings were barely able to fly on April 15. There have been no additional reports of nesting.

Records extend from a November 7, 1987, report of two pairs at RGV (Cynthia Simmons), through the winter, to May 3, 1969 (Wauer). Most of the reports are from the open flats near the Rio Grande, but I found three birds in the Chisos Basin on December 23, 1969, and Charles Callagan reported seven along the Pinnacles Trail on December 30, 1989.

Western Bluebird. *Sialia mexicana*

Rare migrant; fairly common winter visitor.

Records range from October 23 to March 31, and there are two late spring or summer reports: C. Phillip Allen found it at Boot Spring on May 24, 1963, and Bonnie McKinney reported one near the Chisos Basin Amphitheater on July 19, 1983. There is no evidence of nesting. In winter, 20 to 30 birds frequent Boot Canyon, Laguna Meadow, and Emory Peak during mild days and move into the lower Basin during colder days. These birds spend considerable time soaring along the upper ridges and pinnacles. On November 4, 1967, I found a flock of 17 in the pinyon-juniper woodlands above Boot Spring; 12 of those were eating mistletoe berries.

Western Bluebird, *Sialia mexicana*

There also are occasional reports for the lowlands from RGV west along the River Road to SEC.

Mountain Bluebird. *Sialia currucoides*

Casual migrant; sporadic winter visitor.

Records extend from early November through March, and Van Tyne and Sutton (1937) reported specimens taken from Castolon on May 6, 1935, and a male seen at 6,000 feet in Pine Canyon on May 9, 1933. Most of the recent records are from the lowlands, including a high count of 60 to 75 birds on a grassy flat near San Vicente on November 11, 1967 (Wauer). Some winters this species is abundant in the open valleys north of the park; Bonnie McKinney reported a flock of 100 to 150 birds on the grassy flats of the Agua Fria Ranch from October 1980 through March 1981. She told me that some of these birds "roosted in Elf Owl nesting cavities in corral posts."

Townsend's Solitaire. *Myadestes townsendi*

Fairly common migrant and winter resident.

The first of the fall migrants reach the park the first week of October, and the southbound movement continues until late November. Several birds were found eating berries of Texas madrones along the Emory Peak ridge on November 15, 1966 (Wauer). Winter residents never are numerous but usually can be found at preferred localities: along the lower Window Trail, in Laguna Meadow, along the Emory Peak ridge, and in lower Boot Canyon. Spring migrants pass through the Big Bend from the last of March to mid-April, and there is a second movement from late April to mid-May. Except for a single report at Boquillas on April 6, 1991 (Deborah Macmillan), all reports are from the Chisos Mountains.

Veery. *Catharus fuscescens*

Casual spring migrant.

There are only a handful of sightings, ranging from a March 18, 1969, sighting at RGV by George Shier, to three reports at the Old Ranch on May 9, 10, and 12, 1980, by Jim Shiflett and C. C. Wiedenfeld, Richard Derdeyn, and Linda Snyder, respectively; it was photographed by Shiflett and

Wiedenfeld. There are two reports for Boot Spring: Byron Griffen found one on May 3, 1970, and Robert Hopkinson reported one on May 2, 1984.

Gray-cheeked Thrush. *Catharus minimus*
Casual spring migrant.

Records range from three birds reported by Chris White in the Chisos Basin on March 5, 1987, to one found by Linda Snyder at the Old Ranch on May 12, 1980. Except for birds found at Glenn Spring by George Shier on April 17, 1970, and another at SEC by Dave Easterla and Dave Snyder on April 7, 1971, all reports are from the highlands.

Swainson's Thrush. *Catharus ustulatus*
Uncommon migrant; two winter records.

Spring sightings extend from March 19 to May 20, fall records range from September 1 to October 21, and there are two winter reports: Ed Kutac found one at Laguna Meadow on February 19, 1978, and Helen and George Champtax reported one from the Window Trail on December 8, 1978. Except for a May 7, 1971 sighting at RGV (Wauer), all spring records are from the mountains; fall migrants have been recorded at all elevations.

Hermit Thrush. *Catharus guttatus*
Common migrant; fairly common winter resident.

Early fall migrants may reach the Big Bend area by September 8, but the main southward movement does not begin until late September, reaching a peak in the middle of October, and then gradually declining until early November. Late influxes of migrants are not uncommon; many birds were recorded along the Rio Grande on December 22, 1968, and I counted more than 100 along the Window Trail on January 26, 1969; only a few had been seen there a few days earlier. Wintering birds usually can be found along the Rio Grande and throughout the canyons of the Chisos Mountains. Numbers found on recent (1985–94) CBCs at RGV have fluctuated from none in 1989, 1990, 1991, and 1993 to 62 individuals in 1987.

Spring migrants become evident by mid-March; there is a relatively heavy movement through the area that lasts until April 12, then reports decline sharply. This low is followed by a second surge of migrants from April 26 to mid-May, and stragglers have been found as late as June 10, 1969 (Wauer). And there also is a lone July report: Louis Dombroski found one at Boot Spring on July 22, 1969. I have heard the Hermit Thrush sing in migration only twice: two birds were singing at Boquillas during the morning of March 25, 1967, and two or three singing birds were detected on the ridge above Boot Spring during the very rainy morning of May 10, 1969. And Tony Gallucci reported birds singing at Boot Spring in the evening and morning of May 14 and 15, 1975.

Wood Thrush. *Hylocichla mustelina*

Casual spring migrant.

There are a few scattered reports ranging from one at RGV on April 5, 1967 (Wauer), to two observations at the Old Ranch on May 6 and 7, 1985, by Harold Hedges, and Anne Bellamy and Cynthia Simmons, respectively. And there is a very late report of a lone bird at Boot Spring on June 1, 1985 (B. Norris and B. Leske).

American Robin. *Turdus migratorius*

Uncommon migrant; fairly common winter visitor.

Records range from a very early fall post-nesting wanderer on July 19, 1969 (an immature bird fully capable of flight found near the Chisos Basin sewage lagoons by Wauer), several observations in the Basin between August 22 and early September, and more numerous sightings after mid-October and through April. Although most flocks consist of less than a dozen individuals, 15 were found wintering in Laguna Meadow in 1966–67; 45 and 55 were found along the Window Trail on March 21, 1970, and March 21, 1971, respectively (Wauer); and Bonnie McKinney found 100 or more feeding on Texas madrone berries in upper Green Gulch on October 28, 1986. Much larger flocks occur each winter in the Del Norte and Davis mountains to the north. Normally, Big Bend's wintering Robins rarely remain in one place for more than a week or two. Four or five birds frequent RGV and CC each winter, and a few usually can be found in the lower canyons of the Chisos Mountains. There is no apparent increase in numbers in spring, except that one or two birds may appear at Hot Springs, PJ, the Basin, or elsewhere.

Varied Thrush. *Ixoreus naevius*
Casual visitor.

Bryant Pomrenke was the first to record this Western thrush in the park; he found it in upper Juniper Canyon on December 7, 1981. Greg Lasley found what was probably the same bird in Boot Canyon on December 18, and Mark Berrier reported it again in Boot Canyon on January 10, 1982. Berrier's record was later accepted by the TBRC. There are three additional reports: Don and Martha Shearer found one at Castolon on April 12, 1989; Lee Daniel found it there on April 14; and Bonnie McKinney found a female dead on the highway one mile north of PJ on October 18, 1992.

Aztec Thrush. *Ridgwayia pinicola*
Casual in late summer.

An immature bird discovered in Boot Canyon by Mimi and David Wolf on August 21, 1977, represents the first for the park as well as the state of Texas (Wolf 1978). Deborah DeKeyzer, a member of the Wolf party, photographed the bird; the photograph was later verified by ornithologist Dr. Eugene Eisenmann. The bird was again found on August 25 by Peter Scott and Steve West, who watched it feed on the ground, scratching among the leaves like a towhee, and on berries in a nearby Texas madrone tree. There is a second series of reports: Chuck Sexton found one in lower Boot Canyon on July 31 and August 1, 1982, and Mark Lockwood reported a female Aztec Thrush in Boot Canyon on August 7, 1982. Both of these records were accepted by the TBRC. There is an additional unverified report for the Lost Mine Trail on August 14, 1983 (Ed Pace). The nearest known breeding ground of this tropical thrush is in the high mountains of southern Chihuahua and Coahuila.

FAMILY MIMIDAE: MOCKINGBIRDS, THRASHERS AND ALLIES
Gray Catbird. *Dumetella carolinensis*
Rare spring migrant; casual fall migrant and winter visitor.

There are records for every month but August, September, and November. The majority of reports range from April 27 to May 20, and most of those are from the lower Chisos Mountains; the exception was one collected at RGV on May 7, 1971 (Wauer). All of the October and winter reports are from the vicinity of the Rio Grande, except for one found by

Peter Riesz at the Old Ranch on December 25, 1990, and three in the Chisos Basin: I found one on January 16, 1990, and another on February 25, 1971, and Frank Oatman reported one from Oak Creek on January 16, 1989. All of the park records are of lone birds, except for three reported near the Basin sewage lagoons by Dennis Luton on May 20, 1978.

Northern Mockingbird. *Mimus polyglottos*

Abundant summer resident; common migrant and winter resident.

Summertime birds frequent almost every arroyo and patch of vegetation from the Rio Grande floodplain up into the lower edge of the Chisos woodlands. Nesting has been recorded from April through August; breeding birds possess darker plumage than those in winter. A population decline begins in mid-August and continues through the fall and winter; a low is reached from February 22 to mid-March, when wintering birds move out of the area. By March 15 to 17, however, there is a dramatic increase as spring migrants begin to pour into the desert lowlands. This high remains until mid-June, when the first of the nesting birds begin to disperse. Some of Big Bend's Mockers are permanent residents; a bird banded at RGV was recorded all 12 months of the year. Breeding birds at PJ, however, do not remain year-round, although they return each March and stay until at least mid-July.

Sage Thrasher. *Oreoscoptes montanus*

Uncommon spring migrant; sporadic in fall and winter.

Records range from September 14 through April 29, and there is one summer report of a lone bird along the Window Trail on July 24, 1964 (Dick Rasp). Spring migrants are most numerous from March 9 to April 7, and I found lone birds at Persimmon Gap on April 21, 1970, and at Hot Springs on April 27, 1968, and Tony Gallucci reported two along the River Road on April 29, 1978. The earliest fall record is one at Tuff Canyon on September 14, 1974 (Vaughn Morrison). Fall reports are scattered through October, increase during early November, and usually decline by late November. I found 15 to 20 individuals near the Adams Ranch, just northeast of the park, on October 13, 1969, and 50 or more birds on Dog

Northern Mockingbird, *Mimus polyglottos*

Canyon Flat on December 16, 1970. It appears that Sage Thrashers move through the area in numbers, and if adequate food, such as tasajillo cactus fruit, is available, they may remain for several days. I have found birds on the flat just west of Boquillas Canyon parking area almost every year during the first two weeks of November. Some years, birds remain there and at similar areas in the lowlands all winter.

Brown Thrasher. *Toxostoma rufum*

Uncommon migrant and winter resident.

This eastern thrasher has been recorded from September 26 through May 20, and there are two June reports from the Old Ranch: Jim Harvey and Sue and Ted Ulrich found one on June 10, 1978, and Steve Hoffman reported one there on June 24, 1993. Most sightings are from the Rio Grande floodplain at RGV, CC, and the SEC picnic area. Most records are of lone birds, but migrants sometimes are found in twos and threes.

Long-billed Thrasher. *Toxostoma longirostre*

Rare spring migrant; casual summer and winter visitor.

The status of this thrasher has changed in recent years: it was reported for the park only twice prior to 1970; 12 times from 1976 through 1983; and 17 times from 1984 to spring 1994. It is most numerous in late winter and spring, from late January to early May, but there also are scattered reports through early August. Although Bill Bouton, Dave Powell, and Vic Reister tape recorded one singing at Dugout Wells on May 25, 1981, there is no evidence of nesting. There are no reports from late August to late October, until an October 28, 1987, sighting at RGV by Robert Rothe and family; Kelly Bryan found one at RGV on November 7, 1991; then there are no reports again until late January. All of the park records are from brushy areas along the Rio Grande and at mid-elevation, such as at RGV, Dugout, and the Old Ranch. In addition, Bonnie McKinney captured, banded, and photographed one at the Black Gap WMA on June 4, 1983.

The Long-billed Thrasher is native to the Tamaulipian brushlands in Southeast Texas and as far west as Del Rio; increased records in the Big Bend Country may relate to the clearing of brushland in Southeast Texas and adjacent Mexico or to a natural westerly range-expansion.

Curve-billed Thrasher. *Toxostoma curvirostre*

Fairly common summer and winter resident and fall migrant, and common spring migrant.

Summer birds are rather localized. Nesting has been recorded numerous times, including one at Glenn Spring in May 1932 (Van Tyne and Sut-

Curve-billed Thrasher, *Toxostoma curvirostre*

ton 1937), and several times at PJ: I banded juvenile birds, barely able to fly, on June 6, 1971; I had seen adults throughout May for the first time in five years. Anne Bellamy watched begging fledglings on June 25, 1983, and John Gee found a nest with four downy young at the visitor center on July 16, 1990.

Fall migrants reach the park by late August, and the species generally can be found almost anywhere in the lowlands from late October through May; I recorded it consistently at PJ from October 15 until mid-April. Wintering populations may be somewhat sporadic; during ten years (1985–1994) of CBCs at RGV, participants tallied none on three years and three to 26 individuals on seven years. Spring migrants are most numerous from mid-March to mid-June, but a few stragglers can be found until mid-June. Singing birds have been recorded in migration as well as on their wintering grounds. The earliest song I heard was at PJ on February 11, 1969. Although most migrants pass through the lowlands, there are several sightings for the Chisos Basin, and one from Laguna Meadow on December 23, 1967 (Wauer).

Crissal Thrasher. *Toxostoma dorsale*

Uncommon summer and winter resident and migrant.

Nesting has been recorded at a wide range of sites between approximately 3,500 and 6,500 feet elevation. Van Tyne and Sutton (1937) first reported it as a nesting bird only in the Chisos Basin, but it later was found nesting in Blue Creek Canyon on May 8, 1969 (Wauer and Mike Parmeter), in a mesquite at the K-Bar the first week of May 1970 (Ty and Julie Hotchkiss), an adult was found feeding three youngsters along the Window Trail on May 25, 1969 (Wauer), a pair with fledglings was seen at Laguna Meadow on April 20, 1979 (David Wolf and Rose Ann Rowlett), and an adult was feeding young in upper Green Gulch on April 29, 1992 (Wauer). Post-nesting birds wander into the lowlands and may be found along the Rio Grande at RGV and CC during the summer.

The Crissal Thrasher is most numerous as a migrant from mid-March to April 10 in spring and from August 22 to early November in fall. Wintering birds usually can be found among the dense mesquite thickets along the river and in brushy canyons below approximately 6,500 feet in the Chisos Mountains. A search near CC, the flats just north of the SEC picnic area, and along the Window Trail below the sewage lagoons usually will produce at least a few Crissal Thrashers. In spring, also search the slopes below the Blue Creek Canyon parking area, the brushy flat above the Old Ranch, Cottonwood Creek below the Old Ranch, and the Grapevine Hills.

Crissal Thrasher, *Toxostoma dorsale*

FAMILY MOTACILLIDAE: PIPITS

American Pipit. *Anthus rubescens*

Fairly common migrant and winter visitor.

Fall migrants may arrive as early as September 24 but are more numerous from mid-October to late November. Wintering birds are almost totally confined to grassy flats along the Rio Grande, although they occasionally visit grassy areas along upper Tornillo and Terlingua creeks as well. Although most records are of flocks of eight to 20 birds, I found a flock of about 75 individuals at San Vicente on November 11, 1967. Spring migrants are most numerous from mid-March through May 11, and stragglers continue to pass through the area until May 28. Most sightings are from along the Rio Grande floodplain and open washes, but migrants also may occur in the mountains: there are several records from the Chisos Basin, including 12 on October 15, 1982 (Anne Bellamy), and I found lone birds at Boot Spring on May 8, 1968, and at Laguna Meadow on May 10, 1969.

Sprague's Pipit. *Anthus spragueii*
Rare migrant; casual winter visitor.

The earliest fall migrant was reported at RGV by Jeanne Ayers on September 21, 1987, and there are a scattering of reports every month through the winter and spring to one found at Laguna Meadow by Ned Fritz on May 6, 1968. The largest number I recorded in six years was six birds at RGV on October 18, 1968.

This buff-colored ground-dweller prefers rather arid short-grass fields and stays away from wetter tracts more than the preceding species. A walk through the open flats along the Rio Grande is the most likely place to flush out one or more of these very shy birds. When startled, American Pipits will usually fly some distance in a flock before alighting and walking about. The Sprague's Pipit (usually alone rather than in a flock) will suddenly fly up, almost at one's feet, rise into the air for some distance, and then drop suddenly into another site. Its characteristic flight and distinct call note (a loud, squeaky "squeet") readily separate this species from the more common American Pipit.

Family Bombycillidae: Waxwings
Cedar Waxwing. *Bombycilla cedrorum*
Common spring migrant; uncommon fall migrant; sporadic winter visitor.

There are only a few fall records, ranging from a very early sightings at PJ on September 21, 1987 (Jim Carrico), to another at PJ on October 12, 1970 (Wauer), and a few others in late October. Wintering birds occasionally are found along the Rio Grande, at lowland springs, and in the lower mountains. Anne Bellamy reported a flock of 50 birds at the Chisos Basin sewage lagoons on January 13, 1983. Normally, flocks of 10 to 25 birds remain at a particularly good feeding area for a few hours to a few days and then move on. In ten years (1985–1994), CBCs participants at RGV tallied none on seven years and totals of 6, 13, and 241 individuals on the remaining three years. It is most numerous in spring from mid-March to late May. Some years they are numerous along the river, and flocks of a dozen to 200 birds can be found. Flocks of 180 to 200 were seen daily at RGV from April

25 to May 19, 1969; a few remained until May 27 (Wauer). There are no records from May 28 through September 20.

FAMILY PTILOGONATIDAE: SILKY-FLYCATCHERS
Phainopepla. *Phainopepla nitens*
Uncommon early summer and winter resident; rare migrant.

The breeding status of this silky flycatcher has increased in recent years. Although Van Tyne and Sutton (1937) found it nesting near Terlingua on May 10, 1935, and Peter Koch found a nest in lower Green Gulch in 1947, no additional nesting in the park was recorded until Peter Scott discovered two nests in 1986: adults with three fledglings at 3,936 feet elevation in Green Gulch on May 29, and an adult female with three fledglings in Blue Creek Canyon on August 24. Since then, I have found three additional nests: one five feet high on an acacia (with three brown-speckled eggs) in Blue Creek Canyon on May 3, 1991, and two nests in Blue Creek on April 27, 1993. This species now appears to be a regular early summer resident in similar habitats, including Blue Creek Canyon, lower Green Gulch, along the lower Window Trail, and below Pine Canyon.

Most of the park's breeding population appears to move out of the area by early July, although there are scattered reports all summer. Southbound migrants appear in small flocks along the Rio Grande and in the lower Chisos canyons during September and October. By November they seem to remain at localized areas of mistletoe for longer periods of time. Wintering birds are irregular in occurrence but have been reported most often from lower Green Gulch and just west of the Chisos Basin campground. On ten (1985–1994) CBCs at RGV, none were reported for seven years, while two were tallied in 1985 and 1986, and one was found in 1989. By early March there is a slight increase in numbers, and this apparent northbound movement continues through mid-April; Charles Crabtree reported "several" along the Dodson Trail and on Mesa de Anguila, April 7 to 10, 1971. This increase is followed by another lapse of records and then another increase in sightings from late April to May 28.

FAMILY LANNIDAE: SHRIKES
Loggerhead Shrike. *Lanius ludovicianus*
Uncommon summer resident; common migrant and winter resident.

Nesting normally occurs during April, May, and June within the upper desert and sotol-yucca grasslands. I have found two nests near Dugout

Wells, one on a Torrey yucca on May 28, 1968, and another in a mesquite with two barely fledged birds on May 3, 1994. There also is an early nesting report from Persimmon Gap; an unknown reporter found eggs in a nest on February 20, 1978, and fledglings on March 31 (NPS files). Shrikes are extremely shy during the nesting season, but they are more easily found by late summer when post-nesting visitors and early fall migrants begin to move into the lowlands. Populations decline somewhat by November, but wintering birds generally remain common below 4,500 feet. On ten (1985–94) CBCs at RGV, participants tallied as few as two birds in 1989 and as many as 81 in 1987.

FAMILY STURNIDAE: STARLINGS
European Starling. *Sturnus vulgaris.*

Casual spring, fall, and winter visitor.

The first park record was of a lone bird at RGV in January 1965 (Mr. and Mrs. C. Edgar Bedell). I found one there with several Brewer's Blackbirds on April 28, 1967, and an additional three individuals on October 31 and December 10. The next reports are of lone birds at RGV on May 6 and 8, 1968, and at CC on December 22, 1969 (Wauer). Bert Hensel reported it at RGV on November 28, 1979; Jeff Selleck found one at RGV on January 13 and 15, 1988; Orval Lawler found a male on the Window Trail on May 9, 1989; and Carl and Florence Fleming discovered two at PJ on December 31, 1989. Scattered sightings of Starlings can be expected, but it likely will remain only a vagrant in BBNP because of the park's wilderness character.

FAMILY VIREONIDAE: VIREOS
White-eyed Vireo. *Vireo griseus*

Rare spring migrant.

This eastern vireo has been reported in spring from February 16 through May 7. Except for lone birds on the Cattail Falls Trail on April 18, 1983 (Bruce Talbot), and two sightings at the Old Ranch on April 19, 1986 (Jim and Carolyn Stevens), and May 7, 1993 (Peter Reisz), all the reports are from the vicinity of the Rio Grande. There also is one fall report: Johnny Armstrong found one at RGV on November 26, 1982.

Bell's Vireo. *Vireo bellii*

Abundant summer resident on the Rio Grande floodplain, casual elsewhere.

Records extend from a very early report at RGV on February 8, 1994 (Audrey Ashcroft), none again until one at Boquillas on March 8, 1969 (Wauer), and it becomes more numerous after mid-March. The earliest spring arrivals and late summer birds are quiet except for very early morning singing. By March 24, however, their song is one of the most commonly heard along the floodplain. Nesting occurs from April through mid-June; I found fledged birds at RGV on May 10, 1968, a nest with young at Oak Creek on May 14, 1967, and an active nest located 12 feet high in a cottonwood at Castolon on June 7, 1969. And Helen and Max Parker discovered a pair incubating eggs on a nest in a cottonwood at RGV as late as July 25, 1974.

Most years this tiny vireo also can be found at springs and riparian-like habitats to about 3,500 feet elevation. For instance, on five population surveys involving one-mile routes conducted in five years (1990-1994), I recorded 41 territorial birds near Dugout Wells in late April and early May 1994, 37 territorial birds in lower Green Gulch, seven below Pine Canyon, four in upper Green Gulch, and none in Pine Canyon. Most of the summering birds move out of the area by the second week of September, but an occasional individual usually can be found for another couple weeks.

Black-capped Vireo. *Vireo atricapillus*

Rare summer resident.

This little vireo was reported within the park only three times before 1966: Dick Youse found one in upper Blue Creek Canyon on May 20, 1956; Jerry Strickling saw two at Kibby Spring on May 13, 1962; and Ben and Joan Trimble and Malcolm Jenkins reported two along the Window Trail on August 15, 1963. On May 5, 1966, Jon Barlow found it nesting in Campground Canyon on the south slope of Pulliam Ridge. After 1966, it was found in this and adjacent canyons annually until about 1980. Examples include a nest with three eggs in Campground Canyon on May 18, 1967 (Wauer); Dave Easterla found a male feeding fledged birds there on July 5, 1967; and David Wolf and Nicholas Halmi reported two immature

Black-capped Vireo, *Vireo atricapillus*

birds there on August 19, 1977. It also was reported during the same peri-od from the north side of Pulliam Ridge (Jim Liles) and at Panther Canyon (Will Risser), Green Gulch, Blue Creek Canyon, and Juniper Canyon.

The earliest park sighting is April 9, 1993, at PJ (Anne Bellamy). There appeared to be some post-nesting wandering; I found a juvenile within a heavily wooded area below Emory Peak at 6,100 feet on August 7, 1969; David Wolf reported one female and one immature at RGV on September 7, 1973; and John Gee reported a singing male below Laguna Meadow on September 4, 1990.

By the mid-1980s, Black-capped Vireo populations were declining throughout their breeding range. The U. S. Fish and Wildlife Service com-missioned a population survey by Joe Marshall and Joseph Gryzbowski in 1985 to assess their status; the entire U.S. population was listed as "endangered" on November 5, 1987. The Marshall/Gryzbowski report (1985) included the following summary for Brewster County:

> We found six males singing on territories in lower Juniper Canyon on 4–5 May, at least one in lower Pine Canyon on 6 May, and two territorial males in lower Blue Spring [Creek] Canyon on 9 May. Sightings of single birds were reported from halfway down the Window Trail on 13 May, and the head of that trail near the treatment ponds on 28 July, and a singing male in Panther Canyon on 15 June (fide Bonnie McKinney). These may be wanderers as they were in places we had thoroughly searched in May. The Park sustains an abundance of Brown-headed Cowbirds and consequent dearth of small songbirds other than cavity nesters.

The National Park Service has monitored Black-capped Vireo populations in recent years; Resource Management Specialist Carl Fleming told me in May 1994 that "at least 10 to 12 pairs nest annually in the foothills and canyons of the Chisos Mountains." Park Volunteer Carol Edwards told me that a 1995 survey reported a total of 32 Black-capped Vireos. Blue Creek Canyon may now be the most likely place to find this bird.

Although habitat destruction and overuse may be a principle cause of this bird's decline elsewhere in Texas, at BBNP, population decline is undoubtedly due to nest parasitism by the Brown-headed Cowbird. Cowbird populations are directly related to human developments, especially the Chisos Mountain Remuda and the extensive amount of horse use along the park's "wilderness" trails. Concerted efforts to reduce cowbird populations by trapping during spring should be undertaken. And the 1994 closure of the remuda should provide needed relief to breeding Black-capped Vireos.

Gray Vireo. *Vireo vicinior*

Fairly common summer resident; rare migrant and winter resident.

Males arrive on their breeding grounds as early as March 17 and can be easily detected by their distinct three-whistle song. Males vigorously defend their territories throughout the breeding period and are one of the park's most vociferous species at that time. Six singing birds were found

Gray Vireo, *Vireo vicinior*

in Blue Creek Canyon on May 8, 1969; starting from about one mile above the ranch house, territorial birds were detected approximately every quarter-mile (Wauer). I consistently found singing birds in this same area during the early 1990s, as well. A more accessible breeding habitat occurs along Oak Creek Canyon below the Chisos Basin campground. Most of the canyons along the south slope of Pulliam Ridge contain one or two breeding pairs of Gray Vireos from late April through early June. Jon Barlow (1967) studied the Gray Vireo in these canyons during the summers of 1966 and 1967.

There is some post-nesting dispersal: I found lone birds at PJ on June 18, 1967, on the Lost Mine Trail on July 23, 1967, and in Panther Canyon on August 23, 1970. Patty Easterla reported one at PJ on June 6, 1967;

Peter Scott found one at the Grapevine Hills on August 20, 1986; Sandra Darby and Dora Sylvester found one there on October 16, 1982; and Anne Bellamy reported a singing bird at Dugout Wells on October 28, 1993. These later two reports may be migrants, although there is little recognizable influx of fall or spring birds. And wintering birds are also few and far between. However, persistence can result in finding winter Gray Vireos at pertinent sites, where they frequent shrubby flats and arroyos. Jon Barlow and I found birds near the Chimneys and at Robber's Roost on December 30, 1970, and January 3, 1971 (Barlow and Wauer 1971). Bruce Talbot and Jerry Freilich found it at Cross Canyon on February 10, 1984; Brete Griffen reported birds at Dugout Wells, Blue Creek Canyon, and Mule Ears on February 17, 18, and 19, 1984, respectively; and Bryant Woods found it at Grapevine Hills on February 20, 1992.

Solitary Vireo. *Vireo solitarius*

Casual summer resident; fairly common migrant; rare winter visitor.

It appears that this bird nests in a few high, moist mountain canyons during wet years. A pair was found courting at Boot Spring on May 12, 1968; none were seen in the summer of 1969, but I found a male defending a territory at Boot Spring on May 7, 8, and 9, 1970. The spring of 1971 was very dry, and I did not find it in Boot Canyon, although I did discover a pair in upper Campground Canyon on June 16.

Solitary Vireos are most numerous as a migrant, when birds can be found from the Rio Grande floodplain to the highest parts of the Chisos Mountains. I have recorded spring migrants regularly after March 11, and a peak is evident from April 1 through 11, when the majority of the birds are of the small, yellow-green *cassinii* race. There is a paucity of sightings from mid- to late April, when another heavy movement begins and lasts until about May 17, peaking between May 2 and 9. The majority of these latter birds are the larger and lighter *plumbeous* race.

Fall migrants may reach the park as early as August 15 but are most numerous from September 8 through 25; stragglers continue to pass through the area until mid-December. I found lone birds at Laguna Meadow on December 16, 1968, and on the Lost Mine Trail on December 16, 1966. The majority of the fall migrants are large and light, but an occasional yellow-green bird is found as well. There is also a handful of winter reports from RGV and CC. On ten (1985–94) CBCs at RGV, it was recorded only once, a lone yellow-green bird in 1990.

Yellow-throated Vireo. *Vireo flavifrons*
Casual spring migrant.

There are a handful of spring records from various elevations, extending from an April 7, 1978, sighting at RGV by Stuart Tingley, to one at Castolon on June 8, 1993, by Kevin Ramsey and Susan Ortiz. There also is a single fall report: I observed one foraging among the pines with several Townsend's and Orange-crowned warblers in upper Boot Canyon on September 29, 1969.

Hutton's Vireo. *Vireo huttoni*
Common summer resident; uncommon in winter.

Nesting occurs during April, May, and June; a nest was found in a clump of mistletoe on an oak at Laguna Meadow on April 29, 1935 (Van Tyne and Sutton 1937); nest-building was found there on May 17, 1969, and an adult was seen feeding a fledgling at Boot Spring on June 9, 1968 (Wauer). Nesting birds are generally restricted to the upper parts of the Chisos woodlands, above 5,800 feet. I counted 11 singing birds between the upper Chisos Basin and Laguna Meadow on March 30, 1968. Its loud "sweeet" or "siree" call can be heard for more than a hundred feet, and a few loud squeaks or "spishing" in the proper habitat can usually attract one or two birds. Soon after nesting, it moves into lower canyons, where it remains throughout the winter; it can often be found in oak groves, such as those along the lower end of the Window Trail, at the east side of Panther Pass, and in Pine Canyon. Hutton's Vireos may wander below the woodlands on occasion: I found two individuals about 300 feet below the pinyons and junipers in Blue Creek Canyon on February 1, 1969.

Big Bend's Hutton Vireo represents the Mexican race *carolinae*, that reaches its northern limits in West Texas (AOU 1957); it was initially described from specimens taken in the Chisos Mountains by Herbert Brandt (1938).

Hutton's Vireo, *Vireo huttoni*

Warbling Vireo. *Vireo gulvus*

Sporadic summer resident; uncommon spring migrant; rare in fall.

The summering status of this vireo in the park is similar to that of the Solitary Vireo; it nests in the high Chisos canyons during wet years only. I found a pair at Boot Spring on May 3 and 14 and June 11, 1967, and discovered a nest among the foliage of a Grave's oak at Boot Spring on June 8, 1968. And there are three nesting records for the riparian areas at RGV and CC: Harold Holt found nests at both sites on May 12, 1976, and Wayne Gordon reported a nest at CC on June 15, 1982. It is most numerous as a spring migrant from mid-April to late May, when it can be found along the Rio Grande floodplain and at oak groves in the mountains. Fall migrants are not as numerous, and sightings are scattered from late July to early November, primarily in the lowlands.

Philadelphia Vireo. *Vireo philadelphicus*
Casual migrant.

Spring records range from a very early record at Burro Spring on March 4, 1969, by the Wards; a March 30, 1965, report at the SEC picnic area by the Walstons; and scattered records from early April to May 19. Fall sightings extend from a lone bird at CC on August 7, 1977 (Chuck Hunter and Rich Pruett), to one at CC on October 24, 1974 (Wauer and Russ and Marian Wilson). Except for the Burro Spring sighting and one report from PJ on April 31 and May 1, 1980 (Jim Liles), all records are from the vicinity of the Rio Grande.

Red-eyed Vireo. *Vireo olivaceus*
Rare spring migrant.

There are scattered springtime reports that extend from a very early sighting on April 19 (in 1966 at Dugout Wells by Clarence Cottam) to several from April 28 through May 20; there is a late spring sighting at the Chisos Basin on June 21, 1976 (Jimmy Homer). There also is a single early fall report: Steve West found one at Boquillas on August 12, 1977. This bird apparently is silent in migration, and may be more common than current records suggest; I caught and banded two individuals in a mist net at RGV on May 10 and 17, 1970, although none were otherwise detected.

Yellow-green Vireo. *Vireo flavoviridus*
There are two reports.

There is one verifiable record of this tropical vireo: Dave Easterla (1972) collected a singing male at CC on July 13, 1972. It also was reported at RGV on May 7 and 8, 1980, by Mark Tuttle. This bird, earlier considered only a race of the Red-eyed Vireo, breeds in the Mexican lowlands (up to about 4,000 feet) from Tamaulipas to Sonora and south.

FAMILY EMBERIZIDAE; SUBFAMILY PARULINAE: WARBLERS
Blue-winged Warbler. *Vermivora pinus*
Casual spring migrant.

There are scattered records, ranging from one at RGV on April 20, 1971, by Bert and Millie Schaughency, through April to one at RGV on May 11, 1970 (Wauer); there also is a much later report at Castolon on June 8, 1993 (Kevin Ramsey and Susan Ortiz). Except for one found at Boot Spring on May 7, 1983 (Bonnie McKinney and Nancy Flood), and one at the Old Ranch on May 1, 1993 (Wauer), all reports are from the vicinity of the Rio Grande.

Golden-winged Warbler. *Vermivora chrysoptera*
Casual spring migrant.

Reports range only from April 26 to May 12. Charles Crabtree and I found one first among the oaks in Boot Canyon on May 9, 1970. It was next recorded by Peter Scott at RGV on May 3, 1980; Susan Ward found one at Boot Spring on April 26, 1984; Richard Guillett and Bill Bourbon reported a female at RGV on May 1, 1988, and a male was found on the Pinnacles Trail by Jeff Rice on May 12, 1988. In 1990, Joan and Ted Tedford found a male at RGV on May 1, and I observed a male there on April 30, 1991.

Tennessee Warbler. *Vermivora peregrina*
Casual spring migrant.

Records range from April 10 to May 19, and there is a lone winter record; Bruce Stewart reported one at RGV that he saw several times between December 20 and 23, 1978. In the 1980s, Will Risser found one at RGV on May 3, 1980; Ben and Sally Sorensen observed one at Dugout Wells on April 23, 1983; Tom Will found one "with a flock of Black-headed Grosbeaks" at Boot Spring on May 5, 1984; Anne Bellamy, Cynthia Simmons, and Patrick Bolton reported one at RGV from April 27 to May 1, 1985; David Wolf found one there on April 22, 1986; Clair Berkman reported one at Boot Spring on May 19, 1986; and Wilhelmania Howe found one at RGV on April 10, 1987. The most recent sighting is one at RGV on April 25, 1995 (Wauer).

Orange-crowned Warbler. *Vermivora celata*

Fairly common migrant and winter resident.

Fall migrants have been recorded as early as August 12, and a peak is reached from October 18 to November 5. There are a few instances when small flocks were recorded; for example, I found eight birds at RGV on September 5, 1969. Wintering Orange-crowns are fairly numerous until early January, when there is a noticeable decline. CBCs at RGV averaged 15 Orange-crowns in ten years (1985–1994), with a low of one bird in 1993 and a high of 35 in 1987. Spring migrants appear about the second week of March, a peak occurs from March 24 to April 11, and then numbers gradually decline until May 13.

Nashville Warbler. *Vermivora ruficapilla*

Fairly common migrant.

This is one of the earliest of the spring warblers and is a good indicator that the spring migration has begun. Spring records range from March 22 through May 24. Although it is never abundant, small flocks of three to ten birds can usually be found at all elevations. The fall migration ranges from September 5 through October 24; there are scattered sightings to November 25; and there is one late December 29, 1989, report at Castolon (Barbara Weintraub). Southbound migrants seem to move through in larger flocks than they do in spring; Anne Bellamy and Barbara McKinney found a flock of more than 100 birds at RGV on October 10, 1986. Although the majority of the reports are from the lowlands, there also are a few from the mountains.

Virginia's Warbler. *Vermivora virginiae*

Uncommon migrant in spring; rare in fall.

Reports range from April 14 to May 24 in spring and from August 5 to October 10 in fall. Most sightings are from the mountains, but it also has been recorded along the Rio Grande. I found birds at RGV on May 1, 1969, two on May 20, 1967, and one on May 24, 1967; one at the SEC picnic area on May 1, 1967; one at RGV on September 6, 1968; and two at CC on September 15, 1969. Highland birds may be confused with the more numerous Colima Warbler.

Colima Warbler. *Vermivora crissalis*

Fairly common summer resident.

This is Big Bend's most renowned bird. It occurs nowhere else in the United States, and it winters in relatively inaccessible mountainous areas in southwestern Mexico. It has been recorded in the Chisos Mountains as early as March 15 and as late as September 18, although there are three unverified, much later reports. It also is a common nesting bird in the pinyon-juniper-oak woodlands of Mexico's Maderas del Carmen, 50 miles southeast of the Chisos Mountains.

Colima Warbler, *Vermivora crissalis*

Colima Warblers usually arrive in BBNP during mid-March, and, except for one report by Anne Bellamy and Betty and Tom Alex at PJ on March 24, 1993, all park records are from the forested portion of the park. In dry years they are extremely difficult to find until the first or second week of April. Afterward, there is little problem finding birds in the proper habitat. They normally are vociferous; males sing throughout the days prior to nesting but only in the early morning hours and on a few other occasions during the day when nesting. Nests are placed on the ground in leaf litter or under clumps of grass. Both adults build the nest, incubate the eggs, and care for the young. I have banded nestlings ready to leave the nest from May 25 to July 6. Very little attention is given the youngsters after they have been out of the nest a few days. Further details about nesting site preferences are available in an article that appeared in the August 1994 issue of *Birding* (Wauer).

By late June, Colimas may be more difficult to find, but searching among the oaks in suitable mountain locations will surely turn up at least a few individuals. If a birder enters an oak grove and remains for several minutes, he or she often will find Colimas beginning to move about among the heavier foliage of the oaks and other broadleaf trees and shrubs. Post-nesting birds generally remain on their breeding grounds at least until mid-July, although there is some dispersal; Greg Lasley found one in the oaks near the Chisos Basin sewage lagoons on August 31, 1988. Although there is a noticeable decline after mid-July, a few Colimas usually can be found at choice sites, such as just above the cabin at Boot Spring, throughout August and early September; my latest sighting is September 18.

Colima Warblers also occur at a number of other localities within the Chisos Mountains. Annual counts were taken during the second week of May in 1967 through 1970. All locations with suitable habitat were searched. Totals of 92 Colimas were found in 1967, 130 in 1968, 166 in 1969, and 118 in 1970. In all instances they were associated with oak-pinyon-juniper or oak-maple-Arizona cypress habitats. Approximately 85% of the birds tallied were located along narrow and relatively humid canyons with considerable overstory of vegetation, and 15% were found on relatively drier open slopes and ridges. Some localities appeared to offer stable habitats, whereas fluctuation was evident elsewhere. All of the Boot Canyon drainages, including Boot Canyon proper and along the Pinnacles and Colima trails, were heavily used every year, but considerable fluctuation was detected in fringe areas, such as Laguna Meadow and its drainages, Emory Peak, upper Juniper Canyon, and middle and upper Pine Canyon. In general, the distribution of breeding Colimas appears to be determined by the precipitation received during the months just prior to the nesting season. During wet spring months, as in 1968, Colimas were found nesting along the trail below Laguna Meadow and in middle Pine Canyon. During dry years, such as 1969, more were found in the higher canyons, and fewer were detected in the lower and drier canyons such as below Laguna Meadow and in middle Pine Canyon.

Lucy's Warbler. *Vermivora luciae*
Localized early summer resident.

This tiny warbler is the park's newest breeder; it has nested at CC only since 1986: Bob Quinn found a pair of singing birds on March 21, and

Lucy's Warbler, *Vermivora luciae*

Rose Ann Rowlett and Peter Scott observed adults feeding young on May 12 and fledglings on May 19. It was unreported in 1987, but there were numerous sightings at CC in 1988: Peter Scott found two singing pairs on March 26 and April 2; Steve and Lona Flocke reported "at least eight individuals" on April 6 and 7; Hal Wierenga discovered a nest on May 3; and Willie Sekula and John Muldrow reported two adults with two juveniles on August 21. In 1989, David Muth and R. D. Purrington reported "at least four singing, territorial, interacting males, one with a companion," at CC on May 17 and 18. In 1990, John Gee reported a pair at CC on March 23 and 24; Van Remsen found birds "singing steadily" on April 12 and 13; and I found at least four individuals, including a pair carrying nesting materials, on April 25. Each year since, two or more pairs have been recorded nesting there.

Nesting has been expected in the park for several years, as this warbler has progressed eastward along the Rio Grande during the 1970s. Tony Gallucci found it nesting west of the park near Candelaria in April and May 1979, including four fledged birds on May 20. There were several earlier park records: Noberto Ortega and I found the first bird at RGV on April 8, 1970. I collected a singing male at Boquillas on April 17 and observed two additional birds at RGV on May 3 (Wauer 1973a). In 1972, I found lone singing birds at RGV on April 4 and 23. It was not reported in the park again until 1984: Bonnie McKinney recorded a female at Hot Springs on April 12, 1984; and Jeremy Clark found one in Boquillas Canyon on August 18, 1992.

Northern Parula. *Parula americana*

Uncommon spring migrant; rare winter visitor; casual in summer and fall.

It is most numerous from mid-March to early May, and the vast majority of records are from the lowlands along the Rio Grande. There also are a few reports from the Old Ranch, Dugout Wells, and along the Window Trail. From mid-May through summer and early fall, records are few and far between; there is no evidence of nesting despite several reports of singing birds at RGV during the nesting season. There are no October sightings, but it has been reported sporadically at RGV and CC throughout the winter months, although it was not recorded on ten years (1985–1994) of the CBCs centered at RGV.

Tropical Parula. *Parula pitiayumi*

Casual spring and winter visitor.

The first park record is a lone bird found at Boquillas on March 19, 1967 (Wauer); Joanne Kangas next reported one in SEC on March 23, 1967; Scott Carroll and Fred Harris found one on the Window Trail on March 22, 1976; Robert Harms reported one with several Yellow-rumped Warblers at RGV on January 3, 1979; Charles Callagan found one at the Old Ranch on April 26, 1986; and Gordon Fitch reported one in SEC on November 24, 1993. The species was finally verified in 1994, when a singing male was found at RGV from April 30 and May 2: it was first discovered by Alan Wormington, and later observed by Cheryl Johnson, Brad McKinney, Greg Lasley, Mike Pawlick, and myself.

The Tropical Parula is a Mexican species that barely reaches into the United States. The nearest known breeding grounds are in extreme South Texas in the Lower Rio Grande Valley.

Yellow Warbler. *Dendroica petechia*

Fairly common migrant.

Records extend from April 15 to June 1 in spring and from August 11 to September 15 in fall. Except for lone birds on the Lost Mine Trail on May 12, 1968, at Dugout Wells on May 16, 1990, and May 17, 1968, and at the Old Ranch on August 27, 1955, all reports are from the vicinity of the Rio Grande. This bird once was also a fairly common summer resident on the Rio Grande floodplain; Van Tyne and Sutton (1937) found it nesting at Boquillas, Hot Springs, and San Vicente during the 1930s. Although I searched the floodplain for nesting birds from 1966 through 1971, I found no evidence of nesting, but I did find a few singing males (Wauer 1973a). It is likely that Yellow Warblers that once nested there have been extirpated by the expanding population of Brown-headed Cowbirds.

Chestnut-sided Warbler. *Dendroica pensylvanica*

Casual migrant.

There are seven reports in spring between May 1 and June 2, and there are two records in the fall, both at RGV; on October 5, 1969 and October

10, 1970 (Wauer). The spring records include a female at the Old Ranch on May 1, 1991 (Ron and Barb Cavin); one at RGV on May 9, 1985 (John Arvin and Steve Hoffman); a male at RGV on May 9, 1986 (Steve Hoffman, Derek Muschalek, Dale Stahlecher, and Kevin Zimmer); I collected one of two birds seen at RGV on May 13, 1969 (Wauer 1973a); Joe Harrison reported a male from Boot Canyon on May 14, 1993; Rene and Andrew Franks found one at RGV on May 21, 1989; and Gary Berg reported one for the Old Ranch on June 2, 1980.

Magnolia Warbler. *Dendroica magnolia*
Casual migrant.

Records range from April 10 to June 8 in spring and from October 14 to 29 in fall. Except for two reports from the Old Ranch on May 9, 1980 (Jim Shiflett) and May 18, 1969 (Wauer), and one from PJ on May 14, 1970 (NPS files), all are from RGV or CC.

Cape May Warbler. *Dendroica tigrina*
Casual spring migrant.

This lovely warbler has been reported only from April 19 to May 3. The majority of reports are of a lone male that remained at the Old Ranch from April 23 to May 2, 1976; it was seen by (in order of reporting) Barbara Ribble, John Pond, Mr. and Mrs. Glenn Smith, Jean Bensmiller, Donald Billiard, Paul Krapfel, Larry Pearler, Kevin Zimmer, Scott Robinson, Robert Anderson, Charles Gill, Bill Smith, Skip Nichols, David McCorquodale, and Mary Ann Payne. A record on April 19, 1985, is from Dugout Wells, where it was photographed (NPS files) by Lula Gullett and Mary G. Jones. There also is an earlier photograph, taken by L. DeMarch at RGV on May 24, 1979.

Black-throated Blue Warbler. *Dendroica caerulescans*
Rare spring and casual fall migrant.

The majority of reports are from May 3 to 20 from along the Rio Grande, at the Old Ranch, and from Boot Canyon. There also is a March 30, 1979, report at the Old Ranch by Jack and Phyliss Wilburn, and a later spring record at PJ, on June 22, 1971, by Patty Easterla, who found a dead female below the window of her residence after a storm (Easterla 1972).

Fall records range from October 4 to November 18, generally later than most songbirds, all from RGV, Dugout Wells, and PJ. There also are two unverified winter reports at RGV: on January 3, 1979 (Robert Morse) and February 12, 1975 (Jody Miller).

Yellow-rumped Warbler. *Dendroica coronata*

Common migrant and winter resident.There are records for every month of the year, but the vast majority of reports range from early September through late May. Also, both the western "Audubon's Warbler" and the eastern "Myrtle Warbler" occur in the park, and sightings were maintained separately until the two were lumped by the AOU. Therefore, they will be discussed separately. Typical male Audubon's possess a yellow throat and a large, white wing patch, whereas typical Myrtle Warblers have a white throat and two distinct white wing bars. This coloration is rather vague in winter birds and females, but there is another good method of separating the two: the rear of the black cheek patch turns up in the Myrtle but joins the dark on the chest or throat in the Audubon's.

Audubon's Warbler is the more common of the two. It is most numerous as a spring migrant from late March through mid-May. There are several late May records as well, and D. R. Love reported one at Boquillas on June 5, 1962. Moderately large flocks have been seen during the spring migration: C. Phillip Allen found 40 birds at Boot Spring on April 27, 1963, and I counted 58 along Boot Canyon on May 12, 1967. Fall migrants do not seem to be as numerous as they are in spring, but larger flocks or "waves" have been recorded. On August 30, 1966, I found 150 or more individuals with several Ruby-crowned Kinglets, Townsend's Warblers, and White-breasted Nuthatches at Laguna Meadow. On September 25, 1966, I recorded a "wave of birds near the East Rim at 8:30 a.m., including 35 to 40 Audubon's Warblers, and many Townsend's Warblers with a few Hermit Thrushes, Hepatic Tanagers, Ruby-crowned Kinglets, and Vesper Sparrows." A very early fall report of an immature Audubon near the Pinnacles Trail crest on July 23, 1990 (John Gee), is certainly a post-nesting migrant or visitor; there is no evidence of this species nesting in BBNP. The fall movement subsides by early November, but birds remain common along the river and uncommon above 4,500 feet during the first half of the winter, or until the first good series of northers reach the Big Bend. Afterward it is almost impossible to find this bird in the mountains until the first of the spring migrants begin to move into the area in late March.

Myrtle Warblers are generally less numerous and do not arrive in the park until mid-October; reports are few and far between until mid-December when there is a noticeable increase in the lowlands. There also are a few winter reports at higher elevations: Dick Youse found one at the Old Ranch on February 12, 1965, and I saw one at the Chisos Basin on December 22, 1967. Myrtle Warblers begin to increase slightly toward the last of February, and by mid-March are equally abundant as Audubon's in the lowlands. A peak is reached in early April, but stragglers continue to pass through the park until mid-May.

In ten years (1985–1994) of CBCs at RGV, an average of 12 Myrtle Warblers and 20 Audubon's Warblers have been tallied annually.

Black-throated Gray Warbler. *Dendroica nigrescens*

Uncommon fall migrant; rare winter visitor and spring migrant.

Records exist for every month but June and July. It is most numerous in fall from early August to mid-September, after which there are scattered sightings each month until late April, and there are two later reports: Carol Edwards found one along the Pinnacles Trail on May 2, 1995, and Dan and Barbara Williams reported one near Boot Spring on May 21, 1995. The elevations of sightings vary with the seasons: All of the early fall reports are from the high Chisos, but by late August through mid-April most are from along the Rio Grande. Wintering birds appear to be on the increase: A single winter sighting was reported in the first edition of this book (1973) and one remained at RGV from January 1 through February 3, 1965 (Dingus, Mr. and Mrs. C. Edgar Bedell, and Pete Isleib). A "few" winter sightings were included in the 1985 revision, including a male along the Window Trail on January 27, 1974 (Stephen and Janet Hinshaw), and four individuals in the Chisos Basin on January 4, 1975 (Tom Will). Since then it has become a rare but somewhat regular winter visitor, especially at CC.

Townsend's Warbler. *Dendroica townsendi*

Fairly common migrant; casual winter visitor.

Records extend from August 2 through May 13, and the vast majority of these are from the mountains. Fall migrants reach the park by the first week of August but do not become numerous until the end of the month

Townsend's Warbler, *Dendroica townsendi*

and on through mid-September; then it is the most commonly encoun-
tered warbler in the Chisos Mountains. The high fall count was 28 along
the trail between the Chisos Basin Trailhead and the South Rim on September 4, 1966 (Wauer). Stragglers continue to pass through the area until
mid-November. Wintering birds may be somewhat sporadic in occurrence; I found it regularly from December through February on four of
five winters, the exception was 1969–70. Most of the wintertime reports
are from Laguna Meadow and near Boot Spring; it is casual at RGV and

CC. Spring migrants move through the park area from early April through May 13. A peak is reached from May 1 to 10, when Townsend's can be found in numbers at all elevations, although it is most numerous in the mountain woodlands. On May 8, 1967, I heard several singing on the hillside above Boot Spring, but I could not find a single bird the following morning. And Carol Edwards reported that nine individuals were recorded on the May 13, 1995, North American Migratory Bird count, seven in the mountains and two at CC.

Hermit Warbler. *Dendroica occidentalis*
Uncommon migrant; casual winter visitor.

Records of this Western warbler range from April 13 to May 14 in spring and from August 5 to September 28 in fall, and there are two winter reports: lone birds along the Pinnacles Trail on December 28, 1991 (Ken Stinnett), and at Boot Spring on January 2, 1991 (Mark Korducki). All but two of the spring and fall sightings are from the mountain woodlands; the exceptions include one at Dugout Wells on April 22, 1989 (Jesse Grantham) and a lone bird in company of a Townsend's Warbler at RGV on August 31, 1969 (David Simmon).

Black-throated Green Warbler. *Dendroica virens*
Rare spring and casual fall migrant.

Records extend from March 21 to May 12 in spring and from August 8 to September 17 in fall, and there is a later report of two birds at Glenn Spring on October 23, 1989 (James Zabriskie). Except for a male found at Dugout Wells by Ron Spomer on March 21, 1980, and one at RGV on April 7, 1970 (Wauer), all reports are from the higher Chisos woodlands.

Golden-cheeked Warbler. *Dendroica chrysoparia*
Casual migrant.

There are two spring and four fall reports. Fred R. Gehlbach and his students reported it first: a singing male in upper Boot Canyon on April 9, 1968. Next, Chris Seifert and Carol Brubaker found a lone male at Cattail Falls on April 7, 1978, which they observed "for 30 minutes." H. P. Langridge reported a male in Boot Canyon on July 10, 1978; Tyrrell Harvey,

Steve Hawkins, and Richard Schaefer found one at Boot Spring on July 12, 1980; there are no additional reports until 1993, when Elizabeth Seaunght found one at Pinnacles Pass on August 6, and Cricket Rose reported one at Laguna Meadow on September 10. According to Warren Pulich (1976), this bird does not occur in Texas after August 18.

Blackburnian Warbler. *Dendroica fusca*
Casual spring migrant.

Spring records range only from May 6 to 27, and there is a single fall report: Bonnie McKinney observed a lone immature female in the Chisos Basin on September 10, 1986. The May reports include three from RGV: Doyle and Helen Peckham and I found one on May 6, 1970; Mabel Bendixen and Kristin Larson separately reported one on May 9, 1983; and Dennis Luton and Dean Fisher found one on May 22, 1978. There are two later reports from the South Rim: Stephen K. Perry and Susan L. Gawarecki found a male on May 25, 1984, and Ray Heitmann, Nanette Armstrong, and Lin Dahl reported a male there on May 27, 1989.

Yellow-throated Warbler. *Dendroica dominica*
Casual migrant and winter visitor.

There are several spring reports from March 7 through April 29, all from RGV, Dugout Wells, and PJ. In addition, there are one fall and three winter reports, all from RGV: Robert Rothe and family reported one on October 28, 1990; Bryant Woods found one on December 5, 1990; Peter Riesz recorded it on December 29, 1990; and Mark Korducki and Mike Quinn found one on January 1, 1991. The latter three reports are likely of the same bird.

Grace's Warbler. *Dendroica graciae*
Rare migrant.

Records range from April 7 to June 1 in spring and from August 8 to September 24 in fall. All reports are from the Chisos Mountain woodlands, except for one at RGV on April 18, 1979 (Ava Nelson) and a male at CC on May 8, 1983 (Tommy Michael and Bob Honig). The high count is six birds found at Boot Spring on September 5, 1983 (Nick Jackson).

Pine Warbler. *Dendroica pinus*
Casual migrant and winter visitor.

The first park record is one found at Boot Spring on April 27, 1966, by David T. Brown and members of the San Antonio Audubon Society. It was not seen again until Robert and Joan Rothe found one at RGV on February 24, 1991, and Michael Hayes reported it again on March 1. One also was present at RGV from November 19, 1991, through February 15, 1992; it was seen by several birders and photographed by Barry Zimmer. There also is a single fall report at Dugout Wells on October 25, 1993 (R. Siebert).

Palm Warbler. *Dendroica palmarum*
Casual spring migrant; two fall records.

The majority of reports extend from April 1 to May 14, and there are two in the fall: J. R. Barnwell found two at RGV on October 14, 1971, and Jack M. Kiracofe reported one from the Chisos Basin on October 17, 1985. Joe Lunn, Martin Bovey, and I first found a bird of the yellow, eastern race at Boquillas Crossing on April 1, 1970; it was collected and represents the first for West Texas (Wauer 1973a). Ben Feltner next reported one for the Chisos Basin on May 5, 1980, and Jim Shiflett and C. C. Wiedenfeld found three individuals—at RGV, CC, and the Old Ranch—on May 9, 1980. It was reported at RGV on April 27, 1984, by Mel White; David Wolf and Drew Thate discovered a male of the Western race near the Basin sewage lagoons on May 8, 1993; and Don Burt reported one at RGV on May 14, 1994.

Blackpoll Warbler. *Dendroica striata*
Casual spring migrant.

Records range from April 20 to May 15. Carl Swenson reported one first along the river at RGV on May 5, 1960. It was not seen again until 1970, when Dave and Ginger Harwood found one "flycatching" over the RGV silt pond on April 26, 1970. I next found one among the oaks at Boot Canyon on May 8, 1970; Greg Lasley and Chuck Sexton found a male at RGV on May 15, 1979; Bob Merrill reported a male at RGV on April 20, 1991; Rose Ann Rowlett discovered a female at Boulder Meadow on May 7, 1991; and Victor Emanuel found what was likely the same bird along the Pinnacles Trail the following day. The most recent report is a male at the Old Ranch on May 3, 1995 (Wauer).

Cerulean Warbler, *Dendroica cerulea*

There are three reports.

Bonnie McKinney was first to record this little Eastern warbler in the Big Bend Park area; she, along with Katie and Tina Reynolds, found three individuals in brush at a stocktank on the Black Gap WMA on March 29, 1982. It was next recorded on October 5, 1992, at PJ in the visitor center patio; a female was observed by several members of the park staff (Tom Alex, Sarah Bourbon, John Forsythe, and Susie Stewart), and Katie Northrup took two slides (NPS files) for documentation. There is one additional report for RGV on April 27, 1993 (Janet Morgan).

Black-and-white Warbler. *Mniotilta varia*

Uncommon spring migrant; rare fall migrant; casual winter visitor.

This little warbler has been recorded every month. It is one of the earliest spring migrants, sometimes arriving in February; there are two reports for CC: on February 9, 1987 (NPS files), and Carol Edwards found one there on February 17, 1995. It is most numerous from April 20 to May 11, at all elevations. Scattered reports exist during the remainder of May, and there also is a June 6, 1985 report of a bird singing at the Pinnacles (Kevin Karlson). Summer reports include one along the Window Trail on July 1, 1976 (Roger Eastman), and scattered sightings from mid-July to early October, mostly from the lowlands. It has been reported only eight times in winter; five occasions at RGV: November 10 and 18, 1981 (Wauer), December 8, 1983 (Cynthia Simmons), December 28, 1965 (Raymond Fleetwood), and January 4, 1979 (L. A. Deveutt). It also was found near SEC on November 27, 1971 (Wauer). And there is a report along the Window Trail on December 21, 1987 (Nancy Kelley).

American Redstart. *Setophaga ruticilla*
Uncommon migrant; casual late winter visitor.

Reports exist every month but November, December, and January. The earliest fall migrants arrive as early as August 8, a peak is evident from September 5 to 26, and there are a few reports to October 24. Most of the fall birds are either females or immatures. The earliest spring sightings are from RGV on February 7 and 8, 1981 (David Steadman), and Anne Bellamy found a female at the mouth of Mariscal Canyon on February 21, 1984. Afterward there are scattered reports during late March and April from RGV and Boquillas. It is more numerous throughout May, and occasional reported until late June, mostly from along the Rio Grande. There also is a single July record; Joe Buckman and Burt Gurney reported a male at RGV on July 13, 1978.

Prothonotary Warbler. *Protonotaria citrea*
Uncommon spring migrant.

Records range from April 1 through May 15, and there is one fall report: Bill and Sarah Bourbon found one at Buttrill Spring on September 3, 1989. The earliest park record was of an adult bird photographed on a Mexican pinyon in the Chisos Basin campground by Forrest and Aline Romero on April 27, 1971, a very strange habitat for this bird of the Southeastern swamps (Wauer 1973a). Except for the Basin record, one at Boot Spring on May 5, 1985 (E. J. Seedge), and two at Dugout Wells on April 12, 1986 (Kathlyn Rust), all other park reports are from the vicinity of the Rio Grande.

Worm-eating Warbler. *Helmitheros vermivorus*
Rare spring migrant.

Records extend from an early sighting in SEC on March 27, 1987 (Steve Zachary), to a very late observation of a singing bird in Boot Canyon on June 6, 1985 (Kevin and Dale Karlson). The majority of reports range from April 21 to May 6, about half from RGV and the other half from Boot Canyon. A specimen was taken in Boot Canyon (Wauer 1973a) on May 4, 1967.

Ovenbird. *Seiurus aurocapillus*

Rare spring migrant.

Records extend from March 31 through June 2, and there is a single fall sighting of two birds on the RGV nature trail on September 11, 1970 (Wauer). The March 31, 1977, report (in the Chisos Basin in 1977 by M. D. McGhee) is more than three weeks earlier than the next report of one that flew into the window pane at PJ on April 23, 1987 (Ginny Carrico). Several additional reports exist through May 20, and the latest record is from Boot Canyon, by John Egbert on June 2, 1976. Of 15 spring records, seven are from Boot Canyon, three from the Chisos Basin, one from the Old Ranch, and four from RGV.

Northern Waterthrush. *Seiurus noveboracensis*

Uncommon spring and rare fall migrant.

Records extend from a very early report at Castolon on March 18, 1967 (Steve Zachary), one at RGV on April 26, 1971 (Wauer), to several reports from May 1 to 20 in spring, and from August 19 to September 17 in fall; this includes a specimen obtained after it flew into the glass door of the PJ visitor center on September 17, 1977 (Margaret Littlejohn). Migrants can be expected from the Rio Grande floodplain to the upper Chisos canyons. Although most reports are of single birds, I found three in Boot Canyon on May 4, 1967. Also, it may be more numerous in spring than records indicate; from May 3 to 17, 1970, I captured and banded four individuals in 12 net-hours at RGV. During the same period, I saw only one other Northern Waterthrush. There also is a much later report; Rob Pearson found one near SEC, at the mouth of Terlingua Creek, on November 10, 1987.

Louisiana Waterthrush. *Seiurus motacilla.*

Casual migrant.

Records extend from March 26 to May 31 in spring, and from July 12 through September 22 in fall. Reports are distributed about equally between the Rio Grande floodplain, especially at RGV, and the Chisos Mountain. All reports are of lone birds.

Kentucky Warbler. *Oporornis formosus*

Casual spring migrant.

This is a relatively late migrant in spring; reports range from April 17 to May 24, and primarily from middle elevations. Of 14 reported sightings, four are from Dugout Wells on April 19, 20, and 22, and May 6; three from the Old Ranch on April 17 and 18 and May 24; three from the Chisos Basin on April 29 and May 5 and 8; and three from RGV on April 30 and May 1 and 11.

MacGillivray's Warbler. *Oporornis tolmiei*

Fairly common spring migrant; casual in fall.

Records extend from March 28 to June 27 in spring and from August 31 to October 23 in fall; there also is a very early February 18, 1993, report along the Window Trail by Warren Parker. It can be numerous along the Rio Grande floodplain and a few other sites from late April to mid-May; I found five individuals at Dugout Wells on May 16, 1968. Although most sightings are from the lowlands, it also has been recorded in the mountains, at Boot Spring and Laguna Meadow, on a number of occasions.

Common Yellowthroat. *Geothlypis trichas*

Fairly common summer and winter resident; common migrant.

This wetland bird occurs at suitable habitats in cane and cattails along the Rio Grande and adjacent ponds. A few pairs nest regularly at the RGV silt pond and beaver pond along the nature trail; two youngsters were found at the silt pond on July 9, 1968 (Wauer). Migrants are most numerous along the river, but it also has been reported from water areas throughout the park; for example, C. Phillip Allen found one in Boot Canyon on July 31, 1963, and I observed one at Oak Spring on September 9, 1967. Wintering birds usually can be found at areas of heavy vegetation along the Rio Grande floodplain. Participants in RGV CBCs reported an average of seven individuals in ten years (1985–1994), with none in 1990 and a high of 24 in 1992.

Hooded Warbler. *Wilsonia citrina*

Casual spring migrant.

Records extend from April 30 to June 16 in spring, and there are two additional reports: I found one at RGV on September 1, 1971, and Bill Bromberg and Gordon Baumgartner reported one at Boquillas on November 21, 1961. It is most numerous from May 1 to 20, and the majority of these reports are from RGV. Exceptions include one at Dugout Wells on May 1, 1978, by "JM," one at Hot Springs on May 18, 1976 (Jean and Bill Hough and Barbara Ribble); and James Black reported a male at Boot Canyon on May 20, 1990. The late June 16, 1979, report is from Laguna Meadow (Ann Ayers and Marge Eaton).

Wilson's Warbler. *Wilsonia pusilla*

Abundant migrant; casual winter visitor.

Records extend from March 25 through June 4 in spring, and from August 8 through October 12 in fall, and there also are three winter reports: Iris Wiedenfeld found one at RGV on December 27, 1976; one was reported at Hot Springs on January 31 (early NPS records); and Jon Dunn and Guy McCaskie found one at CC on February 8, 1992.

This is the park's most common migrant. A few birds reach the park in late March, and it becomes abundant by the second week of April. A peak is reached from April 22 to 27; more than 85 individuals were counted in mesquites within one 125-square-foot area at RGV on April 22, 1970, and more than 40 were found at Hot Springs on April 27, 1967 (Wauer). The majority of spring migrants pass through the area by May 20. In fall, a peak is reached from August 20 to September 19. Although the vast majority of records are from the lowlands, especially in the vicinity of the Rio Grande, there are numerous sightings at mid-elevations in the mountains as well.

Canada Warbler. *Wilsonia canadensis*

Casual migrant.

Reports are few and far between; they range from May 7 to 27 in spring and from August 12 to 28 in fall, and there also is a much later report on October 9, 1982 at Black Gap WMA (Bonnie McKinney). David Wolf first recorded a female feeding in low, damp brush near the corral at Boot Spring on August 23, 1966.

Charles and Ella Newell next found one at RGV on May 7, 1971. On August 28, 1977, Laurie Yorke reported a male at Laguna Meadow, and on May 19, 1978, Ian McGregor found a male above the Chisos Basin campground. There were three reports during the 1980s: Peter Scott found one at Boot Spring on August 13, 1985; Andrew and Rene Franks reported one there on May 23, 1989; and Tony and Phyliss Frank discovered one at Cattail Falls on May 27, 1989. The most recent sighting is a male at the Old Ranch on May 3, 1995 (Wauer).

Red-faced Warbler. *Cardellina rubrifrons*

Sporadic summer visitor.

It was first reported by Bruce A. Mack at Boot Spring on June 5, 1964, and I listed it as hypothetical in the first edition of this book (1973). Robert Anderson next reported one from Boot Spring on August 10, 1973. And in 1974, Dominic Bartol observed and photographed one at Boot Spring on June 2; Bartol's color print (No. 294 of the Texas Photo Record File) represents the first documented report of this bird for Texas. And on June 5, Glenn Britt found one near the Chisos Basin sewage lagoons.

The Red-faced Warbler was next reported in 1978 on two occasions: H. P. Langridge found one at Boot Spring on July 9, and Julius W. Dieckert reported one there on August 22. There were eight reports, all from Boot Canyon, during the 1980s, including another series of photographs by Greg Lasley in lower Boot Canyon on August 10, 1982. There are an additional eight reports between 1990 and 1994: Jon Dunn found it at Boot Canyon on May 1, 1990; Tom and Calyn Jenns and Mike Bishop reported one (probably the same bird) the following day, as did Tom Boyle, Jim Hayes, Steve Kerr, and Ward Dorsey; and Mark Lockwood found and photographed one in Boot Canyon on August 17, 1991; John Marsh found one in Boot Canyon on August 15, 1992; and there are three reports for 1993: Richard Michael and Thelma Sims recorded it as PJ on April 30; John and Beverly Hargrave reported a pair at PJ on May 1, 1993; and John and Betsy Searight found a lone male at Boot Spring on August 7.

The distribution and status of this brightly marked warbler was documented by Greg Lasley, Dave Easterla, Chuck Sexton, and Dominic Bartol in a comprehensive 1982 article in the *Bulletin of the Texas Ornitho-*

logical Society, which is worth reading. They point out that the species nests in the Sacramento and Sandia mountains of New Mexico and that the Big Bend records likely are migrants. However, its presence in the Chisos should be carefully monitored. Because the habitat in the Chisos Mountains appears similar to that on its known breeding grounds in New Mexico, these increasing records may suggest an eastern movement of its breeding range. This colorful bird would be a welcome addition to Big Bend's breeding avifauna.

Painted Redstart. *Myioborus pictus*

Sporadic summer resident.

Records of this brightly marked warbler extend from March 12 to September 4, all from the Chisos Mountains, with two exceptions: Captain

Painted Redstart, *Myioborus pictus*

and Mrs. E. B. Hurlbert, Becky Wauer, and I found one at RGV on March 20, 1971, and Abbot and Ava Nelson reported a lone male there on March 17, 1978. Van Tyne and Sutton (1937) reported that there appears to be "great fluctuations in the numbers" of this bird, and that

> "in [June] 1901 [Vernon] Bailey, [Louis Agassiz] Fuertes, and [Harry C.] Oberholser saw no Painted Redstarts during their three weeks' exploration of these mountains [the Chisos]. Gaige found the species fairly numerous at Boot Spring, and yet Van Tyne, [Max M.] Peet, and [Edouard C.] Jacot spent the whole of May at the same locality four years later without getting more than an unsatisfactory glimpse of one; and the Carnegie Museum party, in 1933 and 1935, did not record the species at all. On June 24, 1936, however, Tarleton Smith saw an adult male at the head of Blue Creek Canyon."

And on May 13, 1937, Herbert Brandt found a nest with three eggs at Boot Spring. That record was the first documentation of breeding for the Chisos Mountains and Texas (Brandt 1940).

There were no further reports of Painted Redstarts for the park until Harold Brodrick and Richard D. Porter found several at Boot Spring on April 3, 1958; one was collected by Porter (Wauer 1973a). There were five reports during the 1960s: Ralph Raitt found it in Pine Canyon on April 16, 1961; David and Roy Brown reported it at Boot Spring on April 28, 1966; David Simmon found one there on August 27, 1966; I observed two singing birds in Oak Creek, just below the Chisos Basin campground, on March 19, 1967; and Rene Ross, Thelma Fox, Mary Griffith, Maragite Hollar, and Peggy Accord reported one for Boot Spring on May 12, 1969. I found singing birds in Boot Canyon on April 10, 18, and 24, 1971, and those sightings were followed by another period with no records.

Since 1976, however, Painted Redstarts have been reported for the Boot Canyon area every year but 1987, 1990, 1991, and 1994. During this period, nesting was documented on five occasions. John Egbert, who spent May and June 1976 in Boot Canyon studying the Colima Warbler, reported Redstarts from May 18 on, and on June 19 he discovered a nest with four eggs in a grass clump under a mountain sage. Park records show that 1977 was a good Painted Redstart year: Warren Pulich found a pair with two young out of the nest at Boot Spring on July 8, and David and Mimi Wolf reported two fairly young birds at Boot Spring on July 23 and

24; Chuck Hunter, Rich Pruett, and Wesley Cureton found seven birds in Boot Canyon on August 8; and Andrew Stewart and Ron and Marcia Brown reported three adults and one immature bird there on September 4. In 1978, Peter Scott (1978) wrote that "for the third consecutive year," this bird was "common in moist canyons of the high Chisos," and "several singing birds were found May 20." And in 1979, Greg Lasley and Chuck Sexton found and photographed adult birds feeding young in Boot Canyon on May 16 and 17.

During the 1980s, Lasley reported that the species was "more common this year [1982] than last." Joe Kuban found six singing males in Boot Canyon on March 18, 1982, and Bruce and Chris Palmer found a nest with four eggs there on May 13. Three singing males were reported near Pinnacles Pass on March 23, 1984, by Jeffrey Weigal and Mary E. Cowder; and three singing birds were reported for lower Boot Canyon on March 31, 1985, by Kevin Head and John Muller. Later reports include a singing bird near Pinnacles Pass on April 15, 1992 (John Clarkson), and Gail Luckner found several in June 1993 along the Colima Trail. None were reported for 1994, a very dry year, although it was present in 1995, another dry season.

This is a common nesting bird of the forested canyons of Mexico's Maderas del Carmen, 50 miles southeast of the Chisos (Wauer and Ligon 1977). That larger breeding population apparently serves as a recruitment base for the Chisos Mountains some years.

Slate-throated Redstart. *Myioborus miniatus*

There is one verified series of reports.

A lone bird was seen by at least 10 birders at Boot Spring from April 26 to May 15, 1990. Gene Warren was first to find this tropical warbler along the drainage below Boot Spring; Phyllis and Tony Frank and Caroline Coleman located it on April 30; and Mark Lockwood found it on May 15. This record was later reported to the TBRC and accepted (Greg Lasley). This lovely bird breeds in the "mountains from Sonora, Chihuahua, San Louis Potosi south," according to Roger Tory Peterson and Edward Chalif (*A Field Guide to Mexican Birds*), and the nearest known record is one found by Greg Lasley and me "less than 150 airline miles from the Texas border," just south of Monterrey, San Louis Potosi (Wauer 1992).

Rufous-capped Warbler. *Basileuterus rufifrons*

Sporadic visitor.

This little Mexican warbler was first discovered by David Wolf in Campground Canyon on Pulliam Ridge, across from the Chisos Basin campground, on September 9, 1973. It was found again in the same location in May 1974; Bryon Berger, Jerry and Nancy Strickling, Rose Ann Rowlett, and I found it on May 24. There were numerous reports during June and July, including those by William Biggs, Dave Easterla, Dave Goodwin, Larry Hobkins, Ed Kutac, and Joe Taylor. In 1975, it was recorded in Campground Canyon during July and August, and as late as November 23 (Ben Feltner).

Then, in 1976, it was discovered along the SEC nature trail on August 3 by Timothy Thomas and Jack Whetstone (separate reports). It was located there again on April 15, 1977, by Burnell Hill and Laurie Schaetzel, and also observed by an additional 26 individuals during the next two weeks. It was not seen again during 1976, but was reported sporadically in 1978: Travis Beck found one on the SEC nature trail on January 27, and Mary Shannon reported it there on December 17. In 1979, it was recorded there by numerous birders between March 23 (Morgan Jones) and the second week of June, including Greg Lasley, who obtained photographs.

There are two later reports (both accepted by the TBRC): Dick Payne found one on the Lost Mine Trail on March 12 and 13, 1986, and Kinki Koi and others reported one at Dugout Wells on May 8, 1993.

This is a common Mexican warbler of "open woodlands, brushy hillsides, rarely forests; foothills into mts. (to 7000 ft.)," according to *A Field Guide to Mexican Birds* (Peterson and Chalif 1973). Although I have not found it in the Maderas del Carmen Mountains, 50 miles southeast of the Chisos, I have seen it in Sierra de Muzquiz, less than 100 miles southeast of the Maderas del Carmen, and Mike Braun found 70 in the Fraile Mountains, 45 miles south of Falcon Dam, according to Victor Emanuel. This species is likely to occur again within the park, and the chances that it might eventually become established as a breeding bird are good.

Yellow-breasted Chat. *Icteria virens.*

Abundant summer resident; uncommon migrant.

In summer, this large warbler is abundant among the dense vegetation of the Rio Grande floodplain and less numerous at other riparian areas, such

Yellow-breasted Chat, *Icteria virens.*

as Dugout Wells and the Old Ranch, up to about 4,000 feet elevation. In 1995, I recorded two territorial birds just below the sewage lagoons in the Chisos Basin on May 7. It has been recorded from April 10 through September 24, and there are two additional reports: I found one at Boquillas

Crossing on November 3, 1967, and Nancy and Jerry Stickling discovered one in the river cane at RGV on January 8, 1978.

Early spring arrivals are silent, but by the end of April this is the most vociferous bird of the floodplain. Displaying birds can be found every few dozen feet wherever there is heavy growth of vegetation from Lajitas eastward through the Lower Canyons. By the end of July there is some dispersal of early nesters, but others are still feeding young. A sighting of a lone bird in the Chisos Basin on June 26, 1989 (Jeff Selleck), is likely a post-nesting wanderer. In mid-August a definite decline is evident, and they are almost entirely gone from their breeding grounds by the end of the month. The few September sightings are late nesters and migrants. There apparently is some movement of migrants through the mountains: Peter Scott found one on the Window Trail in May 1978, and Walter Boles, Jim Shields, and John St. Julien reported a lone bird at Boot Spring on August 10, 1970.

Olive Warbler. *Peucedramus taeniatus*

Casual spring and late summer visitor.

Charles Bender and Bill Mealy found one first near the South Rim on August 19, 1966. I discovered a lone bird in Boot Canyon on September 19, 1970 (Wauer 1973a); Thelma Dalmas found one at Laguna Meadow on July 4, 1975; and Carolyn and Ray Cuthbertson and George Burns reported one in Blue Creek Canyon on May 3, 1991. There also are two lowland reports at RGV on May 6, 1985 (Larry and Martha Ballard) and July 8, 1991 (J. Hansche), and a lone winter report: Robert Harms found one on the Window Trail, January 4, 1975. This pine forest species is a fairly common breeding bird in Mexico's Maderas del Carmen (Wauer and Ligon 1977), and post-nesting birds should be expected.

FAMILY EMBERIZIDAE
Subfamily Thraupinae: Tanagers
Hepatic Tanager. *Piranga flava*

Uncommon summer resident and migrant.

Records extend from April 12, through the summer, to October 19. Although this liver-red (male) bird is never numerous, it occurs regularly at a few localities. Breeding pairs usually can be found in upper Green Gulch, just above the Chisos Basin cottages, at Juniper Flat, and above

Laguna Meadow almost any morning in May and June. I found a nest on a pinyon pine near the Chisos Mountain Lodge on May 12, 1968, and saw an adult male carrying food above the cottages on June 10, 1967.

Migrants can hardly be separated from early breeding birds and post-nesting wanderers. However, on September 25, 1966, I recorded a "wave of birds near the East Rim at 8:30 a.m." that included at least a dozen Hepatic Tanagers, along with several Ruby-crowned Kinglets, Hermit Thrushes, and Vesper Sparrows.

Lowland reports are questionable: I never have found this tanager below the Chisos woodlands, although there are a few reports. Fall birds can be very confusing because the bill color of the Summer Tanager is sometimes dark at that time of year.

Summer Tanager. *Piranga rubra*

Common summer resident; uncommon migrant; casual in winter.

Males arrive as early as March 25 (Wauer and Carol Edwards at RGV in 1995), and females and subadults follow within a week or two. By the last week of April this bird is abundant at RGV; I counted 40 there on April 23, 1967. However, it does not reach its breeding grounds at higher elevations until late April. Nesting occurs along the Rio Grande floodplain, especially at RGV and CC, and also at areas of deciduous vegetation in the lower mountains; examples include Dugout Wells, the Old Ranch, Cattail Falls, Oak Creek, and Green Gulch. During the summers of 1968 and 1969, the feeding territories of this species and the Hepatic Tanager overlapped along Oak Creek, just below the Chisos Basin campground.

Summer Tanagers are gregarious and, like the Orchard and Hooded orioles that use the same cottonwood groves at RGV and CC, they spend a great deal of time chasing each other around the groves when they first arrive. Nesting gets under way by early May, and young are out of the nest in June, although there is some late nesting as well; nest-building was found at RGV on June 20, 1967, and adults were seen feeding young in a nest at Boquillas Crossing on August 20, 1970 (Wauer). I have detected only minimal post-nesting wandering; for the most part, this species seems to remain on its breeding grounds throughout August and most of September. There is a noticeable decline in birds by the last of September, and I could find only two individuals at RGV on October 5, 1969. A late sighting at Oak Creek on October 10, 1967 (Wauer) may be either a tardy resident or a migrant. And some years it apparently also occurs in winter; there are four reports: Wesley Cureton found one at RGV on November 30 and December 1, 1985; Ron Korosick reported one there on December 30, 1985; Anne Bellamy and Charles Callagan found one there (perhaps the same bird) on January 13, 1986; and Kelly Bryan reported one at CC on November 9, 1991.

Scarlet Tanager. *Piranga olivacea*
Rare spring and early fall migrant and summer visitor.

This lovely Eastern tanager has been reported in BBNP from as early as March 16 (Nancy Baron reported a male at Santa Elena Crossing in 1986), during summer, to August 23 (Eunice Chynoweth and Victor Petty found a molting male at RGV in 1986). Although the majority of reports are from the vicinity of the Rio Grande, it also has been recorded at higher elevations: a pair in upper Oak Creek on May 8, 1986 (Alan Van Valkenburg); a male at Boot Canyon on June 21, 1992 (Bill Bourbon); a singing male at Laguna Meadow on June 23, 1991 (James Peters); and a male at Pinnacles Pass on June 28, 1990 (Michael Evans). It may be more common than the few records suggest; females are difficult to separate from other female tanagers.

Western Tanager. *Piranga ludociciana*
Rare in summer; fairly common migrant.

Tarleton Smith (1936) reported seeing "young birds able to fly" in Pine canyon on July 24, 1936. There is no later evidence of breeding, in spite of a vigorously singing adult male at Juniper Flat on June 7, 1970 (Wauer). Northbound birds do not reach the Big Bend area until mid-April, peak from May 6 to 15, and stragglers have been reported as late as May 26. Afterward, except for the June 7 record, there are no additional reports until July 4, when post-nesting and nonbreeding birds begin to move through the area on their southward journey. I found adult males at RGV on July 4, 1969, and July 12, 1970, and Dave Easterla reported one at PJ on July 9, 1974. However, it is most common in the mountains, where birds can be found throughout the remainder of the summer.

Fall migrants have been recorded regularly from mid-August to late September, numbers decline in early October, and an occasional straggler

Western Tanager, *Piranga ludociciana*

is reported to October 25. The largest number reported was "25-plus" along the Window Trail on September 23, 1971 (Wauer). Winter reports are few and far between: Clyde Glastetter and Nancy Kelley found a male along the Window Trail on December 21, 1988; there are no January records; Keith and Jan Wigger reported a male at RGV on February 10, 1979; Anne LeSassier and C. Philip Allen found two males on the Window Trail on February 27, 1963; and Alan Wormington reported a female at CC on March 3, 1992. There are no further spring reports until April 18.

FAMILY EMBERIZIDAE
Subfamily Cardinalinae: Cardinals, Grosbeaks, and Allies
Northern Cardinal. *Cardinalis cardinalis*

Common year-round resident on the Rio Grande floodplain and less numerous in lowland riparian habitats elsewhere.

It is most numerous at RGV and CC, but breeding birds also usually can be found at Dugout Wells, Government Spring, the Old Ranch, and a few other riparian areas up to about 3,500 feet elevation. Nesting normally occurs in

April and May, but Bill Bourbon found an adult with two fledglings at CC on August 4, 1990. Reports of a lone male at 4,000 feet in Blue Creek Canyon on May 29, 1989 (Sarah Bourbon), and one at the Chisos Basin Amphitheater on June 10, 1989 (Bill Bourbon), may be post-nesting vagrants.

Most sightings away from choice nesting sites from mid-July through October and mid-February through March are probably migrants. Small flocks of 10 to 15 birds were found moving north near RGV on March 21, 1969, and a lone male was found at PJ on March 19, 1967 (Wauer); and Hank Schmidt found one at PJ on September 16, 1960. Wintering Cardinals are most numerous along the Rio Grande, although one stayed at PJ from November 29, 1967, to December 13, 1968, and was banded on December 9 (Wauer). In recent years (1985–94), CBC participants at RGV have recorded it every year; average counts numbered 14 birds, including a low of two individuals in 1989 and a high of 26 in 1985.

Pyrrhuloxia. *Cardinalis sinuatus*

Common year-round resident.

This is a bird of the desert arroyos; the closely related Northern Cardinal prefers riparian areas. Pyrrhuloxias usually can be found at mesquite-acacia thickets in the drier parts of the Rio Grande floodplain and in arid side-canyons up to about 4,500 feet. Lowland birds are mostly permanent residents. Nesting occurs in April, May, and June; I found adults feeding young at RGV on May 21, 1968, and an active nest seven feet high in a mesquite there on June 14, 1968. Pyrrhuloxias are fairly shy while nesting but become easier to find soon afterward. Except for the resident birds of the floodplain, there appears to be considerable wandering after nesting; numbers increase at PJ and in the Chisos Basin during late July and August. By October, birds may even be found in the higher parts of the mountains as well; I found two in upper Boot Canyon on October 22, 1967, and one near the South Rim on November 22, 1967. Wintering birds generally remain below 5,000 feet. Lowland residents often congregate in flocks of 10 to 30 individuals from late September until the first of March. Those in the lower mountain canyons seldom flock, but usually are found in smaller family groups.

Pyrrhuloxia, *Cardinalis sinuatus*

Rose-breasted Grosbeak. *Pheucticus ludovicianus*
Rare spring migrant; casual in summer and fall.

Spring reports are scattered from March 23 through April, and more numerous from May 1 to 20. There is a single summer report: William M. Shepard found an adult male at the Old Ranch on June 15, 1993. Fall records include an adult male at the Chisos Basin sewage lagoons on July 21, 1989 (Kelly Bryan); Mark Lockwood found one at Boot Spring on August 28, 1990; and Paul Saraceni reported an immature male at Dugout Wells on September 24, 1994. The majority of reports are from middle elevations, such as Dugout Wells and the Old Ranch, but there also are a few sightings from along the Rio Grande and in the higher Chisos Mountains. And, except for a pair found at Dugout on June 8, 1974 (Ken Able), and two males in the Chisos Basin on May 20, 1978 (Fred Dalby), all reports are of lone birds.

Black-headed Grosbeak. *Phaucticus melanocephalus*
Common summer resident; uncommon migrant.

This bird summers in the deciduous woodlands above 4,500 feet. It reaches the Big Bend the last week of April and begins to nest almost immediately; I found it nest-building in the Chisos Basin on May 2, 1967, and Tarleton Smith (1936) reported a nest with two well-feathered young in the Basin on July 11, 1936. Breeding birds begin to move out of the area by early September, and by the middle of the month only migrants can be found. I discovered a late southbound bird along the Window Trail on October 4, 1968, and an immature bird visited my feeder at PJ on November 4 and 5, 1969. One reported by Theodore M. Sperry and Gladys C. Galliger in the Basin on December 21, 1960, was surely a very late vagrant. Most of the park's Black-headed Grosbeak records are from the mountains, but there also are a handful from the lowlands: I found lone males at RGV on May 8, 1968; May 6, 1970; September 14, 1968; and September 26, 1969. And Robert Rothe and family reported one at RGV on October 4, 1987. There also is one very early spring report: Bonnie McKinney found a lone male along the Rio Grande at Rooney's on March 4, 1987.

Black-headed Grosbeak, *Phaucticus melanocephalus*

Blue Grosbeak. *Guiraca caerulea*

Fairly common summer resident; uncommon migrant; casual winter visitor.

Like the Black-headed Grosbeak of the mountains, this bird is one of the late spring arrivals. Migrants begin to move along the Rio Grande in mid-April (the earliest report is April 16 at Castolon), but they do not become regular until the first of May. The vast majority of migrants stay in the lowlands, but John Egbert found one at Boot Spring on May 19, 1976. It nests in riparian thickets along the river, at a few of the dense mesquites bosques in the desert arroyos, and along open mountain canyons to about 5,000 feet. It almost always can be found in late spring and summer along the RGV nature trail, at the Old Ranch, and along lower Oak Creek Canyon below the Chisos Basin campground. Some years territorial birds occur at a few additional sites, such as Blue Creek Canyon and lower Pine Canyon. Nest-building was reported at RGV on June 10, 1970 (Dave Easterla).

By early August, southbound birds begin to appear at all elevations; Chuck Sexton found a molting male at 7,100 feet in Boot Canyon on August 8, 1992, and Gloria Saylor reported a male there (perhaps the same bird) on August 20, 1992; and Greg Lasley found one at the South Rim on August 18, 1990. Fall migrants generally replace the summer residents by late August and reach a peak the first few days of September. Stragglers continue to pass through the area until October 1. And only during the 1990s has this species begun to appear in winter: Beverly Carlisle was first to report a male at Castolon on January 1, 1991, and Robert Rothe reported a male at RGV on February 10, 1991. On December 28, 1991, Ken Stinnett, Jane Gray, and Bryant Woods found a male at RGV, and six individuals were recorded near the Castolon store by M. Gustafson and Barbara Peterjohn on January 17, 1992. Chuck Hill reported one at RGV on January 25, 1992, and Greg Lasley found and photographed one at CC on January 29, 1992.

Lazuli Bunting. *Passerina amoena*

Rare spring migrant; casual in summer and fall.

Records of this Western bunting extend from two very early spring (or late winter) reports at SEC on February 8 (a female by Alan Wormington and Bill Lamond in 1992) and along the Window Trail on March 18 (female by Russell Fraker in 1992), to three reports in late April, several from May 1 to 12, and a few scattered reports to June 9. There are no further reports until July 30 (a male and two females at the Chisos Basin sewage lagoons by Nick Jackson in 1984), there are seven sightings from mid-August to September 20, and there are no reports for October, November, December, and January.

Indigo Bunting. *Passerina cyanea*

Uncommon spring migrant; rare in summer and fall.

The earliest spring report is from RGV on March 10, 1978 (A. Brander and H. Schulz), and Jim Liles found a male in Juniper Canyon on April 14, 1983. The majority of reports range from April 24 through May; it is most numerous from May 1 to 13, and there is a second surge of migrants from May 18 to 26, followed by a few scattered reports through June. Many of the June sightings are of singing birds. Those found along the Window Trail appear to be competing for territories with Varied Buntings, which are very vocal there at that time of year. Perhaps the presence of singing Varied Buntings keeps the Indigo Buntings longer. In 1970, singing male Indigos also were found at RGV from May 22 to June 10, in the same area with singing Painted Buntings. The Indigo Buntings vacate both areas during July, although an occasional bird is reported as late as July 25. There is no evidence of nesting.

Indigo Buntings next appear during mid- to late August: Stanley Auker found one in the Basin on August 18, 1981, and Willie Sekula reported one at the Basin sewage lagoons on August 22, 1988. All later reports are from RGV: I found an immature male on September 18, 1970; Robert Rothe reported lone birds on October 2 and 29, 1989; and there is a lone winter report—M. Gustafson and Barbara Peterjohn found a female at RGV on January 6, 1992. The vast majority of reports are from mid-elevations and the lowlands, but Doug Evans found a lone male in Boot Canyon on May 5, 1984.

Varied Bunting. *Passerina versicolor*

Fairly common summer resident; migrant; casual in winter.

The earliest spring reports include lone birds at Hot Springs on March 25, 1994 (Dorthy Hagewood), and at RGV on April 4, 1972 (Wauer and

Varied Bunting, *Passerina versicolor*

Russ and Marian Wilson). Reports are more numerous after mid-April, including one caught in a mist net at PJ on April 18, 1969 (Wauer); it was banded and released. During the first two weeks of May, Varied Buntings become fairly common in weedy arroyos and along the roadways. Males arrive on their breeding grounds at mid-elevations first, and the females join them a few to 10 days later. On April 29, 1970, I found four singing males along the Window Trail, but no females. A male was actively defending a territory in this same area on May 24, 1968, and a male was seen feeding two youngsters there on July 19, 1969. I found a nest containing three nestlings in Blue Creek Canyon on June 4, 1968, and seven singing males along a one-mile stretch of Cottonwood Creek, just behind the Old Ranch, on July 13, 1968. I also found four singing males and one nest on a squaw bush along one mile of Blue Creek Canyon, just above the Homer Wilson Ranch house, on June 4, 1968. It also can be found during the nesting season in the brushy drainage below Government Springs, in the shallow drainage above Dugout Wells, and, on June 5, 1970, I found four singing birds among the rather open mesquite thickets north of the roadway northeast of Todd Hill.

There appears to be double brooding or late nesting some years. I found an adult male feeding two fledged young along the Window Trail on August 28, 1966; and on August 23, 1970, I found nine singing males and several females and juveniles along a two-mile stretch on lower Panther Canyon. A visit there on September 13 turned up only two adult males, but one was feeding three very recently fledged youngsters.

Varied Buntings are most numerous during wet years and less abundant during years of little winter/spring precipitation. During the wet summer of 1968, I found a singing male in a thicket of mesquite and cane along the Rio Grande, just two miles below SEC. And on August 11, 1971, Red and Majorie Adams and Rose Ann Rowlett found an adult male feeding young below the SEC overlook. There appears to be some postnesting wandering; Kevin and Dale Karlson reported an immature male at Juniper Flat on June 7, 1985.

Varied Buntings usually can be found with some searching in the proper weedy habitats below approximately 5,000 feet through the second week of September. There are no reports from mid-September through November, but there are several wintertime sightings: Rick LoBello reported one from the Old Ranch on December 3, 1976; I found one below the Basin campground on December 28, 1968; Glenn Cureton reported a male behind the Chisos Remuda on December 30, 1976; there is a report for Castolon on January 3 (NPS file); and four in February—Anne Bellamy found a male at the Basin sewage lagoons on February 6, 1987; Francis Williams reported one there on February 12, 1975; Mark Lockwood observed a male at CC on February 19, 1992; and Jesse Boyce and Cathy Moitoret found one at SEC on February 22, 1976.

Painted Bunting. *Passerina ciris*

Common summer resident; uncommon spring and rare fall migrant.

This is another rather late spring arrival, not usually present on its breeding grounds until April 22. However, there are four earlier spring reports: Jim Hurst reported a pair at RGV on February 21, 1995; Bill and Sarah Bourbon found one at Terlingua on March 9, 1991; Kathy Fox reported one near the Chisos Basin Trailhead on March 15, 1994; and Dave Easterla found one at RGV on April 5, 1971. Nesting occurs during June, July, and August, including one very late nest with two nestlings at Boquillas on August 29, 1970 (Wauer). Males normally desert their breeding grounds during the first two weeks of August. Only the greenish females and juveniles are likely to be seen afterward. By early September, females and immatures also are hard to find, but a search through weedy patches at RGV and Castolon usually will turn up a few. Immature birds can be found at such places until October 5.

Fall migrants are rare; an adult male found on the RGV nature trail on September 21, 1970, was assumed to be a migrant because it was the first adult seen there since August 22. There also are two extremely late sightings at RGV: I found a lone female on November 19, 1970, and Georgia Callagan and Jeff Miller reported an adult male on December 27, 1984. There are no January and February reports.

Dickcissel. *Spiza americana*

Rare spring and uncommon fall migrant.

There were no records of this bird prior to 1967, when one appeared at my feeder at PJ on May 14. Since then, it has been reported regularly from April 26 through May 27 in spring and from August 5 to October 22 in fall. The spring reports are widely scattered and, except for two at PJ, all are from the vicinity of the Rio Grande. There are twice the number of fall reports, including two from the Chisos Basin: P. D. Hulce found an immature bird at the campground on August 4, 1994, and I found one there on August 26, 1969. The latest fall record is one banded by Bonnie McKinney at Black Gap WMA on October 22, 1983. All of the reports are of one to five birds.

FAMILY EMBERIZIDAE
Subfamily Emberizinae: Towhees, Sparrows, and Longspurs
Green-tailed Towhee. *Pipilo chlorurus*

Fairly common migrant and winter resident.

Tarleton Smith (1936) reported a nest containing eggs from 4,600 feet in the Chisos Basin on July 10, 1936. The only other evidence of nesting is an apparently territorial bird seen above Laguna Meadow, May 28, 1971, by Ted Parker and Harold Morrin. Fall migrants reach the Big Bend area by September 19, but it is not reported regularly until mid-October, when it may be numerous along weedy arroyos to 5,000 feet. Fall migration subsides by early November, but stragglers and winter residents usually can be found at thickets almost anywhere below the pinyon-juniper-oak woodlands.

Wintering birds can be found most easily at the Old Ranch, Dugout Wells, and in brushy areas in lower Green Gulch and along the Rio Grande. It was recorded on nine of ten (1985–1994) of CBCs in the Chisos Mountains, including a high of 34 birds in 1986; and on seven of ten years (1985–1994) of CBCs centered at RGV, where a high of 17 birds was reported in 1986. Spring migrants begin to appear about mid-March; they reach a peak during the second week of April; there is a short lapse in reports during mid-April, followed by another peak from April 26 to May 6; stragglers continue to pass through the area until May 17; and there is one very late sighting at Laguna Meadow on June 24, 1995, by Victor Emanuel, Forrest Rowlands, and others.

Rufous-sided Towhee. *Pipilo erythrophthalmus*

Common summer resident and spring migrant; uncommon fall migrant; fairly common winter resident.

Breeding birds are confined to the wooded canyons of the Chisos Mountains and nest during May, June, July, and August. The majority seem to remain on their breeding grounds most of the year; one banded at Boot Spring on January 26 was recaptured there on May 7. However, some fall dispersal is evident in September, when some of the high country birds apparently move into the lower canyons. Fall migrants have been recorded until the middle of October; the earliest sighting along the Rio Grande is one at RGV on October 18, 1969 (Wauer). Afterward it becomes regular at localized places for the remainder of the winter.

Rufous-sided Towhee, *Pipilo erythrophthalmus*

Robert DeVine found six Rufous-sided Towhees, along with three Canyon and two Green-tailed towhees, at his feeder at PJ on January 20, 1979. Spring migrants reach the Big Bend area by mid-March, a peak is evident during the second week of April, and there is only one report for the lowlands after April 21; I found one at RGV on May 15, 1968.

Canyon Towhee. Pipilo fuscus

Common permanent resident.

This is the very plain brown, ground-loving bird, earlier known as "Brown Towhee," that is numerous in the Chisos Basin campground and around the lodge and accommodations. Nesting occurs from April throughout the summer and fall, especially during wet years; in 1966, I found an adult bird feeding a spotted youngster on the Lost Mine Trail on November 6.

There seems to be some altitudinal movement to lower areas during some winters; I found it more numerous than usual at RGV from September 21 through April in 1969–70, but I did not detect increased numbers during other winters. From 1985 through 1994, CBC participants tallied an average of 61 birds on the Chisos Mountain count and only six on ten RGV counts.

Cassin's Sparrow. Aimophila cassinii

Sporadic summer resident; fairly common migrant; uncommon winter resident.

This is one of Big Bend's most interesting sparrows because of its almost complete dependence upon the spring and summer rainy season for nesting. Although it is a regular nesting sparrow on the grasslands in northern Brewster County and north to Fort Stockton and Fort Davis, where singing birds usually can be found every May, June, and July, and during August and September in wet years, it is a very sporadic nesting bird within BBNP. In 1967, three skylarking males were observed in lower Green Gulch on June 3, and 15 singing birds were counted there on July 30, several days after heavy showers. In 1968, cool and moist weather prevailed from April through September. A few singing birds were heard in Green Gulch as early as June 27, and an estimated 35 skylarking birds were recorded there on July 4. The summer of 1969 was exceptionally dry; it was found singing only in spring, including five to seven individuals singing on the flats near Dog Canyon on June 6. Searches for nesting birds in Green Gulch during the dry period of June, July, and August 1969 proved fruitless. In 1970, I did not find any singing birds during the relatively dry spring and early summer, but after rainy periods in July and August, the Cassin's Sparrow was the most numerous singing bird on grassy areas below 4,000 feet throughout the park. In fact, numerous sky-

Canyon Towhee, *Pipilo fuscus*

larking birds were even recorded at RGV and along the River Road all during August; I found an estimated 30 singing birds along the River Road on August 21. Only a few singing birds were detected in the area by mid-September, but these apparently remained at grassy places throughout the fall and winter. In addition, Peter Scott reported that he found none during the dry seasons of 1977 and 1978, but that from March to early June, 1979, was another good season for Cassin's Sparrows. And in 1982, Brete Griffen reported three skylarking birds below PJ on June 6, and Jo Williams III found four singing birds near the Fossil Bone Display on Tornillo Flat on June 28.

In years when nesting birds are not already numerous in August and September, there is a distinct movement of fall migrants into the park during the first week of September. This influx is usually over by September 20. Afterward, a few birds usually can be found at choice weedy places along the Rio Grande floodplain as well as in the grassy, open canyons of the lower mountains during the remainder of the winter. I found a high of 58 birds on the December 28, 1968, Chisos Mountains CBC; it was found only three times from 1985 to 1994, including a high of 12 birds in 1986; none were found on ten (1985–1994) CBCs centered at RGV. By the second week of March, singing birds often can be detected at wintering sites, but later reports depend upon precipitation. As soon as the rains begin it is only a few days before singing birds are evident.

Rufous-crowned Sparrow. *Aimophila ruficeps*

Common permanent resident.

This upland sparrow maintains a fixed territory year-round; a bird banded at Boot Spring on January 26, 1968, was seen there on February 23 and May 8, 1968, and on June 7, 1970 (Wauer). Nesting occurs during April and May and again during the summer rainy period in July, August, and September. In fact, in the lower portion of its range, nesters are far more active during wet summers than they are in spring. Ten (1985–1994) Chisos Mountains CBCs tallied an average of 54 individuals, with a high of 219 in 1986 and a low of 16 in 1989. There are no reports below approximately 3,500 feet elevation.

Chipping Sparrow. *Spizella passerina*
Common migrant; fairly common winter visitor.

This is probably the park's most numerous sparrow from October to mid-May. It has been recorded every month; there is an absence of reports only from June 6 through July 18. Fall migrants can be expected any time after July 19; I banded one on that date at PJ in 1970. There are scattered reports during the remainder of July and the first half of August, after which it becomes more numerous, reaching a peak in early October, when mixed flocks of Chippers and Clay-colored Sparrows and a few Brewer's Sparrows usually are common along the lowland roadways and on the Rio Grande floodplain. Most flocks of *Spizella* sparrows in the mountains are dominated by Chippers.

Wintering birds are most numerous below 5,500 feet, but they usually also can be found in the pinyon-juniper woodlands on the South and East rims during warm winter days. They also can be found in the lower Chisos Basin, and small flocks are fairly common on the Rio Grande floodplain. Northbound migrants begin to move into the area in early March, and the spring migration is well under way by the third week of March, when flocks of 30 to 50 birds often can be found feeding under the cottonwoods at RGV and CC, as well as on open ground in the Basin. The spring movement does not subside until the middle of May, and stragglers have been recorded to June 5 (Wauer).

Clay-colored Sparrow. *Spizella pallida*
Uncommon migrant; sporadic winter resident.

Some years this bird is almost as numerous as the Chipping Sparrow; other years it is rare. Records are almost totally confined to the open desert and arroyos below 4,000 feet; I have found it in the mountain woodlands only a few times. In September 1968 it was abundant; only one was seen at Dugout Wells on September 10, but on the morning of September 17, thousands were found scattered over the desert. These birds were in the company of Lark Buntings and an occasional Field or Lincoln's sparrow. The wave of sparrows subsided by late afternoon, and I found only a few individuals there on September 19. The winters of 1968–69 and 1970–71 were good "sparrow winters," and Clay-coloreds could be found at weedy fields along the river all winter. Conversely, the fall, winter, and spring of 1969–70 represented an all-time low: Only a few were recorded from September 19 through October; none were seen from November 1 through February; and there were only a few reports from March 18 to May 6. Normally, northbound migrants begin to move into the area by mid-March, a peak is reached during the first week of April, and there are fewer reports during the remainder of the month, followed by another influx from May 1 to 9, which is followed by scattered sightings until June 1.

Brewer's Sparrow. *Spizella breweri*

Fairly common spring migrant; sporadic fall migrant and winter visitor.

Records range from October 20 through May 23. Like the Clay-colored Sparrow, Brewer's rarely occur above 4,500 feet. Fall migrants are somewhat sporadic and are almost always in association with Chippers or Clay-coloreds. Wintering birds can be found at weedy fields along the Rio Grande during "sparrow years": I found it during the winters of 1966–67, 1968–69, and 1970–71 at RGV and Castolon. It was present within the sotol grasslands all winter in 1970–71 as well. During the spring migration, it can be found with certainty only from mid-March through mid-April. A peak is reached from March 15 to 27, and flocks of 10 to 50 birds often can be detected by their choruses of musical trills.

Field Sparrow. *Spizella pusilla*

Sporadic migrant and winter visitor.

Records range from September 15 through the winter to March 22, and there is a very late report at PJ on April 24, 1994 (Wauer). Like the other Spizella sparrows, this little bird may be numerous some winters and hard to find others. During 1967–68 it was present in substantial numbers throughout the grassy slopes of the Chisos Mountains below 5,000 feet. Nine were banded at PJ on the following dates: December 31; January 10 (two) and 15; February 3, 6, and 27; and March 15 and 17 (Wauer). In 1968–69, several were found on grassy flats along the Rio Grande from September 15 to March 15. But I found only one during the entire fall, winter, and spring of 1969–70—at Castolon on December 21. And during the winter of 1970–71 they were present in small numbers up to about 4,000 feet.

Black-chinned Sparrow, *Spizella atrogularis*

Black-chinned Sparrow. *Spizella atrogularis*

Fairly common summer resident; uncommon migrant; sporadic winter resident.

There are reports of this colorful little sparrow every month but October. Singing birds have been recorded as early as March 17 in the Chisos Basin, where they usually can be found along the upper portions of the Window Trail and adjacent to the campground. It nests there, as well as along the north and west slopes below Casa Grande, in the chaparral-like vegetation surrounding Laguna Meadow, along upper Green Gulch, and in lower Blue Creek Canyon. Some years it is abundant at Laguna Meadow; 12 singing birds were counted there on May 7, 1970 (Wauer). During dry years it apparently waits until the summer rainy season before nesting.

Wintering Black-chins may be fairly common at weedy patches in the canyons between 4,400 and 5,400 feet elevation, but other winters they are difficult or impossible to find. In 1967, 15 were found in Maple Canyon on January 20, and 12 along the Window Trail on January 21. There is a defined downward movement most winters; none have been recorded above 5,400 feet from November 6 through mid-April. If enough rain falls in the summer to produce a good grass crop, Black-chins usually can be found wintering in weedy areas along the Window Trail (just below the sewage lagoons), near the Basin campground, and in middle Green Gulch. Populations may be somewhat cyclical. Chisos Mountains CBC participants tallied four in 1985, 14 in 1986, eight in 1987, one in 1988, none in 1989 and 1990, 15 in 1991, eight in 1992, three in 1993, and 16 in 1994.

Vesper Sparrow. *Pooecetes gramineus*

Common migrant; sporadic winter resident.

Fall migrants reach the park area in mid-September and become more numerous during October. At times they are abundant at weedy areas almost everywhere below 5,400 feet, and less numerous in the highlands. I found several near the East Rim on September 25, 1967. Wintering birds generally are restricted to the lower, weedy flats. I have found them most numerous during certain "sparrow winters," after summer rains have produced good grass crops. An example was 1967–68, when I banded 24 individuals at PJ between January 13 and April 18. During that same period, except for Chipping Sparrows, it was the most common sparrow banded. Northbound birds usually appear by mid-March, a peak occurs during the first two weeks of April, and stragglers can be expected until May 23.

Lark Sparrow. *Chondestes grammacus*

Fairly common migrant; casual summer visitor.

Spring migrants can be found as early as March 19, they become more numerous from early April to early May, followed by scattered reports to May 19, and there are four much later sightings: Ken Bass and Jerry Rogers found one at the Chisos Basin ranger station on May 31, 1976; I found one at PJ on June 6, 1967; and Dave Easterla reported one from PJ on June 12, 1973 and another from Ernst Tinaja on June 29, 1968. Most records are from the desert lowlands and arroyos below 4,000 feet.

Although this sparrow nests at weedy thickets in northern Brewster County, there is no good evidence of nesting in the park, although it is possible. Small flocks of three to ten birds begin to appear in late July and become regular at weedy areas from mid-August until October 24; a peak is evident from August 19 to mid-September. And there are two later reports: I found lone birds near Solis on November 11, 1967, and at Gano Spring on December 29, 1970. There are no reports for January, February, and the first half of March.

Black-throated Sparrow. *Amphispiza bileata*

Abundant permanent resident.

This is the park's most commonly seen desert sparrow. It is most numerous within the shrub desert to about 4,200 feet elevation, and less numerous along the open Rio Grande floodplain. I detected 35 to 48 individuals on four one-mile breeding bird surveys near Dugout Wells in late April and early May 1994. Nesting occurs from April to June and again in July, August, and September, if the summer rains arrive and produce an adequate seed crop. Non-nesting birds usually occur in flocks of five to 30 individuals, and often are detected first by their tinkling calls. It is somewhat shy while nesting, but usually can be attracted with squeaking or "spishing" sounds. Juveniles lack the typical black throat of adults; this difference can be confusing, but they almost always are accompanied by adults.

Sage Sparrow. *Amphispiza belli*

Sporadic winter visitor.

This Western sparrow may be more common within BBNP in winter than records indicate; they frequent sparse grasslands, such as those on Tornillo Flat, where few birders spend time. However, there are several reports that extend from December 27 through May 22, plus a very early sighting at RGV on October 24, 1970 (Wauer and Russ and Marian Wilson). The vast majority of reports are from Tornillo Flat, east of the Fossil Bone Display. Steve Carroll reported 50 to 100 birds there on December 28, 1991; I found small flocks in the same area on January 5 and January 18, 1969; Dick Payne reported it there on March 13, 1986, and Steve Carroll found flocks of about 50 and 10 birds there on December 28, 1991.

Black-throated Sparrow, *Amphispiza bileata*

Lark Bunting. *Calamospiza melanocorys*
Fairly common migrant; sporadic winter visitor

Fall migrants have been reported as early as July 10 (a lone male found at Persimmon Gap in 1985 by Phil Gordon), but the majority of the southbound migrants do not reach the Big Bend area until early August. A peak is evident from early September to mid-October, and scattered reports continue through November. Wintering birds are never abundant, although they are more numerous some years than others; the majority of the winter records are from the PJ area. Spring migration can be detected by early March, and the bulk of the northbound birds are found in the lowlands, especially in the Boquillas/RGV area and along the road between RGV and PJ, from mid-March to mid-April; on March 22 and 23,

1969, I found thousands of Lark Buntings along the Rio Grande between RGV and Boquillas Canyon. After mid-April, the spring migration progresses at a slower pace until the end of May; there are no June reports.

Savannah Sparrow. *Passerculus sandwichensis*

Uncommon migrant and winter visitor.

Fall migrants do not reach the park until mid-September; it is more numerous during the latter half of October, and there are scattered reports during November, December, January, and February. Wintering birds usually can be found at weedy patches and grassy flats along the Rio Grande and in open arroyos up to 4,500 feet. It was recorded only once on ten (1985–1994) CBCs centered at RGV. Spring migrants begin to move through the area by mid-March and may be quite numerous along the river. The latest reports are at RGV on May 24, 1967 (Wauer) and at the Old Ranch on May 29, 1989 (Richard Jeffers). The majority of reports are from the lowlands, but there also are a few up to the Chisos Basin. At least two races of Savannah Sparrows visit the park. They look considerably different, and this variation can lead to confusion; the wintering resident and early spring migrant is smaller and lighter than the large, dark form, which is present only as a migrant.

Baird's Sparrow. *Ammodramus bairdii*

Casual migrant; sporadic winter visitor.

Records extend from September 6 to May 21. There are widely scattered reports from September 6 to January 25, none in February and March, one in April at PJ on April 2, 1967 (Wauer), and several reports from May 2 to 22. Except for one found at the Chisos Basin sewage lagoon by David Wolf and Drew Thate on May 8, 1993, all the reports are from weedy areas in the lowlands. I have found it most often at old fields between Castolon and SEC from mid-October to late December.

Grasshopper Sparrow. *Ammodramus savannarum*

Uncommon spring and rare fall migrant; sporadic winter visitor.

It has been recorded as early as September 26, but southbound birds cannot be expected with regularity. During the winter of 1967–68 this bird was present at weedy places in Green Gulch and in Panther Canyon, as well as in old fields at Castolon from December 5 through March 19. But I could not find it at these locations during the next two winters. More recently, Chisos Mountains CBC participants tallied it only twice in ten years (1985–1994), one in 1991 and two in 1994. Spring migrants pass through the park area from early March to April 4, and there are two later reports: lone birds in the Chisos Basin on May 18, 1967 and at RGV on June 5, 1967 (Wauer).

Le Conte's Sparrow. *Ammodramus leconteii*

Casual migrant and winter visitor.

There are widely scattered reports from late August through the winter until early March, all from the Rio Grande floodplain. It was first found at RGV on March 10, 1963, by Mr. and Mrs. Edgar Bedell. I found one there on August 29 and two on October 24, 1966. Ben Feltner next reported one in the weedy fields at Castolon on January 3, 1972. David Wiedenfeld found six at San Vicente on December 27, 1976; Eric and Mildred Hartman and Carroll and Lucy McEathron reported 14 individuals along the River Road on February 16, 1977; Peter Scott observed the species throughout the 1967–77 winter in old fields at San Vicente and reported that the birds left the area by mid-March. And G. S. Taylor reported one at RGV on January 12, 1994.

Fox Sparrow. *Passerella iliaca*

Sporadic winter and spring visitor.

There are several reports between November 11 and April 16. Except for a lone sighting in the Chisos Basin on February 13, 1987 (Anne Bellamy), all the reports are from the vicinity of the Rio Grande. The earliest park record is one found at Boquillas on November 11, 1967 (Wauer). The largest number recorded was seven at RGV on February 24, 1977, by Alan Wormington and Brian Wylie. A specimen, taken at the SEC picnic area on February 1, 1967, was identified as the race *zaboria* (Wauer 1969b).

Song Sparrow. *Melospiza melodia*

Uncommon migrant and winter visitor.

Except for one very early mid-September report by Bonnie McKinney in the Chisos Basin on September 12, 1987, fall birds do not reach the park area until October 10; a peak is reached from October 24 to 28; and late migrants usually can be found throughout December. There are a number of reports during January and February, all from swampy and overgrown places along the Rio Grande. Northbound birds begin to move along the river by the second week of March, and they become most numerous from April 1 to 11; a high of five birds was seen at RGV on April 8, 1970 (Wauer). Stragglers have been reported to May 10. Specimens taken by Adrey Borell at Hot Springs on November 9, 1936 (Borell 1963), and at Boquillas on February 14, 1967 (Wauer), were both of the race *juddi*.

Lincoln's Sparrow. *Melospiza lincolnii*

Fairly common migrant and winter resident.

This perky little sparrow has been recorded in the park as early as September 15 and as late as the first of June; S. A. Stedman found one at the end of the Window Trail on June 2, 1983. Fall migrants reach a peak from October 19 to 26, and they can be found at weedy patches on the Rio Grande floodplain and in mountain canyons up to 5,300 feet almost any time during migration and in winter. Spring migrants become numerous from March 15 to April 11, and stragglers continue to pass through the area until the first of June.

Swamp Sparrow. *Melospiza georgiana*

Uncommon migrant; fairly common winter resident.

Fall migrants do not reach the Big Bend area until October 5, and it has been recorded as late as May 20 in spring. This bird is usually more numerous than the related Song Sparrow, which utilizes the same habitat. It usually can be found at the beaver dam area and the silt pond at RGV, as well as at weedy places elsewhere along the Rio Grande and up to the mountain canyons, especially following rainy periods. Swamp Sparrows usually can be squeaked out of hiding at these places throughout the winter and spring. An average of five individuals were found on ten (1985–1994) CBCs at RGV, including none in 1986 and 1987 and a high of 17 in 1994.

White-throated Sparrow. *Zonotrichia albicollis*

Uncommon migrant and winter visitor.

Records range from November 2 to May 10. Although this sparrow is never numerous, it occurs regularly at lowland, brushy areas during winter. I have found it most often along the Rio Grande and less often at higher elevations, such as at Dugout Wells, Grapevine Spring, and the Old Ranch. It also occurs irregularly in the lower mountain canyons, such as lower Green Gulch and along the Window Trail. CBC participants in the Chisos Mountains and at RGV tallied it only four and five times, respectively, from 1985 through 1994. During migration, it can occur anywhere below approximately 5,000 feet.

Golden-crowned Sparrow. *Zonotrichia atricapilla*

Casual winter visitor.

On December 9, 1971, I netted and banded an immature bird found with a flock of several hundred White-crowns in the Alamo Creek drainage near Castolon. I saw it there again on December 28, and Ben Feltner observed an unbanded juvenile there on January 3, 1972. Larry May and I next found one at Boquillas Canyon parking area on January 15, 1974; Larry took several photographs, one of which I later submitted to the TBRC. It was next reported at RGV on January 12, 1982 (Tex Sordahl); Harold Wellander reported one from Panther Canyon on April 3, 1985; and Gerhard and Beverly Thiem found one at RGV on April 10, 1988.

White-crowned Sparrow. *Zonotrichia leucophrys*

Common migrant and winter resident.

It has been recorded from September 15 through June 4. Early fall migrants are restricted to the Rio Grande lowlands and do not appear in the higher elevations until mid-October, when the species may be common along the river, uncommon in the mid-elevation grasslands, and rare in the lower Chisos woodlands. Wintering birds usually are common all along the Rio Grande but sporadic at higher elevations. During the 1966–67 winter, I banded 472 White-crowns at PJ, but only 112 in 1967–68, 105 in 1968–69, none in 1969–70, and 22 in 1970–71. This species is most numerous at RGV and CC, where wintering birds may remain until late May. Spring migrants begin to move through the park area by mid-March and may be numerous along the floodplain and at adjacent mesquite thickets until mid-May. Stragglers have been reported in the lowlands until early June.

Harris' Sparrow. *Zonotrichia querula*

Casual winter visitor.

Records range from October 31 (an immature bird found at RGV in 1990 by Stuart Dechka and C. L. Skulski) through February 22. Captain and Mrs. E. B. Hurlbert were first to find one at SEC picnic area on February 25, 1965. Mr. and Mrs. Edgar Bedell reported one at RGV from February 15 to 22, 1966. And a lone adult visited my feeder at PJ from November 30 to December 6, 1968; it was netted, photographed, banded, and released. The species was not reported again until James Stewart found one at RGV on December 3, 1985; Cynthia Simmons and Anne Bellamy found it (apparently the same individual) again on December 9. On January 21, 1986, Bellamy recorded one at PJ. And Laura Greffenius found one with a flock of White-crowns at RGV on February 4 and 15, 1987; Bellamy found it on February 18, and Shirley Sink reported it there on February 19.

Dark-eyed Junco. *Junco hyemalis*

Three easily recognized races of Dark-eyed Juncos—known as the Slate-colored, Oregon, and Gray-headed Juncos before they were lumped together by the AOU—occur in the park. The species as a whole is a fairly common migrant and winter resident, particularly in the middle elevations of the park, and is rarely reported in the lowlands. I will discuss the three forms separately.

The Slate-colored Junco is an uncommon migrant and winter resident. Records range from October 20 to April 9. It has been reported from the Rio Grande floodplain up to Boot Canyon, but the only place I have found it consistently is along the Window Trail between December 1 and March 25. It almost always is seen either alone or with a small flock of Oregon or Gray-heads.

The Oregon Junco is a fairly common migrant and winter resident. It arrives as early as October 20 and remains until April 18. Most sightings are of two to eight birds along the Window Trail or in the higher canyons, such as Boot Canyon, and migrants are often in the company of Slate-colored or Gray-headed Juncos.

The Gray-headed Junco is an uncommon migrant and fairly common winter resident. Fall birds arrive as early as October 10, and the latest spring report is John Egbert's sighting of one at Boot Spring on June 11, 1976. On May 27, 1968, I banded five birds from a flock of about 25 at Boot Spring, where I had previously recorded what I believed to be the same flock on October 22, 1967; February 13 and 23, 1968; and March 31, 1968. Three birds of this same flock were recaptured at Boot Spring on October 20, 1968; that flock remained at least until May 9, 1969. This is the most numerous wintering junco in the mountains.

Yellow-eyed Junco. *Junco phaeonotus*
Casual spring visitor.

Records range from March 19 to June 17, and there also is a single fall report in the Chisos Basin on October 26, 1985 (Bonnie McKinney). Although there is an old undated record (prior to 1966) in the park files for along the Window Trail, the first modern report was of 10 to 15 birds at Boot Spring by Mr. and Mrs. W. L. Erwin on April 3, 1980; and Paul Baicach and Ron Naveen reported one there on June 17. On March 19, 1986, Jonathan and Dorothy Carter reported five or six at the Chisos Basin Trailhead; Kathy Johnson found one in Boot Canyon on March 25, 1987; John Selle and Robert Rothe reported one there on April 29, 1990; Victor Emanuel discovered one on the Colima Trail on May 5, 1990; and Joe and Addie Bolser found one at Laguna Meadow on April 6, 1991. This is a common nesting bird in Mexico's Maderas del Carmen, 50 miles southeast of the Chisos Mountains.

Smith's Longspur. *Calcarius pictus*
There is a single park record.

Rich Stallcup and Gary Rosenberg found a lone male, in "near breeding plumage," at PJ on April 29, 1986. It was photographed by Stallcup and Sam Fried, and a photograph (TBRC No. 394) was submitted to and accepted by the TBRC. There also are two previous, unverified reports: J.

W. Leach first found one at Dugout Wells on May 2, 1962, and Richard P. Curt reported one at SEC on April 28, 1988. This bird is an irregular winter visitor to West Texas.

Chestnut-collared Longspur. *Calcarius ornatus*
Rare spring migrant.

Records range from February 10 through May 5, and there is a late spring report and photograph of a male that Bonnie McKinney netted and banded at Black Gap WMA on May 26, 1983. I also photographed one at RGV on March 23, 1990. Except for a lone bird found in the Chisos Basin on March 23, 1995 (Wauer), all reports are for the lowlands, including PJ, and most are of single birds. Exceptions include 30 birds (three of which were males) found by Bruce Talbot along the River Road near La Clocha on March 17, 1983. There also is a December 1, 1994, report of a lone male 8.5 miles east of PJ by Starr Saphir and Bob Machover.

FAMILY EMBERIZIDAE
Subfamily Icterinae: *Blackbirds and Orioles*
Red-winged Blackbird. *Agelaius phoeniceus*
Uncommon migrant and probable nester.

Records occur for every month but December, January, and July. It is most numerous in migration from mid-April to mid-May in spring; there are a few reports in June; and it is numerous again from mid-August to mid-September, with scattered reports to November 19. There are two possible nesting records: Dave Easterla and Rod Leslie found a singing male and a female carrying nesting material at RGV on June 8, 1973, and Jeff Selleck observed a female nest-building at the Chisos Basin sewage lagoons on June 28, 1988; no male was seen. Most reports are of one, two, or three individuals, sometimes with Yellow-headed Blackbirds, but Robert DeVine found more than 25 birds at the Rosillos Ranch on September 19, 1981.

Eastern Meadowlark. *Sturnella magna*
Rare migrant and winter visitor.

The Eastern and Western meadowlarks are so similar that it is difficult to tell them apart without a specimen or hearing them sing. The Eastern

Meadowlark's song is five or six clear whistles, while that of the Western Meadowlark is loud and flutelike, the song heard in Western movies. (As a child growing up in Idaho, I was told that the Western Meadowlark sang, "Salt Lake City is a pretty lit-tle city.") The Eastern Meadowlark's range in West Texas is rather complicated, and breeding birds overlap with Westerns. Their ranges were described by Gordon Orians (1985) thusly:

> In the southern Great Plains, eastern meadowlarks extend westward as breeding birds along the Canadian, Red, and Brazos rivers of western Texas, but they stop where the flood plains become narrow and the rivers are confined to rugged canyons. Father west, after a gap of eighty miles or more, another race of eastern meadowlark, Lilian's meadowlark, breeds in the dry-desert grasslands of western Texas, New Mexico, and Arizona, south into extreme northern Mexico. . . . The western meadowlark breeds throughout this area and over the entire range of Lilian's meadowlark as well . . . Lilian's meadowlarks are as different in shape from the eastern race of the eastern meadowlark as either is from western meadowlarks, and they may actually belong to a third species of meadowlark.

Although Lilian's Meadowlarks nest throughout the open grasslands from Marathon to Fort Stockton and Alpine to Balmorhea, and although they have not been found to nest within the park, they do occur there rarely in winter. Lilian's prefers sotol grasslands and grassy flats in the lowlands. Roadkills examined on September 26, 1967, October 6, 1968, December 21, 1967, and January 27, 1968, from PJ to upper Tornillo Creek bridge, proved to be this species. In addition, Van Tyne and Sutton (1937) collected a Lilian's Meadowlark on the South Rim, May 20, 1932, and 12 to 14 meadowlarks at RGV in March 1967 were identified by their songs as Easterns by Russ and Marian Wilson. Some ornithologists (Sibley and Monroe 1990) believe that Lilian's Meadowlark represents a distinct species.

Western Meadowlark. *Sturnella neglacta*

Fairly common migrant and winter resident.

This species has been reported within the lower sotol grasslands and on the grassy flats along the Rio Grande during fall, winter, and spring;

records extend from October 9 through May 4, and peaks are evident from mid- to late May in spring and from early October to mid-November in fall. It nests side-by-side with the Lilian's Meadowlark north of the park, and it also may nest in the park: Dale Zimmerman found what he believed to be a nesting bird near K-Bar the second week of April 1971. Nesting should be expected as the park's grasslands, which were severely damaged by years of overgrazing prior to park establishment, continue to recover. Roadkills found from PJ to RGV on October 15 and December 2, 1967; February 1, 1969; and March 14, 1967 proved to be this species. Wintering birds sometimes can be found in rather large flocks: 65 or more were found near San Vicente on November 11, 1967 (Wauer).

Yellow-headed Blackbird. *Xanthocephalus xanthocephalus*

Fairly common migrant; casual winter visitor.

This large blackbird has been reported every month but February and March. The earliest spring migrants may appear along the Rio Grande during the second week of April and can be numerous from April 25 to May 11, after which there are scattered reports until June 1. Flocks sometimes can be extensive; I found 129 individuals (all males) at RGV on April 25, 1969, and Bonnie McKinney reported 800 in six to eight flocks at Nine Point Draw on April 22, 1987. They sometimes occur in mixed flocks with Brewer's Blackbirds or Brown-headed Cowbirds. Although the majority of the spring sightings are from the lowlands, Ty and Julie Hotchkiss reported a lone male at the top of the Lost Mine Trail (6,850 feet elevation) on May 20, 1970.

After June 2 (a 1977 report of a lone male at RGV by Sheriton Burr), there are no further reports until June 28, except for a lone bird at Grapevine Spring on June 14, 1956 (James Dixon). Southbound migrants begin to appear along the river the last week of June, and they can occur in numbers by mid-July; Robert DeVine reported 45 at Laguna Meadow on July 15, 1978, and Harold Brodrick found a flock of more than 100 at PJ on July 23, 1957. There are several reports of larger flocks in September: I observed more than 235 birds at PJ on September 12 and 24, 1961; David Wolf reported more than 320 birds at RGV on September 7, 1973; and Robert DeVine found 250-plus birds at the mouth of Boquillas Canyon on September 14, 1978. After late September, reports are widely scattered but persist to January 10. Bill Bourbon reported a male at RGV on November

Yellow-headed Blackbird, *Xanthocephalus xanthocephalus*

8, 1988; Robert Tanhope found one near Black Dike on December 4, 1969; Ellen Vogal found one eating birdseed at Terlingua on December 23, 1993; and Bruce McHenry reported one at PJ on January 10, 1955.

Rusty Blackbird. *Euphagus carolinus*
Casual late fall visitor.

The first Rusty Blackbird recorded in the park was one collected along an irrigation ditch at RGV on December 10, 1967 (Wauer 1969b). John

Galley observed one at Hot Springs on December 27, 1967; I saw two
with a flock of ten Brewer's Blackbirds and eight Brown-headed Cowbirds at RGV on October 24, 1968, and another one near the beaver pond
on December 23, 1970. This bird may be more common than the few
records indicate, as it easily can be confused with the more numerous
Brewer's Blackbirds.

Brewer's Blackbird. *Euphagus cyanocephalus*
Common migrant; rare winter visitor.

Fall migrants reach the park area during the first week of September, a
peak is evident from mid-September through early November, and there
are scattered reports to January 21. There are no records for February, but
early spring migrants begin to move along the river by the second week of
March and become more common later in the month. The northbound
migrants are most numerous from mid-April to mid-May, and stragglers
continue to pass through the area until June 9. There also is a late report
of one male at PJ on June 27, 1973 (Dave Easterla). Migrants often occur
in flocks of 10 to 25 birds, and although most reports are from the lowlands, it has also been found on numerous occasions at higher elevations:
There are several reports in the Chisos Basin, I found a lone male at the
end of the Lost Mine Trail on March 21, 1967, and it is a fairly common
visitor at PJ in late April and early May—I banded seven birds there from
April 17 to May 1, 1970, but only two in the fall (September 21, 1970, and
October 3, 1969).

Great-tailed Grackle. *Quiscalus mexicanus*
Uncommon spring migrant; casual in summer, fall, and winter.

The majority of reports are from April 1 to June 12, and nesting has been
recorded: Robert DeVine found two nests at RGV on May 12, 1983. It also
is present at Lajitas year-round. Additional park reports include one on
June 30, 1970, at RGV (Wauer); two females at the Chisos Basin on August
3, 1988 (Charles Callagan); four at Santa Elena, Chihuahua, on November
9, 1967 (Wauer); one at Government Spring on November 15, 1987 (Jeff
Selleck); and I have found it twice at CC in December: a flock of 22 on
December 22, 1968, and six on December 30, 1969. There are no reports
in the park for January, February, March, July, September, and October.

Brewer's Blackbird, *Euphagus cyanocephalus*

Common Grackle. *Quiscalus quiscula*

Casual spring and fall visitor.

Reports range from April 2 to May 27 in spring and from October 25 to November 28 in fall. Several of these birds were observed close up. Examples include one at PJ on May 27, 1986 (Rich Stallcup and several Point Reyes Observatory tour participants); another at a PJ bird feeder on November 27 and 28, 1978, by Robert DeVine and James Stovall; and one at PJ with Brown-headed Cowbirds on October 30, 1986 (Anne and Jim

Bellamy). Except for one reported for the Chisos Basin campground on May 24 and 25, 1980 (Jacob Miller), and one at Boot Spring on November 26, 1991 (Peter Gottschling), all records are from mid- to lower elevations.

Bronzed Cowbird. *Molotrhus aeneus*

Uncommon summer resident and spring migrant.

This red-eyed cowbird was first reported in the park on June 9, 1969; Dave Easterla found four males and two females at RGV. One of the males was courting the females; it was last seen on July 4 (Easterla and Wauer 1972). It was next found on June 8, 1970 (Easterla), and at least six males and four females stayed in the RGV campground area until July 3. On July 12, I found a Hooded Oriole nest hanging on a tamarisk near the Daniels house at RGV and containing two juvenile Bronzed Cowbirds (one was collected). On July 18 the nest was empty and a juvenile Bronzed Cowbird was found 55 feet away being fed by both adult Hooded Orioles. And on July 28, I discovered another young Bronzed Cowbird at an Orchard Oriole nest at RGV; Easterla and I watched the youngster being fed by the adult female Orchard Oriole on July 30.

In 1971, an adult male Bronzed Cowbird appeared at PJ on May 22 and remained until May 29, when it was banded and released; it did not return. I found four males and four females at RGV on May 29, and at least a few of these individuals remained through July 13; a juvenile was seen begging from an Orchard Oriole on August 4. Also in 1971, I found the species present at CC from June 5 through July 10.

Since these early sightings, it has been reported annually along the Rio Grande and at higher elevations with regularity; Kelly Bryan and Joseph Ford found one with Brown-headed Cowbirds in the Chisos Basin on May 21, 1979. It also has been recorded in migration; I found a flock of five individuals flying northward near Dugout Wells on May 3, 1994. My 1985 prediction that its presence at BBNP likely would lead to a decline of breeding Orchard and Hooded orioles along the Rio Grande floodplain apparently has come true.

Brown-headed Cowbird. *Molothrus ater*

Abundant summer resident and migrant.

Records extend from March 17 to October 27, and there are two additional sightings: an immature male at my feeder at PJ on February 26,

1968, and another immature bird that arrived at PJ with a cold front on December 28, 1969 (Wauer). Spring migrants begin to move into the park area in mid-March. Early migrants are usually alone or in small flocks, but many large flocks can be found once the northbound movement gets under way, from the first of April to mid-May; Bonnie McKinney found a flock of more than 600 birds, predominantly males, on Tornillo Flat on April 22, 1987; and during the early mornings of April 28 and May 3, 1994, I recorded several flocks of eight to 25 birds flying north near Dugout Wells. Although the majority of the spring migrants are found in the lowlands, there also are a number of reports for Laguna Meadow, Boot Canyon, and the South Rim in late May and early June.

Breeding birds belong to the small *obscurus* race of cowbirds that sometimes is referred to as the "Dwarf Cowbird." They are known to parasitize a great number of the park's nesting birds, including the Blue-gray and Black-tailed gnatcatchers; Bell's, Black-capped, and Gray vireos; Yellow-breasted Chat; Summer Tanager; Blue Grosbeak; Painted Bunting; Black-throated Sparrow; and House Sparrow. All of the breeding Cowbirds above 2,500 feet may be one huge flock; birds banded at PJ were regularly found in the Chisos Basin, especially in the vicinity of the Chisos Remuda, where they were able to feed on seeds from horse droppings. The adult Dwarf Cowbirds move out of their breeding grounds the last week of July but are replaced immediately by a larger race (*artemisae*) during the first week of August. Some of the local youngsters intermingle with the larger birds, which may remain until early September. By mid-September, only an occasional migrant is still present. Fall migrants have not been reported above 5,500 feet elevation. Brown-headed Cowbirds winter with Brewer's Blackbirds throughout the northern portion of the Big Bend Country.

Black-vented Oriole. *Icterus wagleri*

One series of sightings.

A single adult female was regularly seen at RGV between mid-April and early October in 1969 and 1970 (Wauer 1970b). It was first discovered on the morning of September 27, 1968; I watched it for several minutes among the foliage of a thicket along the nature trail. Later in the day I identified it from reading descriptions by Emmet Blake (1953) and

MᶜGOWAN

Black-vented Oriole, *Icterus wagleri*

George M. Sutton (1951), but I could not find it the following morning or on several followup visits to the area.

On April 28, 1969, I again saw an adult Black-vented Oriole less than 300 feet from the location of the first sighting. For more than 40 minutes I watched it and six other orioles (adult female and an immature Hooded Oriole, and two females, one adult, and one immature male Orchard Orioles) chase each other from tree to tree within the campground. The Black-vented Oriole appeared to be in close association with the immature male Hooded Oriole, which nicely fit Sutton's description of a female *wagleri*. Although I have since learned that the species is monomorphic (having a single color pattern), I assumed that I was observing a possible nesting pair.

On May 1, as I was again observing *I. wagleri* at the same location (with, presumably, the same six orioles), I met Ty and Julie Hotchkiss, who were camped at RGV. When I informed them of the bird's identity, they graciously offered to photograph the bird for further documentation. During the following three weeks, they took more than 50 feet of 16mm movie film and eight color slides. *I. wagleri* was further verified by several additional birders: Mr. and Mrs. H. T. Hargis (who also obtained excellent photographs), Terry Hall, Kay McCracken, Doris Maguire, Russ and Marian Wilson, Doyle and Helen Peckham, Warren and Bobby Pulich, Charles and Betty Crabtree, David Wolf, Jim Tucker, Doug Eddleman, and Mike Parmeter in May; Dave Easterla, Guy McCaskie, Cliff Lyons, and Ginger Coughran in June; and Bob Smith and Paul Sykes in July.

These sightings represent the first authenticated records of the Black-vented Oriole for the United States, although there is a questionable sighting by Herbert Brown from the Patagonia Mountains of Arizona in 1910 (Phillips 1968). South of the border, it occurs "from Sonora, Chihuahua, and Nuevo Leon, south through Guatemala and Honduras to El Salvador (in winter) and northern Nicaragua" (Freidmann, Griscom, and Moore 1957). Mexican breeding records nearest BBNP are from 15 miles south of Gomez Farias, Coahuila, where Charles Ely (1962) studied the avifauna in the southeastern part of the state. Gomez Farias is approximately 350 miles from BBNP.

By mid-May, it was evident that the Black-vented Oriole at RGV was not nesting, and that it was not paired. Its behavior gave no indication that it was defending a territory. Yet by midmorning it would usually disappear into the dense floodplain vegetation and often would not return to the campground portion of its range until late afternoon or evening. By 6:30 a.m. it was always back in the campground with many immature Orchard Orioles or the one or two immature Hooded Orioles that still were present. All these seemed to prefer the fruits of the squaw bush, which was ripening throughout May and June. On May 19, I watched *I. wagleri* feed on flowers of desert willow for several minutes, and on June 28 it caught a cicada, tore the wings off, and consumed the softer parts of the body, dropping the rest to the ground.

In order to obtain close-up photographs for racial identification, as well as to band the bird so that it could be recognized if it returned again, I made several attempts to net it between June 28 and July 4. On July 1, I placed a mounted Great Horned Owl, a species that occurs commonly in the immediate vicinity, on the ground next to a mist net. *I wagleri* perched ten feet above the stuffed bird and watched while a pair of Northern

Mockingbirds launched attack after attack on the owl until both were caught in the netting. I even drew a Black-vented Oriole on cardboard, colored it with the proper colors, and mounted the drawing on a stick next to the net. This, too, was a failure—*I wagleri*'s only reaction was one of vague curiosity.

Yet it did show interest in people on a number of occasions. Several times I observed it watching campers going about their routine duties, and on one occasion it flew into a tree above two children who were rolling a red rubber ball around on the ground. It sat there watching this activity for about four minutes before flying off to another perch. On only two occasions did I observe it showing any aggression toward another bird, and then only two very short chases (15–20 ft.) of female Orchard Orioles. Although *I. wagleri* usually could be detected by the very low, rasping call it gave, like that of a Yellow-breasted Chat or a Scott's Oriole, a song was never heard.

Finally, by moving the nets each time *I. wagleri* changed positions, I succeeded in capturing it on July 4. Closer examination showed that it was in nonbreeding status; it clearly lacked evidence of a brood patch and had no cloacal protuberance. Close examination of the bill and cere showed no indication that the bird had been caged at any time. Close-up photographs of the chest were sent to Allan Phillips, who identified the bird racially as the *wagleri* form of eastern Mexico. The chest had a light chestnut tinge.

After carefully photographing the major features of the bird, I placed a band (no. 632-25253) on its right leg and released it. It immediately flew south to the floodplain portion of its territory, dove into the dense vegetation, and was not seen the rest of the day. By July 10, however, it was right back in the same habits and allowed good binocular examination for the first half of each morning.

In early August, it became quite shy and had to be searched for among the dense foliage along the nature trail. I last saw it that year on September 19, exactly one year after the original date of discovery. In 1970, I found it again in the same locality from April 17 through September 21 and again on October 10. A good number of birders observed the same banded bird throughout the summer, but it has not been reported since.

Orchard Oriole. *Icterus spurius*

Common summer resident.

This is a very gregarious species that spends the early part of its breeding season chasing each other around their territories. It is especially numerous in the open cottonwood groves at RGV and CC. Only males are known to sing; second-year males sing and nest as well. Nesting occurs during May, June, and July; I found an adult Orchard Oriole feeding a juvenile Bronzed Cowbird at RGV on July 28, 1970.

There is considerable post-nesting wanderings, particularly among immature birds, and they may be found to 4,500 feet. One was seen along

Orchard Oriole, *Icterus spurius*

the lower part of the Window Trail on July 9, 1962, and they are regular at PJ and adjacent arroyos from late July to early September. Females and immature birds were banded at PJ on July 21, 1970; August 6 and 20, 1967; September 7, 1967; and September 20, 1969. By early September this bird becomes rare on its breeding grounds; I have seen only one adult male later than the first of September, although adult females and immatures usually can be found with some effort. There is one wintertime record: M. S. Croft reported a lone male at RGV on December 24, 1980.

Hooded Oriole. *Icterus cucullatus*

Uncommon summer resident; rare migrant.

It has been recorded from March 16 and throughout the summer to October 1. Adult males arrive on their breeding grounds from mid-March to early April; it is several days before females and subadults put in their appearance. Like the Orchard Oriole, Hooded Orioles are very gregarious at first and often can be found chasing other orioles. Nest-building begins in mid-May; the earliest nest-building I found was at RGV on May 11, 1970. Young are fledged in June and July: Adults were found feeding nestlings on May 24, 1969; two fledged birds were seen at RGV on July 17, 1968; and a nest containing two young Bronzed Cowbirds was discovered there in a tamarisk on July 12, 1970 (Wauer). Apparently, there also is some late nesting; I found a nest under construction near the top of a tall cottonwood at RGV on July 18, 1970.

This lovely bird has declined at least at a few localities in the park during the past 20 years. That decline directly correlates with the appearance and increase of Bronzed Cowbirds. For example, from 1966 through 1972 I found Hooded Orioles common in the riparian habitats along the Rio Grande, from the date palms at Hot Springs to the thickets at RGV and near Boquillas Crossing. In recent years (1990–94), I have found it uncommon to rare in these same locations; it is still common only at CC.

Post-nesting birds do not seem to wander as much as Orchard Orioles, although there appears to be some movement into the mountains; I found an adult male feeding at a century plant near the Chisos Basin campground on August 1, 1966, and one female at Juniper Flat on August 10, 1969. Migrants have been recorded on only a few occasions. It is assumed that early birds in mid-March are migrants; I found adult males at PJ on March 19, 1967, and April 17, 1970; Robert Rothe found one drinking at a hummingbird feeder there on March 10, 1990; the Field Biology Class from Abilene Christian University reported one at Dog Canyon on April 8, 1993; and Jeff Selleck found a male at PJ on April 11, 1988. Further, one found in the Chisos Basin on October 1, 1966 (Wauer), undoubtedly represents a fall migrant.

Altamira Oriole. *Icterus gularis*

Casual visitor.

There are six reports from late March to early October. It was first recorded by Bonnie McKinney, who watched one at the Black Gap WMA headquarters throughout March 29, 1982, following several days of severe winds; that bird also was seen by Katie, Tina, and Garvis Reynolds. Kathaleen Stewart next reported a pair at RGV on October 12, 1982. Then on April 25 and 26, 1990, Chris and Ida Whitten reported a juvenile female at Hot Springs. And on October 5, 1990, Mary and Leonard Olmsted found a pair at Boquillas Canyon. On April 6, 1991, Cynthia Rankin reported one at mile 798 in the Lower Canyons that she was able to compare with a smaller Hooded Oriole that was "20% smaller." And finally, J. J. Arnold and Elizabeth Henze reported one at CC on June 8, 1991.

Northern Oriole. *Icterus galbula*

This is another case of two identifiable birds being lumped into one species by the AOU, although the next AOU checklist is likely to separate the two forms again. And because they can readily be distinguished in the field, I will discuss them separately.

The Baltimore Oriole is a casual spring migrant only. Dixon and Wallmo (1956) first collected one at Black Gap WMA on June 20, 1955; Bobbie Pettit and Ruth and Harvey Williams observed a male at RGV on April 29, 1978; Vermille Ruff reported a male at Castolon on May 21, 1979; D. Buck recorded it at Persimmon Gap on April 3, 1986; Jeff Selleck found one at the Chisos Basin sewage lagoons on June 22, 1989; and Bryant Woods reported one at RGV on April 19, 1990.

The Bullock's Oriole in an uncommon summer resident and migrant. This bird has nested at CC annually at least since 1989, when Bill Bourbon reported a nest with two chicks on June 18. There also is one earlier summer report: Tarleton Smith found one at Boquillas on June 21, 1936. Spring migrants may reach the park area by mid-March, but they do not become regular until early April to mid-May. Fall migrants have been reported from July 29 (a female collected at PJ in 1970) to October 3, with a peak evident from mid-August through the second week of September. The majority of the park sightings are of lone birds, but five (two adults and three females or immatures) were found at RGV on August 20 and 22, 1970 (Wauer). And although the majority of records are from the lowlands, there are four from the mountains: Boot Spring on April 12, 1956 (Harold Brodrick); Laguna Meadow on May 6, 1968 (Ned Fritz); and the Chisos Basin on August 31, 1967 and the Lost Mine Trail on September 19, 1967 (Wauer).

Scott's Oriole. *Icterus parisorum*

Common summer resident and migrant; casual winter visitor.

This black-and-yellow oriole has been recorded every month. Adult males arrive first in spring: Carol Edwards found an early bird at Cross Canyon in Mariscal Canyon on March 4, 1995; singing males were

Scott's Oriole, *Icterus parisorum*

recorded in lower Green Gulch on March 19, 1968 (Wauer); and Anne Bellamy found the "first of the year" at PJ on March 23, 1984. Females and subadults arrive a few days later, and nesting begins immediately rather than being preceded by a period of play, which is typical for Orchard and Hooded orioles. Nests have been reported at PJ as early as March 23, 1960 (Harold Brodrick); I found a nest on a Torrey yucca near SEC on April 28, 1968, and banded three nestlings at the Chisos Basin on June 8, 1970; and Van Tyne and Sutton (1937) reported a youngster already out of the nest at Boquillas on May 16, 1933. The Basin nest was located on a beaked yucca in front of the motel unit, and a second nest later was built within a few inches of the first one, with young present on August 9; I assumed it belonged to the same adults.

The post-nesting period appears to be the main time for play for this oriole, and there is some flocking; a flock of 15 birds (five adults and ten immatures) was seen along the Window Trail on September 10, 1967 (Wauer). Family groups of three to seven birds are more common and sometimes are found considerably above their nesting grounds. I recorded lone birds at Laguna Meadow (6,300 ft.) on September 4, 1967, and September 8, 1969, and an adult male and two females at 6,850 feet at the end of the Lost Mine Trail on October 24, 1968. Some birds remain on their breeding grounds throughout the fall and early winter. Seven individuals were seen along Oak Creek just below the Basin campground on December 1, 1968, and three were found there on December 23. Apparently, it may even remain throughout some winters; I found an immature male on the open mesquite flats below Boquillas Canyon on December 29, 1970, and January 16, 1971; Bob Straub reported a female at Boquillas on December 24, 1990; and Betty and Tom Alex and Lorn Williamham found one near the Basin Junction on December 29, 1985.

FAMILY FRINGILLIDAE: FINCHES
Purple Finch. *Carpodacus purpureus*

There are four records.

It was first reported on April 13, 1972, by Joel Greenberg and P. Phillips, who observed two singing males and one female at RGV. H. E. Poindexter next reported one at RGV on August 26, 1975; Rick LoBello found one female, which he observed from 15 feet, at PJ on December 20,

1976; and Cliff Stogner found and photographed a lone male at RGV on December 30, 1982. Stogner's photograph was submitted to and accepted by the TBRC.

Cassin's Finch. *Carpodacus cassinii*
Sporadic visitor.

Although this finch has been recorded every month but September, it cannot be expected at any one time or place. It was reported several times in 1966–67: Leon Bishop found a "flock of about one dozen" in the pines on the Lost Mine Trail on October 20; and I found two there on November 6, two more at the South Rim on January 29, one at Boot Spring on March 30, one flying over the Chisos Basin on April 2 and 6, and one at Boot Spring on June 8. It was not reported again until July 20, 1969, when I found a lone male near Laguna Meadow. Tony Gallucci next reported a pair on the Window Trail on May 16, 1975, and Wesley Cureton found four females at Laguna Meadow on December 29, 1977. It was next reported on March 22, 1985, when Herb Hausman found a lone male at Laguna Meadow. Garrett and Kathie Albright found one on the Window Trail on July 30, 1992, and Lillian and Roberta Scherer reported one at Government Spring on May 16, 1994.

House Finch. *Carpodacus mexicanus*
Common full-time resident and spring migrant.

At least a few can be found almost anywhere below 5,500 feet at any time of the year. Nesting begins early on the desert, and fledged birds can be found by late April or early May. During wet years, it may also nest in July and August. Of special interest was a nest built in an abandoned Cliff Swallow nest at Hot Springs on March 29, 1968 (Wauer). Post-nesting birds occasionally wander into the higher canyons, such as Boot Canyon, where I found it on August 10, 1968, but the species is generally restricted to lower areas. Family groups become the nucleus of flocks that may number from 50 to 150 birds during fall, winter, and spring. There is an increase in House Finches from mid-March through mid-April, indicating a northerly migration, but there is no evidence of a fall migration.

House Finch, *Carpodacus mexicanus*

Red Crossbill. *Loxia curvirostra*
Sporadic visitor.

This high mountain species was first reported for BBNP by Harry Oberholser (1902) who found it in the Chisos Mountains in June 1901 and considered it to be a probable breeding bird. Although it may nest during wet or invasion years, there is no evidence of nesting. Sightings usually are few and far between. The winter of 1967–68 was apparently an invasion year; I found Crossbills present in the mountains from August 13 through June 11: 12 birds were foraging on pinyons at Laguna Meadow on November 15; four were present along the East Rim on January 28; 12 near Pinnacles Pass on May 3; and 40 were recorded in Boot Canyon on May 25. A specimen taken on May 3 represents the *bentii* race that breeds in the Rocky Mountains from northern New Mexico to Utah and Montana (AOU 1957). More recent reports include two males at RGV on November 9, 1985 (Joseph Ondrejko), and one at PJ on May 21, 1985 (Jim Bellamy and Tina Pearson); and in 1992, Jon Dunn heard one at RGV on November 22; Jeff Selleck, Bill Bourbon, Rob Arnberger, and John Forsythe found two in Boot Canyon on July 27; and Chuck Sexton found two in Boot Canyon on August 7 and 9. The Red Crossbill nests in Mexico's Maderas del Carmen, 50 miles southeast of the Chisos (Wauer and Ligon 1977).

Pine Siskin. *Carduelis pinus*
Fairly common migrant; rare winter visitor.

It has been reported every month but July. The earliest fall records include "several" at the Chisos Basin sewage lagoons on August 9, 1987 (Rob Pearson), Dave Easterla found one in the Basin on August 16, 1973, David Wolf reported a flock of 17 there on August 19, 1968, and I found one at RGV on August 25, 1969. It becomes more numerous from mid-October to early November, and there also are scattered reports in December, January, and February. Sightings increase again by late February, and a peak is evident from early April through mid-May, after which reports are spotty to June 22. The largest flock recorded was 34 birds at RGV on December 30, 1969 (Wauer). This bird nests to the north in the Davis and Guadalupe mountains and is a "probable" nester in Mexico's Maderas del Carmens (Wauer and Ligon 1977).

Lesser Goldfinch. *Carduelis psaltria*

Common year-round resident.

This is the common goldfinch of the Big Bend area. Although it usually can be found in the mountains and along the Rio Grande any time of year, it is most numerous in the mountains in summer and along the river in winter. Nesting occurs from May through September. It prefers areas

Lesser Goldfinch, *Carduelis psaltria*

of broadleaf trees and shrubs but can be found on conifers as well. I found a nest in Pulliam Canyon on May 18, 1967, and singing males among the Arizona cypress in Boot Canyon during the second week of August in 1968 and 1969. Gerry Wolfe reported a nest with two young on a cypress tree next to the Boot Spring cabin on September 16, 1982.

American Goldfinch. *Carduelis tristis*

Fairly common spring migrant; uncommon in fall and winter.

Records range from August 31 to June 10. Fall records include a specimen taken at Oak Creek on September 8, 1956 (Texas A&M University); it does not occur regularly until the last of October, after which a few individuals usually can be found along the Rio Grande and in the mountain canyons throughout the winter. Flocks of 15 to 30 birds are most common, but I found a flock of about 60 birds in Boot Canyon on November 4, 1967. CBC participants recorded it six of ten years (1985–1994) on the RGV count and only twice on the Chisos Mountains count. Spring migrants begin to move into the area during the second week of March; they can be numerous to mid-May. Afterward, sightings are scattered, but all are from PJ and the Chisos Basin.

Evening Grosbeak. *Coccothraustes vespertinus*

Casual spring and fall visitor.

There are only a handful of widely scattered reports from March 31 to May 20 in spring and two in fall. Karl Haller first reported this northern finch in the Chisos Basin on the 1951 CBC (December 30). Mr. and Mrs. Don Troyer next found it "between the Basin Trailhead and Boulder Meadow" on November 13, 1972. Jack Tyler reported a female at Boot Spring on May 20, 1974; Bonnie McKinney found six males at the Chisos Remuda on October 31, 1983; and a lone female was reported twice at Boot Spring in 1987: Steve Zachary reported it first on March 31, and Carolyn and Tom Jervis found it "drinking from a pool" on April 4. And Bill and Sarah Bourbon reported a lone male at CC on April 28, 1993.

FAMILY PASSERIDAE: OLD WORLD SPARROWS
House Sparrow. *Passer domesticus*

Common permanent resident.

One collected at Glenn Spring on July 26, 1928 (Van Tyne and Sutton 1937), represented the first park record. It is of some interest that this species no longer resides at Glenn Spring, probably because that old U. S. Army Post was vacated. This may be one of the few instances on record when the House Sparrow deserted an area; records are usually of invasions. The next reports were by Tarleton Smith (1936), who found it present at Boquillas and other settlements along the Rio Grande, but "none have found our camp in the basin." The area of the Chisos Basin campground and lodge is now one of the House Sparrow strongholds in the park. In 1963, C. Phillip Allen reported that he found only "4 pairs" of House Sparrows at PJ. A conservative estimate of the 1970 population exceeded 200 birds, and it appears that estimate is valid 25 years later. It is impossible to guess how long the species has been in the greater Big Bend area, but Montgomery (1905) reported it common at Alpine, in northern Brewster County, as early as June 1904.

House Sparrows in the park are surprisingly mobile. Birds banded at PJ also frequent the Basin. RGV House Sparrows spend most of their time there in winter and spring, when the campground is most active, but they apparently move to Boquillas, Coahuila, during summer and fall.

BIRDS OF UNCERTAIN OCCURRENCE

The following birds are not included in the regular annotated list because they need further verification; they have not been documented by either a specimen or photograph or by unquestionable reports by five or more individuals or parties.

Western Grebe. *Aechmophorus occidentalis*

Rich Simmons reported this bird at RGV, about 150 yards above the river gauge, on May 25, 1984. It occurs in winter at both Amistad Reservoir, below the Lower Canyons, and at Lake Balmorhea, north of the Davis Mountains.

Brown Pelican. *Pelecanus occidentalis*

A lone bird was found "circling over RGV, above TVs (Turkey Vultures)" by Napier Shelton on April 16, 1994. There are a handful of earlier records for the Trans-Pecos, including occasional winter visitors at Lake Balmorhea.

Anhinga. *Anhinga anhinga*

Wildlife photographer Bert Schaughency and his wife, Millie, saw one flying over the river at Hot Springs on April 23, 1970. It was next reported by Charles and Louise Gambill at RGV on September 17, 1988. And there are two records in the Lower Canyons in 1990: George Simmons, Betty Moore, and Marcos Paredes reported one on March 30 and April 5, and Paredes and Moore reported one at Dryden Crossing on April 8. This bird is listed as a "rare" visitor all four seasons at Del Rio and vicinity (TPWD 1992).

Reddish Egret. *Egretta rufescens*

There are two reports: Victor Emanuel, Dan Kluz, and Barry Lyon observed one on the Rio Grande from the RGV nature trail on May 18, 1992, and Larry Carpenter reported one at CC on July 13, 1994.

Roseate Spoonbill. *Ajaia ajaja*

This large, distinct wader was reported on three occasions in 1994: Gary Kempf found one "4–5 miles below Mimi Tanaha Canyon in shade of overhang" in the Lower Canyons on August 10; Ronald Feischer and Cynthia Grant reported one at Hot Springs on September 10; and Mike Gerber, Ed Claypoole, and N. A. Morgan found it there on September 13. Spoonbills are well known for their wandering habits.

Wood Stork. *Mycteria americana*

It was first reported at Dugout Wells on May 18, 1962; Jerry Strickling found one perched on a cottonwood; it "flew toward Boquillas area" when he approached. A second report is of an immature bird in the Lower Canyons on May 12, 1983; Kristin Larson observed it along the river and "paddled her kayak to within 10–15 feet" of it before it flew. And on July 17, 1994, Bonnie McKinney found one at the Black Gap WMA headquarters. Like the previous species, this large wader is well known for its wandering behavior.

Fulvous Whistling-Duck. *Dendrocygna bicolor*

It was first reported at RGV by birders known only as Hanlon, McCarroll, Meyer, Kuehn, and Rowe on April 18, 1967. And in 1988, one was observed on several occasions on the Rio Grande from Reed Camp to San Vicente by George Simmons on May 9, 10, and 12; on one occasion it "landed in snags 20 feet above the Rio."

Black-bellied Whistling-Duck. *Dendrocygna autumnalis*

Patty and Paul Moser reported a pair of these colorful birds "standing on sand bar. Long legs (reddish), also same bill color," on the Rio Grande above Lajitas on March 6, 1989. At Del Rio and vicinity, it is listed as "rare" in spring, summer, and fall (TPWD 1992).

Muscovy Duck. *Cairina moschata*

There are four records during the 1980s, all of lone birds from the Rio Grande near RGV and Boquillas. It was first reported at RGV by Glen Otteson and Bruce Talbot on February 24, 1984; Homer and Jamie Waite observed one from the RGV nature trail on March 15, 1984; Doris Giewald reported one at the RGV beaver pond on March 8, 1985; and Bill Bourbon found one at Boquillas Crossing on February 22 and 23, 1989. This large tropical duck has became a resident on the Rio Grande below Falcon Dam since the 1980s.

American Black Duck. *Anas rubripes*

On the morning of December 10, 1967, I found an individual with a Mallard and a Gadwall on a pond at RGV; nearby was a Rusty Blackbird, another first sighting for the park. The previous day had been very stormy; snow had fallen on the nearby Del Carmen and Chisos mountains, and a strong southeastern wind had blown all day. Apparently, these birds had arrived with the cold front. It was next reported at the entrance to SEC by Keith and Peggy Nusbaum on January 28, 1989; and Jack and Norma Howard reported two "below SEC" on February 20, 1991. This bird of northeastern North America is extremely rare in Texas; there are only four accepted reports (Lasley and Sexton 1994).

Masked Duck. *Oxyura dominica*

There are two reports of this little tropical duck in the park. A pair was first seen in SEC by Bill Mealy, Dave Mobley, and Michael Allender on March 29, 1978, and on April 11, 1978, C. E. Hall reported three females at Hot Springs.

Northern Bobwhite. *Colinus virginianus*

Chuck Sexton reported flushing a male Bobwhite and hearing two birds singing their "covey call" at RGV on August 3, 1982. Bonnie McKinney informed me that J. P. Bryan, owner of Chalk Draw Ranch (west of Persimmon Gap), had introduced this species to his ranch prior to the above report. McKinney also reports that the Northern Bobwhite is a reasonably common resident on the ranchlands in northern Coahuila, south of La Linda.

Black Rail. *Laterallus jamaicensis*

Verma Starts reported that she identified this bird from a "close look" at RGV on March 5, 1978. The nearest records of this bird in Texas are from the Gulf Coast.

Whooping Crane. *Grus americana*

Jim Liles reported three Whoopers flying over RGV on the morning of October 23, 1982; they circled three times before flying eastward toward Boquillas Canyon.

Semipalmated Plover. *Charadrius semipalmatus*

I found two birds on a mud bank of the Rio Grande just upriver from Boquillas Crossing on April 26, 1970. This shorebird is rare in the Big Bend Country, and seen regularly only in the vicinity of Lake Balmorhea.

Mountain Plover. *Charadrius montanus*

There are two reports of this grassland bird: Bonnie McKinney first found one at a stock tank at the south end of Black Gap WMA on August 27, 1982, and Steve Swanke reported one with three Killdeer along the Rio Grande at mile 807 on April 20, 1990.

Red Knot. *Calidris canutus*

There is a single record of this bird: I observed one at a pond at RGV on September 3, 1966. There are a few other fall reports from the western half of Texas (Oberholser 1974).

Semipalmated Sandpiper. *Caladris pusilla*

Jan and Will Risser reported a lone bird along the Rio Grande at CC on April 23, 1995. It is rare in West Texas (Oberholser 1974).

White-rumped Sandpiper. *Caladris fuscicollis*

Robert Rothe reported a lone bird at RGV on August 20, 1988. There are a handful of other records in the Trans-Pecos, according to Oberholser (1974): near El Paso in spring and fall, and at Lake Balmorhea in spring and summer.

Pectoral Sandpiper. *Calidris melanotos*

Lovie May Whitaker reported this bird at Hot Springs on July 19, 1942. There are five additional records for the Trans-Pecos, including a spring specimen taken from Pecos County (Oberholser 1974).

Stilt Sandpiper. *Calidris himantopus*

Bonnie McKinney reported this bird at a stock tank on Maravillas Road at Black Gap WMA on September 29, 1982. Oberholser (1974) reported two additional West Texas sightings near El Paso in spring and fall.

Buff-breasted Sandpiper. *Tryngites subruficollis*

This grassland bird was reported by Bonnie McKinney at Black Gap WMA headquarters on August 24, 1982. There is one earlier Trans-Pecos sighting in fall from near El Paso (Oberholser 1974).

American Woodcock. *Scolopax minor*

Coleman Newman and Dan Beard first found two birds along an irrigation ditch at RGV on November 2, 1965. W. V. Combs reported a lone bird there on November 15, 1972; McRae Williams and Albertine Bauguess found one on the RGV nature trail on November 24, 1973. And Robert Huggins and J. Stovall Smith reported one at RGV on October 6, 1983.

Herring Gull. *Larus argentatus*

G. Ledbetter reported finding this large gull at Reagan Canyon in the Lower Canyons on November 20, 1984. In the Del Rio area, it is uncommon in spring and fall and common in winter (TPWD 1992).

Common Tern. *Sterna hirundo*

There are two separate reports in May 1978: G. Craig McIntyre first found it at the "Calvary Post ponds, Lajitas" on May 5; and Jeanne Farmer reported one at RGV on May 9, 1978. There are no other records for the Trans-Pecos.

Least Tern. *Sterna antillarum*

Maxilla Evans first observed a lone bird flying over the Rio Grande near Talley, just west of Mariscal Canyon, on April 4, 1969. Helen Nelson next reported one at RGV on May 8, 1978; Bill Bourbon and Robert DeVine found one at RGV on May 16, 1989, and Bourbon located it again on May 28; and Kent Nelson reported one near Castolon on April 21, 1992.

Red-billed Pigeon. *Columba flavirostris*

There is one report of this topical pigeon. Alexander Sprunt, Jr., and John H. Dick reported two flying over their cottages in the Chisos Basin on July 21, 1951; it was seen "in good light and at low elevation, which revealed characteristics perfectly."

White-tipped Dove. *Leptotila verreauxi*

There are three park reports of this tropical species. It was first reported from Dugout Wells and the Chisos Basin by Alexander Sprunt, Jr., on June 10 and 12, 1956. And I found a lone bird at RGV on June 30, 1970. The nearest known breeding grounds of this bird is in Starr County, below Falcon Dam.

Ferruginous Pygmy-Owl. *Glaucidium brasilianum*

There are two park reports: Ada Foster heard one calling "8 or 9 single notes" at RGV on April 11, 1980, and Don and Ruthie Melton reported birds at Buenos Aires and Johnson's Ranch on March 29 and 30, 1991. This little tropical owl is common on the Norias Division of the King Ranch in Kenedy County (Wauer, Palmer, and Windam 1994), and reaches the western edge of its range below Falcon Dam. Bonnie McKinney also told me that she has found this bird during bird surveys on ranchlands south of La Linda in northern Coahuila, Mexico.

Spotted Owl. *Strix occidentalis*

There are two reports from the area: Bonnie and Pat McKinney first observed birds on June 25 and 30, 1982 at the Black Gap WMA; one was "feeding on a dead rabbit" along Farm Road 2627. And on October 20, 1981, Del DuBois reported one at Alamo Creek, on the Mexican side of the Rio Grande.

Barred Owl. *Strix varia*

There are two reports. Mr. and Mrs. Robert Foster reported hearing one calling several times in Reagan Canyon, below La Linda in the Lower Canyons, during the night of November 25, 1971. And Mr. and Mrs. H. E. Poindexter reported one sitting in the roadway in Green Gulch during the evening of August 27, 1975. At Del Rio and vicinity, it is considered "irregular" in winter and spring (TPWD 1992).

Black Swift. *Cypseloides niger*

Alexander Sprunt, Jr., and John H. Dick first reported "five or six individuals" from the South Rim Trail over Blue Creek Canyon on July 22, 1951. And Fran Nuebel and Ruth Carter reported one at SEC on May 9, 1968.

White-collared Swift. *Streptoprocne zonaris*

On May 5, 1989, Pat and Hilton Hagan and Millie Bilotta found a swift "much larger than White-throated Swifts" over the Chisos Basin campground, which they identified as this tropical species. There are only three accepted (Lasley and Sexton 1994) Texas records: at Rockport on December 4, 1974; Padre Island on March 8, 1983; and Freeport on December 20, 1987.

Violet-crowned Hummingbird. *Amazilia violiceps*

Rob Pearson reported this tropical hummingbird from the Chisos Basin, where he watched it through a scope, on November 9, 1987. His later report to the TBRC was not accepted (Lasley and Sexton 1994).

Berylline Hummingbird. *Amazilia beryllina*

One reported by John Trochet for Juniper Canyon, below Juniper Spring, on August 8, 1991, is the first for Texas. This record was reported to the TBRC and accepted (Lasley and Sexton 1994). The nearest known breeding grounds of this tropical hummingbird is in southern Chihuahua.

Allen's Hummingbird. *Selasphorus sasin*

There are a handful of records, ranging from a July 24, 1984, report in the Chisos Basin by Jeffrey W. Kirk, to an October 5, 1970, sighting of a male on the Window Trail (Wauer), and there is one very early report by Margaret Littlejohn of a male on the Window Trail on May 18, 1978. Also, Brad McKinney photographed one feeding on a century plant near the Chisos Basin campground on August 12, 1989. This is an extremely difficult bird to identify, and care must be taken not to confuse it with an immature Rufous Hummingbird. Some green-backed Rufous Hummers apparently occur; "at our present state of knowledge it will take a specimen or hand-held measurements of tail feathers to have a record accepted" (Greg Lasley).

Ringed Kingfisher. *Ceryle torquata*

This huge, tropical kingfisher has been reported in the park on three occasions. Bill Mealy and Dave Mobley found one first in SEC on March 29, 1978; Robert DeVine and Ted, Bob and Karen Jones found one at Hot Springs on July 28, 1981; and C. G. Potter reported one at the entrance to SEC on April 25, 1988. This bird has expanded its range in recent years; it is found regularly along the Rio Grande to Falcon Dam and considered "irregular" at Del Rio and vicinity (TPWD 1992).

Downy Woodpecker. *Picoides pubescens*

It has been reported on four occasions. Doyle and Helen Peckham found it first at RGV on May 17, 1969; a male was reported there by Robert Coalston on March 22, 1992, and Dale Evans found one there on April 14, 1992; and Cliff and Maryjane Davenport reported one at RGV on April 3, 1994.

Hairy Woodpecker. *Picoides villosus*

There are four park reports. Harold Brodrick (1960) reported it first for an unrecorded location on March 10, 1950. T. Paul Bonney next found a female at RGV on May 12, 1973. Bonnie Herdel observed one at PJ on March 17, 1986; and Jennifer Gongaware reported five from the South Rim on April 15, 1994. There is an additional record of one at Black Gap WMA headquarters on April 13, 1983 (Bonnie McKinney). This woodpecker is a common nesting bird in Mexico's Maderas del Carmen, 50 mile southeast of the Chisos Mountains.

Northern Beardless-Tyrannulet. *Camptostoma imberbe*

Len Robinson and Eleanor Beal reported this little flycatcher at two locations on April 2, 1975: Green Gulch and the Window Trail. And Buck and Linda Carpa reported it again for Blue Creek Canyon on May 1, 1991. This tropical species is resident in Texas only in the lower Rio Grande Valley.

Buff-breasted Flycatcher. *Empidonax fulvifrons*

There are two reports of this Southwestern flycatcher. It was first reported by Dr. and Mrs. R. C. Smith in the Chisos Basin on August 12, 1969; and Doris Harden reported a pair near the Chisos Basin Trailhead on April 17, 1994.

Nutting's Flycatcher. *Myiarchus nuttingi*

Jim Tucker, Benton Basham, Barbara and John Ribble, and Willie Sekula observed this bird from as close as six to eight feet along the RGV nature trail on January 23, 1987. The bird was also photographed by Basham. This report and photograph was later submitted to the TBRC, but was not accepted (Lasley and Sexton 1994).

Great Kiskadee. *Pitangus sulphuratus*

There are four reports. Roy and Jean Hudson reported it first along the Rio Grande at Boquillas on May 21, 1964; N. Dobbins found one at RGV on December 30, 1979; Pierce reported one near the start of the SEC trail on May 18, 1983; and J. A. Barnes found a pair at Boquillas Crossing on April 12, 1985. It is listed as "uncommon" in spring, summer, and fall at Del Rio and vicinity (TPWD 1992).

Pinyon Jay. *Gymnorhinus cyanocephalus*

Sheriton Burr reported seeing a lone Pinyon Jay with a flock of Mexican Jays on the Lost Mine Trail on May 5, 1978. This species is a sporadic late fall/winter visitor in northern Brewster County.

Black-billed Magpie. *Pica pica*

Phil and Charlotte Spencer reported that a magpie flew across the road at the Old Ranch on February 15, 1981. And C. G. Potter reported it near SEC on April 15, 1988; that sighting was submitted to the TBRC but was not accepted. The nearest known Texas record is one from El Paso on February 6, 1990 (Lasley and Sexton 1994).

American Crow. *Corvus brachyrhynchos*

There are three reports of this farmland corvid. Barbara Ribble reported seeing two birds flying over Castolon on December 27, 1970; D. Brooks found one at RGV on September 14 and 17, 1984; and Joyce Dolch reported one there on October 3, 1990.

Chickadee. *Parus* sps.

Bernard Browerhand first reported seeing five or six chickadees that sang a "coarse chickadee call" in Boot Canyon on June 26, 1974; Mr. and Mrs. F. P. Elby reported six to twelve "very noisy chickadees" on the Lost Mine Trail, August 21, 1975; Bonnie McKinney found one at Black Gap WMA following a severe cold front on January 13, 1982; and Roger Mitchell reported a lone "Mt. Chickadee" with "white line above eye, black beneath eye," on the Strawhouse Trail, January 3, 1991. The Mountain Chickadee nests in the Davis and Guadalupe mountains north of the park.

Bridled Titmouse. *Parus wollweberi*

This Southwestern tit has been reported for the park on five occasions, but only three of the reports are from the proper habitats. Henry West and M. E. Gibson first reported five individuals with Bushtits in the Chisos Basin on May 12, 1981; Bonnie McKinney found two along the Window Trail on November 16, 1981; and Dr. and Mrs. Bernard Shadoin reported three in Pine Canyon on March 20, 1989. Two additional reports are from Hot Springs and PJ "with Black-throated Sparrows."

Clay-colored Robin. *Turdus grayi*

Mr. and Mrs. R. N. Hewitt first reported one with several American Robins at RGV on March 6, 1977, and Joan Babbitt reported one on the Window Trail, May 8, 1990. This tropical species is a rare Lower Valley resident and is "irregular" in spring at Del Rio and vicinity (TPWD 1992).

Rufous-backed Robin. *Turdus rufopalliatus*

There is one series of sightings. I found a lone bird among the dense mesquite and seepwillow thicket at the Gambusia Pond at RGV on October 23, 1966. It was found again on October 25 and 30, but it was extremely shy after the initial observation. This was the first sighting of this tropical bird in Texas, but it has since been reported below Falcon Dam on December 29, 1975, at Langtry on November 11 and 18, 1976, two near Ft. Davis on February 2, 1992, and at El Paso on October 27, 1993.

Bendire's Thrasher. *Toxostoma bendirei*

This western thrasher has been reported on nine occasions, but none of the sightings has been verified, nor is the species accepted anywhere in Texas (Lasley and Sexton 1994). It was first reported by Laurie Yorke, who watched one "singing occasionally" at Dugout Wells on August 27, 1977. It was next reported on December 28, 1978, when R. J. Bullock and Mary Louise and Bruce Stewart found one at Hot Springs. In 1980, Nancy and Jerry Strickling reported one at Dugout on January 8, and Bruce Stewart reported one at Boquillas on December 26. None were reported in 1981 and 1982, but there were three 1983 reports: Jeanne Pratt found one on Dagger Flat on January 30; Brete Griffen, Ann Tews, and Mark Kirtley discovered one at PJ on February 27; and Gerry and Vicki Wolfe found one in the Chisos Basin on August 21. Bonnie McKinney next reported one at Black Gap WMA on July 19, 1982. None were reported in 1983, but Catherine Hillman found one in the Basin campground on May 20, 1984. The only additional report is a singing bird found in lower Pine Canyon by Jan and Bill Bolte on January 28, 1991. Further verification by taped song or photograph is necessary.

Crescent-chested Warbler. *Parula superciliosa*

Libby and Ronald Wolfe reported this bird in upper Boot Canyon on June 2, 1993; their report was later submitted to the TBRC and accepted (Lasley and Sexton 1994). The nearest breeding grounds for this tropical warbler is in the pine-oak woodlands of southern Tamaulipas and Nuevo Leon.

Prairie Warbler. *Dendroica discolor*

The first report of this bird was a male found at RGV on April 28, 1990, by Mike Austin, Peter Gottschling, Stephen Gast, and Lynne Aldrich; David Mandell, Star Saphir, and Bob Machover found a male at the Old Ranch on June 15, 1990; Tim Brush next reported one he observed and heard singing at Grapevine Spring on May 26, 1992; and Ross Taylor found one on the Pinnacles Trail on April 17, 1993.

Bay-breasted Warbler. *Dendroica castanea*

A lone female was reported at RGV on May 10, 1978, by "D. & D. W."; David Johnson found one next at Glenn Spring on May 14, 1979; Geth and Ed White reported a lone male at the Old Ranch on April 11, 1980; and T. and L. Army and Jeff Chynoweth (separate reports) found a male there on May 27, 1986.

Swainson's Warbler. *Limnothlypis swainsonii*

There is a lone report: Christina and Renee Laubach found one at Boot Spring on April 26, 1986.

Connecticut Warbler. *Oporornis agilis*

There is one report: Henry Childs found one in the Chisos Basin on the Pinnacles Trail on April 28, 1985. This is an extremely rare migrant in the western half of Texas.

Mourning Warbler. *Oporornis philadelphia*

There are two reports: I found one along the RGV nature trail on April 18, 1972, and Peter Riesz found a female in Pine Canyon on May 6, 1993. Oberholser (1974) considers it a "casual" migrant only in the Trans-Pecos.

Golden-crowned Warbler. *Basileuterus culicivorus*

Bill Mealy reported finding a lone bird of this species near Laguna Meadow, "just below the saddle," on April 18, 1982. There are several other Texas records, all from the lower Rio Grande Valley (Lasley and Sexton 1994). The nearest known breeding grounds for this tropical warbler are in southern Tamaulipas and Nuevo Leon.

Yellow Grosbeak. *Pheucticus chrysopeplus*

There are three reports of this West Mexican species. Art Prickett first reported one from below the saddle at Laguna Meadow on May 24, 1985; it was "yellow with black-and-yellow wings and a grosbeak beak." Karen Boucher and Sonja Paspal next found a female at Buttrill Spring on May

24, 1990; they described it as "dull yellow with large grosbeak bill. Darker crown, yellow 'eyebrows,' white on black wings." And Kat and Steve Perry reported one near Boulder Meadow on September 9, 1992. They described it as a "heavyset, yellow-and-black bird" with "a stark black tail, brilliant yellow belly, and striking black wings with strong white bar in the middle and a shorter bar towards the shoulder." The nearest known breeding grounds of this tropical bird is "southern Sonora, southwestern Chihuahua, Sinoloa and western Durango" (AOU 1983).

Blue Bunting. *Cyanocompsa parellina*

This beautiful little bird has been reported three times. Walt Burch reported it first in the Chisos Basin campground on April 25, 1991. Fred Lebseck and Cornelius Alwood next reported one below the Basin campground, describing it as "all blue body, dark bill, same size and shape as Varied Bunting. Samè color on body and head. No wing bars and smaller than Blue Grosbeak." And a male Blue Bunting was again reported along the Window Trail on July 29, 1993, by Elliot Tramer, who later sent a report to the TBRC; at this writing (March 1995) it is still under review. This bunting is common in brushlands along the central Gulf Coast of Tamaulipas.

Olive Sparrow. *Arremonops rufivirgatus*

There are three reports. Scott Robinson found it first at the Old Ranch on April 30, 1976; Bonnie McKinney reported one at Laguna Meadow on July 25, 1985; and Florence Hurst reported one at RGV on April 20, 1986. This species is common in the Tamaulipian brushland of South Texas; it is irregular in winter and spring at Del Rio and vicinity (TPWD 1992).

McCown's Longspur. *Calcarius mccownii*

Steve Johnson and Nancy Saulsbury reported two birds at the K-Bar on March 8, 1981, and Bonnie McKinney reported one at Black Gap WMA headquarters on January 13, 1982. Oberholser (1974) included only five records for the Trans-Pecos.

Lapland Longspur. *Calcarius lapponicus*

There is a single report: John Coons and Rose Ann Rowlett found a lone female about 200 yards west of PJ on May 2, 1988. Oberholser (1974) included no reports of this species in the Trans-Pecos.

Snow Bunting. *Plectrophenax nivalis*

Tom and Helen Nelson and Bob and Myra Braden found a lone male, in full breeding plumage, at the Chisos Basin sewage lagoon on May 9, 1988. A report was prepared for the TBRC and accepted. There are three other Texas records: at Lake Livingston on December 21–23, 1977; two birds near Dalhart on December 29, 1983; and two birds at Lake Balmorhea on November 27, 1993 (Lasley and Sexton 1994).

Bobolink. *Dolichonyx oryzivorus*

There are two reports: Cynthia Womack found one at the RGV amphitheater on May 15, 1993, and David Young independently reported one nearby two days later. This is an extremely rare spring and fall visitor to the Trans-Pecos.

Audubon's Oriole. *Icterus graduacauda*

This black-headed oriole has been reported in the park for several years, but all of the sightings that I or other park officials checked out have always been Scott's Orioles. The eight park reports range from May 13 to October 5, primarily from the Chisos Basin, Laguna Meadow, and two reported from Dugout Wells. This bird does occur along the Rio Grande Valley and nesting records exist up to Del Rio (Oberholser 1974).

Pine Grosbeak. *Pinicola enucleator*

There are three reports: Clara and Harold Spore reported it first in Green Gulch on April 24, 1951; Jane Hamilton reported one at RGV on May 5, 1982; and Garrett and Kathie Albright reported one from the Lost Mine Trail on July 30, 1992. This is a bird of the far north that appears only rarely in North Texas.

Lawrence's Goldfinch. *Carduelis lawrencei*

Doug Bernard reported one at his Chisos Basin residence on March 26, 1977, and Lee Daniel reported one at CC on April 6, 1989. The later bird was reported to the TBRC, but the report was not accepted. This West Coast finch winters in southern Arizona, and a record of one at Hueco Tanks on December 7, 1984 is the only accepted Texas record (Lasley and Sexton 1994).

BIRDS WITH QUESTIONABLE REPORTS

The species below are included to document reports that, although they are extremely unlikely, are considered possible. The questionable species are not included as part of the park's total species count.

Spotted Rail. *Pardirallus maculatus.*

There is one report on the Boquillas Canyon Nature Trail in February 1978.

Plain-capped Starthroat. *Heliomaster constantii.*

This hummingbird of Mexico's Pacific Slope was reported at Laguna Meadow on July 8, 1989.

Three-toed Woodpecker. *Picoides tridactylus.*

There is a lone report at PJ on May 15, 1983.

Pacific-slope Flycatcher. *Empidonax difficilis.*

There is a lone report of a singing bird at RGV on February 15, 1992.

Fork-tailed Flycatcher. *Tyrannus savana.*

There is a lone report at PJ on June 10, 1989.

Black-capped Gnatcatcher. *Polioptila nigriceps.*

There are two reports in 1993: at the Old Ranch on April 25, and at Hot Springs on April 29.

Bohemian Waxwing. *Bombycilla garrulus.*
There is a lone report at RGV on May 8, 1975.

Five-stripped Sparrow. *Amphispiza quniquestriata.*
There is one report from the mouth of Boquillas Canyon on April 20, 1989.

Streak-backed Oriole. *Icterus pustulatus.*
There are two reports in 1986, at RGV on April 15 and September 20.

Hooded Grosbeak. *Hesperiphona abeillie.*
There is a lone report in upper Green Gulch on July 30, 1982.

BIBLIOGRAPHY

Allen, T. M. "A Survey of the Avifaunal Associates of Agave havardiana trel. in Big Bend National Park." Master's Thesis, University of Texas at Arlington, 1977.

Allen, T. M., and Neil, R. L. "Avifaunal Associates of Agave havardiana trel. in Big Bend National Park." In: *Proceedings of the First Conference on Scientific Research in the National Parks,* Vol. 1. U.S. Department of the Interior, National Park Service, Transactions and Proceedings Series, No. 5, 1979, pp. 479–482.

American Ornithologists' Union (AOU). *Check-list of North American Birds, 5th ed.* American Ornithologists' Union, Maryland: The Lord Baltimore Press., Inc., 1957.

American Ornithologists' Union (AOU). *Check-list of North American Birds, 6th ed.* American Ornithologists' Union, Washington, D. C., 1983.

American Ornithologists' Union (AOU). "Thirty-fifth supplement to the American Ornithologists' Union Check-list of North American Birds." *Auk,* Vol. 102, 1985, pp. 680–686.

American Ornithologists' Union (AOU). "Thirty-seventh supplement to the American Ornithologists' Union Check-list of North American Birds." *Auk,* Vol. 106, 1989, pp. 532–538.

American Ornithologists' Union (AOU). "Thirty-ninth supplement to the American Ornithologists' Union Check-list of North American Birds." *Auk,* Vol. 110, 1993, pp. 675–682.

Arnold, Keith A. "Olivaceous Flycatcher in the Davis Mountains of Texas." *Bulletin of the Texas Ornithological Society,* Vol. 2, 1968, p. 28.

Bailey, Vernon. *Biological Survey of Texas.* North American Fauna, No. 25. Washington, D. C., 1905.

Baker, James K. "Association of Cave Swallows with Cliff and Barn Swallows." *Condor,* Vol. 64, 1962, pp. 326.

Barlow, Jon C., "Nesting of the Black-capped Vireo in the Chisos Mountains, Texas." *Condor,* Vol. 69, 1967, pp. 605–606.

Barlow, Jon C., "Effects of Habitat Attrition on Vireo Distribution and Population Density in the Northern Chihuahuan Desert." In: *Transactions of the Symposium on the Biological Resources of the Chihuahuan Desert Region, U.S. and Mexico,* eds. Roland H. Wauer and David H. Riskind. U. S. Department of the Interior, National Park Service, Transactions and Proceedings Series, No. 3, 1977, pp. 591–596.

Barlow, Jon C., and Johnson, R. Roy. "Current Status of the Elf Owl in the Southwestern United States." *Southwestern Naturalist, Vol.* 12, 1967, pp. 331–332.

Barlow, Jon C., and Wauer, Roland H. "The Gray Vireo (Vireo vicinior Coues; Aves: Vireonidae) Wintering in the Big Bend Region, West Texas." *Canadian Journal of Zoology,* Vol. 49, 1971, pp. 953–955.

Beckham, C. W. "Observations on the Birds of Southwestern Texas." *Proceedings from the U.S. National Musuem Bulletin,* Vol. 10, 1888, pp. 633–696.

Bellamy, Anne Henley. "Colima Warbler: Rare Bird of the Chisos." *Texas Parks and Wildlife,* July 1987, pp. 40–42.

Blair, W. Frank. "The Biotic Provinces of Texas." *Texas Journal of Science,* Vol. 2, 1950, pp. 93–116.

Blake, Emmet R. "The Nest of the Colima Warbler in Texas." *Wilson Bulletin,* Vol. 61, 1949, pp. 64–67.

Blake, Emmet R. *Birds of Mexico.* Illinois: University of Chicago Press, 1953.

Bolen, Eric G., and Flores, Dan. *The Mississippi Kite.* Austin: Univeristy of Texas Press, 1993.

Borell, Adrey E. "New Bird Records for Brewster County, Texas." *Condor,* Vol. 40, 1938, pp. 181–182.

Borell, Adrey E. Birds Observed in the Big Bend Area of Brewster County, Texas. Report to National Park Service, 1963.

Brandt, Herbert W. "Two New Birds from the Chisos Mountains, Texas." *Auk,* Vol. 55, 1928, pp. 269–270.

Brandt, Herbert W. *Texas Bird Adventures*. Cleveland: Bird Research Foundation, 1940.

Brodkorb, Pierce. "A New Flycatcher from Texas." *Occasional Papers, Museum of Zoology, University of Michigan*, No. 306, 1935.

Brodrick, Harold. "Check-list of the Birds of Big Bend National Park." Mimeographed. Big Bend National Park, Texas, 1960.

Brodrick, Harold, Allen, C. Phllip, and LeSassier, Anne. *Check-list of Birds of Big Bend National Park*. Big Bend Natural History Association, 1966.

Brownlee, W. C. "Nesting Peregrine Falcons in Texas." Texas Parks and Wildlife Department Report No. W-103-R-071, 1977.

Bryan, Kelly, Gallucci, Tony, and Moldenhauer, Ralph. "First Record of the Snow Bunting for Texas." *American Birds*, Vol. 32, 1978, p. 1070.

Bryan, Kelly, et. al. *A Checklist of Texas Birds*. Austin: Texas Parks and Wildlife Department, 1991.

Castro, Stanley, and Garner, Herschel W. "Photographic Evidence for the occurrence of the Dipper in West Texas." *Bulletin of the Texas Ornithological Society*, Vol. 3, 1969, p. 29.

Correll, Donovan S. and Johnson, Marshall C. *Manual of Vascular Plants of Texas*. Renner: Texas Research Foundation, 1970.

Cottam, Clarence, and Trefenthen, J. B., eds. *Whitewings: The Life History, Status, and Management of the Whitewing Dove*. New York: D. Van Nostrand Co., 1968.

Cruickshank, Allen. "Records from Brewster County, Texas." *Wilson Bulletin*, Vol. 62, 1950, pp. 217–219.

Cully, Jack F., Jr. "Mobbing Behavior of Mexican Jays (Aphelecoma ultramarina) and Scrub Jays (A. coerulescens)." Master's Thesis, University of New Mexico, 1972.

Dixon, Keith L. "Ecological and Distributional Relations of Desert Scrub Birds of Western Texas." *Condor*, Vol. 61, 1959, pp. 397–409.

Dixon, Keith L., and Wallmo, O. C. "Some New Bird Records from Brewster County, Texas." *Condor*, Vol. 58, 1965, p. 166.

Easterla, D. A. "Specimens of Black-throated Blue Warbler and Yellow-green Vireo from West Texas." *Condor*, Vol. 74, 1972, p. 489.

Easterla, David A., and Wauer, Roland H. "Bronzed Cowbird in West Texas and Two Bill Abnormalities." *The Southwestern Naturalist*, Vol. 17, No. 3, 1972, pp. 293–312.

Ely, Charles A. "The Birds of Southeastern Coahuila, Mexico." *Condor*, Vol. 64, 1962, pp. 34–39.

Fox, R. P. "Plumages and Territorial Behavior of the Lucifer Hummingbird in the Chisos Mountains, Texas." *Auk*, Vol. 71, 1954, pp. 465–466.

Friedmann, Herbert, Griscom, L., and Moore, R. T. *Distributional Check-list of the Birds of Mexico, Part II*. Pacific Coast Avifauna, Vol. 33, 1957, pp. 1–435.

Fuertes, Louis Agassiz. "With the Mearn's Quail in Southwestern Texas." *Condor*, Vol. 5, 1903, pp. 113–116.

Galley, John E. "Clark's Nutcracker in the Chisos Mountains, Texas." *Wilson Bulletin*, Vol. 62, 1951, p. 188.

Gallucci, Tony. "The Biological and Taxanomic Status of the White-winged Doves of the Big Bend of Texas." Masters Thesis, Sul Ross State University, Alpine, 1978.

Gehlbach, F. R. "New Records of Warblers in Texas." *Southwestern Naturalist*, Vol. 12, 1967, pp. 109–110.

Griffen, Brete Garland. "Habitat Correlates of Foraging Behavior at Two Levels of Temporal Resolution in the Gray Vireo (Vireo vicinior)." Masters Thesis, University of Toronto, 1986.

Hardy, William John. "Studies in Behavior and Phylogeny of Certain New World Jays." *University of Kansas Science Bulletin*, Vol. 27, 1961, pp. 13–14.

Hector, D. P. "Our rare falcon of the desert grassland." *Birding*, Vol. 12, No. 3, 1980, pp. 92–102.

Hector, D. P. "The habitat, diet, and foraging behavior of the Aplomado Falcon, Falco femoralis (Temminck)." Masters Thesis, Oklahoma State University, 1981.

Hill, K. B., and Schaetzel, L. J. "Peregrine Falcons in Big Bend National Park: 1977 Breeding Season." Report to National Park Service by Chihuahuan Desert Research Institute, 1977.

Hitchcock, Mark A. "A Survey of the Peregrine Falcon Population in Northeastern Mexico, 1976–77." Report by Chihuahuan Desert Research Institute, Contribution No. 40, 1977.

Howell, Steve N. G., and Webb, Sophie. *A Guide to the Birds of Mexico and Northern Central America.* Oxford: Oxford University Press, 1995.

Hubbard, John P. "The Relationship and Evolution of the Dendroica Complex." *Auk,* Vol. 86, 1969, pp. 393–432.

Hunt, W. Grainger. "The Significance of Wilderness Ecosystems in Western Texas and Adjacent Regions in the Ecology of the Peregrine Falcon." In: *Transactions of the Symposium on the Biological Resources of the Chihuahuan Desert Region U.S. and Mexico,* eds. Roland H. Wauer and David H. Riskind. U.S. Department of the Interior, National Park Service, Transactions and Proceedings Series, No. 3, 1974, pp. 609–916.

Hunt, W. Grainger. 1975. "The Chihuahuan Desert Peregrine Falcon Survey, 1975." Report to National Park Service.

Hunt, W. Grainger. "Peregrine Falcons in West Texas: Results of the 1976 Nesting Survey." Report to Texas Parks and Wildlife Department, 1976a.

Hunt, W. Grainger. "The Peregrine Population in the Chihuahuan Desert and Surrounding Mountain Ranges: An Evaluation Through 1976." Report to National Park Service, 1976b.

Hunt, W. Grainger, et. al. "Nesting Peregrines in Texas and Northern Mexico," in *Peregrine Falcon Population Their Management and Recovery.* Idaho: The Peregrine Fund, 1988, pp. 115–121.

Johnson, Brenda S. "Continuing Studies of Raptors in Two National Parks in Western Texas." Report to National Park Service by the Chihuahuan Desert Research Institute, 1976.

Johnson, Brenda S., and Hunt, W. G. "DDT and the Diet of Texas Peregrine Falcons." Report to National Park Service by the Chihuahuan Desert Research Institute, 1977.

Keefer, Mary Belle. "Varied Thrush in Texas." *Wilson Bulletin,* Vol. 69, 1957, p. 114.

Key, J. J. *Peregrine Falcon Breeding Status in Texas National Parks,* 1980. Chihuahuan Desert Research Institute, Contribution No. 97, 1980.

Kowaleski, C. T., and Wade, V. R. "Texas Peregrine Eyrie Search, 1977" Report to National Park Service by Chihuahuan Desert Research Institute, 1977.

Kuban, Joe F., Jr. "The Ecological Organization of Hummingbirds in the Chisos Mountains, Big Bend National Park, Texas." Masters Thesis, University of Texas at Arlington, 1977.

Kuban, Joseph F., and Neill, Robert F. "Feeding Ecology of Hummingbirds in the Highlands of the Chisos Mountains, Texas." *Condor*, Vol. 82, 1980, pp. 180–185.

Kuban, Joseph F., Lawley, John, and Neill, Robert F. "The Partitioning of Flowering Century Plants by Black-chinned and Lucifer Hummingbird." *Southwestern Naturalist*, Vol. 28, No. 2, 1983, pp. 143–148.

Lanning, Dirk V. "Status Report: Vermivora crissalis (Salvin and Godman) Colima Warbler." Report to National Park Service, 1983, pp. 48.

Lasley, Gregory W., et. al. "Documentation of the Red-faced Warbler (*Cardellina rubrifrons*) in Texas and a Review of its Status in Texas and Adjacent Areas." *Bulletin of the Texas Ornithological Society*, Vol. 15, Nos. 1 & 2, 1982, pp. 8–14.

Lasley, Greg W., and Sexton, Chuck. "Texas Region." *American Birds*, Spring 1989a, pp. 127–133.

Lasley, Greg W., and Sexton, Chuck. "Texas Region." *American Birds*, Fall, 1989b, pp. 502–510.

Lasley, Greg W., and Sexton, Chuck. "Texas Region." *American Birds*, Summer, 1990a, pp. 288–290.

Lasley, Greg W., and Sexton, Chuck. "Texas Region." *American Birds*, Fall, 1990b, pp. 458–465.

Lasley, Greg W., and Sexton, Chuck. "Texas Region." *American Birds*, Winter, 1990c, pp. 1154–1160.

Lasley, Greg W., and Sexton, Chuck. "Rare Birds of Texas Master List of Review Species." Photocopied report, 1994, pp. 1–118.

Marshall, Joe T., Jr. *Parallel Variation in North and Middle American Screech-Owls.* Los Angeles, Calif. Monographs of the Western Foundation of Vertebrate Zoology, 1967.

Marshall, Joe T., Clapp, Roger B., and Grzybowski, Joseph A. "Status Report: Vireo atricapillus Woodhouse." Report to U.S. Fish and Wildlife Service, 1985, pp. 1–54.

Martin, Robert F. "Syntopic Culvert Nesting of Cave and Barn Swallows in Texas." *Auk*, Vol. 91, 1974, pp. 776–782.

Maxon, George E. "Military Oologing in Texas." *Oologist*, Vol. 33, No. 10, 1916a, pp. 172–173.

Maxon, George E. "A Soldier Ornithologist." *Oologist*, Vol. 33, No. 12, 1916b, pp. 205–06.

McKinney, Bonnie R. "Brown-headed Cowbird (Molothrus ater) Trapping Program 1986, Big Bend National Park." Report to National Park Service, 1986, pp. 1–8.

Miller, Alden H. "The Avifauna of the Sierra del Carmen of Coahuila, Mexico." *Condor*, Vol. 57, 1955, pp. 154–178.

Montgomery, Thomas H., Jr. "Summer Resident Birds of Brewster County, Texas." *Auk*, Vol. 22, 1905, pp. 12–15.

Neill, R. L., and Allen, T. M. "Concentrated Avian Utilization of an Early Flowering Century Plant (Agave havardiana)." In: *Proceedings of the First Conference on Scientific Research in the National Parks*, Vol. 1. U. S. Department of the Interior, National Park Service, Transactions and Proceedings Series, No. 5, 1979, pp. 475–478.

Nelson, Richard Clay. "An Additional Nesting Record of the Lucifer Hummingbird in the United States." *Southwestern Naturalist*, Vol. 15, 1970, pp. 135–136.

Oberholser, Harry C. "Some Notes from Western Texas." *Auk*, Vol. 19, 1902, pp. 300–301.

Oberholser, Harry C. *The Bird Life of Texas.* Austin: University of Texas Press, 1974.

Ohlendorf, Harry F. and Patton, Robert F. "Nesting Record of Mexican Duck (*Anas diaza*) in Texas." *Wilson Bulletin*, Vol. 83, 1971, p. 97.

Orians, Gordon. *Blackbirds of the Americas.* Seattle: University of Washington Press, 1985.

Palmer, Ralph S. *Handbook of North American Birds,* Vol 1, New Haven, CT: Yale University Press, 1962.

Parker, K. C. "The Structure of Bird Communities in North American Deserts." Ph.D. Dissertation, University of Wisconsin, Madison, 1982.

Peterson, Jim J., et. al. "Additions to the Breeding Avifauna of the Davis Mountains." *Bulletin of the Texas Ornithological Society,* Vol. 24, No. 2, 1991, pp. 39–48.

Peterson, Roger Tory. *A Field Guide to the Birds of Texas.* Boston: Houghton-Mifflin, 1960.

Peterson, Roger Tory, and Chalif, Edward L. *A Field Guide to Mexican Birds.* Boston: Houghton-Mifflin, 1973.

Phillips, Allan R. "The Instability of the Distribution of Land Birds in the Southwest." In: *Papers of the Archeological Society of New Mexico,* Vol. 1, 1968, pp. 129–162.

Phillips, Allen R., Marshall, Joe, and Monson, Gale. *The Birds of Arizona.* Tucson: University of Arizona Press, 1964.

Pulich, Warren M. *The Golden-cheeked Warbler.* Austin: Texas Parks and Wildlife Department, 1976.

Pulich, Warren M., Sr., and Pulich, Warren M., Jr. "The Nesting of the Lucifer Hummingbird in the United States." *Auk,* Vol. 80, 1963, pp. 370–371.

Quillin, Roy W. "New Bird Records from Texas." *Auk,* Vol. 52, 1935, pp. 324–325.

Raitt, Ralph J. "Relationship Between Black-eared and Plain-eared Forms of Bushtits (*Psaltriparus*)." *Auk,* Vol. 84, 1967, pp. 503–528.

Robinson, S. M. "Ethological Study of Vermivora crissalis in the Chisos Mountains, Texas." Master's Thesis, Sul Ross State University, Alpine, 1973.

Rooney, Walter. Interview taped by Doug Evans for National Park Service, 1966.

Scott, Peter E. "The Last Five Years at Big Bend." Talk presented to the Texas Ornithological Society, May 18, 1978.

Scott, Peter E. "Peregrine Falcon Observations in Big Bend NP in 1979." Report to National Park Service, 1979.

Selleck, Jeff. "Hypothetical or Interesting Accidental Bird Reports in Big Bend National Park Since May 1988." Photocopied Report, 1992, pp. 1–3.

Sibley, C. G., and Monroe, B. L., Jr. *Distribution and Taxonomy of Birds of the World.* New Haven, Conn: Yale University Press, 1990.

Smith, Tarleton F. "Wildlife Report on the proposed Big Bend National Park of Texas." Report to National Park Service, October 11, 1936.

Snyder, D. E. "A Recent Colima Warbler Nest." *Auk,* Vol. 74, 1957, pp. 97–98.

Sprunt, Alexander, Jr. "The Colima Warbler of the Big Bend." *Audubon Magazine,* Vol. 52, 1950, pp. 84–91.

Stevenson, John O. "General Wildlife Considerations of the Big Bend Area of Texas." Report to National Park Service, 1935.

Stevenson, John O., and Smith, Tarleton F. "Additions to the Brewster County, Texas, Bird List." *Condor,* Vol. 40, 1938, p. 184.

Sutton, George M., "An Expedition to the Big Bend Country." *The Cardinal,* Vol. 4, 1935, p. 107.

Sutton, George M. *Birds in the Wilderness.* New York: Macmillan Co., 1936.

Sutton, George M. *Mexican Birds—First Impressions.* Norman: University of Oklahoma Press, 1951.

Sutton, George M., and Van Tyne, Josselyn. "A New Red-tailed Hawk from Texas." *Occasional Papers,* Museum of Zoology, University of Michigan, No. 321, September 23, 1935.

Taylor, Walter P., McDougall, W. B., and Davis, W. B. "Preliminary Report of an Ecological Survey of Big Bend National Park." Report to National Park Service, March–June, 1944.

Texas Bird Records Committee. *Checklist of the Birds of Texas.* Austin: Texas Ornithological Society, 1995.

Texas Parks and Wildlife Department. *Birds of Del Rio and Vicinity.* Austin: Wildlife Division, TPWD, 1992.

Thompson, Ben H. "Report upon the Wildlife of the Big Bend Area of the Rio Grande, Texas." Report to National Park Service, April 18, 1934.

Thompson, William Lay. "The Ecological Distribution of the Birds of the Black Gap Area, Brewster County, Texas." *Texas Journal of Science,* Vol. 2, 1953, pp. 158–177.

Van Tyne, Josselyn. "Notes on Some Birds of the Chisos Mountains of Texas." *Auk,* Vol. 46, 1929, pp. 204–206.

Van Tyne, Josselyn. *The Discovery of the Nest of the Colima Warbler (Vermivora crissalis).* Miscellaneous Publications, University of Michigan, No. 33, 1936.

Van Tyne, Josselyn. "Geographical Variation in the Blue-throated Hummingbird (Lampornis clemenciae)." *Auk,* Vol. 70, 1953, pp. 208–209.

Van Tyne, Josselyn, and Sutton, George M. *The Birds of Brewster County, Texas.* Miscellaneous Publications, University of Michigan, No. 37, 1937.

Wallmo, O. C. "Ecology of Scaled Quail in West Texas." Photocopied Report, 1956, p. 134.

Wauer, Roland H. "Report on the Colima Warbler Census." Report to National Park Service, May 29, 1967a.

Wauer, Roland H. "Winter and Early Spring Birds in Big Bend." *Bulletin of the Texas Ornithological Society,* Vol. 1, No. 1, 1967b, p. 8.

Wauer, Roland H. "Further Evidence of Bushtit Lumping in Texas." *Bulletin of the Texas Ornithological Society,* Vol. 1, Nos. 5–6, 1967c, p. 1

Wauer, Roland H. "Colima Warbler Census in Big Bend's Chisos Mountains." *National Parks Magazine,* Vol. 41, 1967d, pp. 8–10.

Wauer, Roland H. "First Thick-billed Kingbird Record in Texas." *Southwestern Naturalist,* Vol. 12, 1967e, pp. 485–486.

Wauer, Roland H. "The Groove-billed Ani in Texas." *Southwestern Naturalist,* Vol. 13, 1968, p. 452.

Wauer, Roland H. "Hummingbirds of the Big Bend." *Bulletin of the Texas Ornithological Society,* Vol. 3, 1969a, p. 18.

Wauer, Roland H. "Winter Bird Records from the Chisos Mountains and Vicinity." *Southwestern Naturalist,* Vol. 14, 1969b, pp. 252–254.

Wauer, Roland H. "The History of Land Use and Some Ecological Implications, Big Bend National Park, TX." Report to National Park Service, November 25, 1969c.

Wauer, Roland H. "Upland Plover at Big Bend National Park, Texas." *Southwestern Naturalist,* Vol. 14, 1970a, pp. 361–362.

Wauer, Roland H. "The Occurrence of the Black-vented Oriole, Icterus wagleri, in the United States." *Auk,* Vol. 82, 1970b, pp. 811–812.

Wauer, Roland H. "A Second Swallow-tailed Kite Record for Trans- Pecos Texas." *Wilson Bulletin,* Vol. 82, 1971a, p. 462.

Wauer, Roland H. "Ecological Distribution of Birds of the Chisos Mountains, Texas." *Southwestern Naturalist,* Vol. 16, 1971b, pp. 1–29.

Wauer, Roland H. "Status of Certain Parulids of West Texas." *Southwestern Naturalist,* Vol. 18, 1973a, pp. 105–110.

Wauer, Roland H. *Naturalist's Big Bend*. College Station: Texas A&M University Press, 1973b.

Wauer, Roland H. "Bronzed Cowbird Extends Range into the Texas Big Bend Country." *Wilson Bulletin*, Vol. 85, 1973c, pp. 343–344.

Wauer, Roland H. "Report on Harlequin Quail Release, Big Bend National Park, Texas." Report to National Park Service, 1973d, pp. 1–6.

Wauer, Roland H. *Birds of Big Bend National Park and Vicinity*. Austin: University of Texas Press, 1973e.

Wauer, Roland H. "Significance of Rio Grande Riparian Systems upon the Avifauna." In: *Importance, Preservation, and Management of Riparian Habitats: A Symposium*. U.S. Department of Agriculture, Forest Service, General Technical Report RM-43, 1977a, pp. 165–174.

Wauer, Roland H. "Changes in the Breeding Avifauna Within the Chisos Mountains System." In: *Transactions of the Symposium on the Biological Resources of the Chihuahuan Desert Region, U.S. and Mexico*, eds. Roland H. Wauer and David H. Riskind. U.S. Department of the Interior, National Park Service, Transactions and Proceedings Series, No. 3, 1977b, pp. 597–608.

Wauer, Roland H. "Interrelations Between a Harris' Hawk and Badger." *Western Birds*, Vol. 8, 1977c, p. 155.

Wauer, Roland H. The Birds of the Lower Canyons of the Rio Grande. Report to National Park Service, 1978, pp. 1–49.

Wauer, Roland H. "Colima Warbler Status at Big Bend National Park, Texas." In: *Proceedings of the First Conference on Scientific Research in the National Parks*. U.S. Department of the Interior, National Park Service, Transactions and Proceedings Series, No. 5, 1979, pp. 474–496.

Wauer, Roland H. "The Sierra del Carmens—Mexico's Forgotten Wilderness." Paper presented at the meeting on Wildlife and Range Research Needs in Northern Mexico and Southwestern United States, Rio Rico, Arizona, April 20–24, 1981.

Wauer, Roland H. *A Field Guide to Birds of the Big Bend*. Austin: Texas Monthly Press, 1985.

Wauer, Roland H. *Naturalists' Mexico*. College Station: Texas A&M University Press, 1992.

Wauer, Roland H. *The Visitor's Guide to the Birds of the Rocky Mountains National Parks, United States and Canada*. Santa Fe, NM: John Muir Publications, 1993a.

Wauer, Roland H. "Birder's Guide to Big Bend National Park, Texas." *WildBird*, September, 1993b, pp. 34–39.

Wauer, Roland H. "Rare, Local, Little-Known, and Declining North American Breeders A Closer Look: Colima Warbler." *Birding*, August, 1994a, pp. 250–253.

Wauer, Roland H. "Report on Five Breeding Bird Study Plots at Big Bend National Park, Texas." Report to National Park Service, 1994b, pp. 1–47.

Wauer, Roland H., and Davis, Donald G. "Cave Swallows in Big Bend National Park, Texas." *Condor*, Vol. 74, 1972, p. 482.

Wauer, Roland H., and Ligon, J. David. "Distributional Relations of Breeding Avifauna of Four Southwestern Mountain Ranges." In: *Transactions of the Symposium on the Biological Resources of the Chihuahuan Desert Region, U.S. and Mexico*, eds. Roland H. Wauer and David H. Riskind. U.S. Department of the Interior, National Park Service, Transactions and Proceedings Series, No. 3, 1977, pp. 567–578.

Wauer, Roland H., and Rylander, M. K. "Anna's Hummingbird in West Texas." *Auk*, Vol. 85, 1968, p. 501.

Wauer, Roland H., and Scudday, James F. "Occurrence and Status of Certain Charadriiformes in the Texas Big Bend Country." *Southwestern Naturalist*, Vol. 17, 1972, pp. 210–211.

Wauer, Roland H., Palmer, Paul C., and Windham, Anse. "The Ferruginous Pygmy-Owl in South Texas." *American Birds*, Vol. 47, 1993, pp. 1071–1076.

Wetmore, Alexander, and Friedmann, Herbert. "The California Condor in Texas." *Condor*, Vol. 35, 1933, pp. 37–38.

Whitson, Martha A. "Field and Laboratory Investigation of the Ethology of Courtship and Copulation in the Greater Roadrunner." Ph.D. Dissertation, University of Oklahoma, Norman, 1971.

Wolf, David E. "First Record of an Aztec Thrush in the United States." *American Birds*, Vol. 32, 1978, pp. 156–157.

Wolfe, Col. L. R. *Checklist of the Birds of Texas*. Kerrville, TX: personal publication, 1956.

Zimmer, Barry, and Bryan, Kelly. "First United States Record of the Tufted Flycatcher." *American Birds*, Vol. 47, 1993, pp. 48–50.

Zimmerman, Dale A. "Range Expansion of Anna's Hummingbird." *American Birds*, Vol. 27, 1973, pp. 827–835.

Appendix A

TEXAS BIRD RECORDS COMMITTEE REPORT FORM

This form is copied with permission of the Texas Bird Records Committee. Please use this format for reporting any of the birds listed below with an asterisk to the TBRC. This list also includes species that need further verification within the park, but already may be well-documented elsewhere in Texas. Therefore, please report any of the birds listed in this section to the National Park Service; several of these birds have not yet been recorded for the park:

Red-necked Grebe	Crane Hawk*
Western Grebe	Roadside Hawk*
Clark's Grebe	Short-tailed Hawk*
Brown Pelican	White-tailed Hawk
Anhinga	Aplomado Falcon*
Reddish Egret	Plain Chachalaca
Roseate Spoonbill	Chukar
Wood Stork	Northern Bobwhite
Fulvous Whistling-Duck	Yellow Rail
Black-bellied Whistling-Duck	Black Rail
Trumpeter Swan*	Spotted Rail*
Muscovy Duck*	Whooping Crane
American Black Duck*	Semipalmated Plover
Eurasian Wigeon*	Mountain Plover
Barrow's Goldeneye*	Northern Jacana*
Masked Duck*	Red Knot
Northern Goshawk*	White-rumped Sandpiper

Pectoral Sandpiper
Sharp-tailed Sandpiper
Stilt Sandpiper
Buff-breasted Sandpiper
Ruff*
American Woodcock
Herring Gull
Common Tern
Least Tern*
Red-billed Pigeon*
Ruddy Ground-Dove*
White-tipped Dove
Northern Pygmy-Owl*
Ferruginous Pygmy-Owl*
Mottled Owl*
Spotted Owl
Barred Owl
Northern Saw-whet Owl*
Pauraque
Black Swift*
White-collared Swift*
Chimney Swift
Green Violet-ear*
Broad-billed Hummingbird*
White-eared Hummingbird*
Berylline Hummingbird*
Violet-crowned Hummingbird*
Plain-capped Starthroat*
Costa's Hummingbird*
Allen's Hummingbird*
Elegant Trogon*
Ringed Kingfisher
Lewis' Woodpecker*
Red-headed Woodpecker
Williamson's Sapsucker*
Downy Woodpecker
Hairy Woodpecker
Pileated Woodpecker

Northern Beardless-Tyrannulet
Greater Pewee*
Yellow-bellied Flycatcher
Buff-breasted Flycatcher*
Dusky-capped Flycatcher*
Nutting's Flycatcher*
Great Kiskadee
Social Flycatcher*
Sulphur-bellied Flycatcher*
Tropical Kingbird*
Fork-tailed Flycatcher*
Rose-throated Becard*
Masked Tityra*
Gray-breasted Martin*
Pinyon Jay*
Clark's Nutcracker*
Black-billed Magpie*
American Crow
Mountain Chickadee*
Bridled Titmouse*
Pygmy Nuthatch
Spot-breasted Wren*
American Dipper*
Black-capped Gnatcatcher*
Veery
Gray-cheeked Thrush*
Clay-colored Robin*
White-throated Robin*
Rufous-backed Robin*
Varied Thrush*
Aztec Thrush*
Bendire's Thrasher*
Bohemian Waxwing*
Gray Silky-Flycatcher*
Yellow-green Vireo*
Tropical Parula*
Crescent-chested Warbler*
Pine Warbler

Golden-cheeked Warbler
Bay-breasted Warbler
Blackpoll Warbler
Swainson's Warbler
Kentucky Warbler
Connecticut Warbler*
Mourning Warbler
Gray-crowned Yellowthroat*
Red-faced Warbler*
Slate-throated Redstart*
Golden-crowned Warbler*
Rufous-capped Warbler*
Olive Warbler*
Crimson-collared Grosbeak
Yellow Grosbeak*
Blue Bunting*
Olive Sparrow
White-collared Seedeater
Yellow-faced Grassquit*
Rufous-winged Sparrow*
Five-striped Sparrow*

Baird's Sparrow
Henslow's Sparrow*
Yellow-eyed Junco*
McCown's Longspur*
Lapland Longspur*
Smith's Longspur*
Snow Bunting*
Bobolink
Rusty Blackbird
Common Grackle
Shiny Cowbird*
Black-vented Oriole*
Streak-backed Oriole*
Altamira Oriole
Audubon's Oriole
Pine Grosbeak*
Cassin's Finch
White-winged Crossbill*
Lawrence's Goldfinch*
Hooded Grosbeak*
Evening Grosbeak

TEXAS ORNITHOLOGICAL SOCIETY
Texas Bird Records Committee Report Form

This form is intended as a convenience in reporting observations of rare or unusual birds. It may be used flexibly and need not be used at all except as a guideline. Attach additional sheets as necessary. PLEASE PRINT IN BLACK INK OR TYPE. Attach drawings, photos, etc., if possible. When complete, mail to: Greg W. Lasley, Secretary, Texas Bird Records Committee, 305 Loganberry Ct., Austin, TX 78745, OR Dr. Keith Arnold, Dept. of Wildlife and Fisheries Sciences, Texas A&M University, College Station, TX 77843-2258. Thank you!

1. Common and Scientific name: _____

2. Number of individuals, sexes, ages, general plumage (e.g. two adults in breeding plumage): _____

3. Location: _____
   _____ County: _____ , TX

4. Date and Time when observed: _____

5. Reporting observer and address: _____

6. Other observers: _____

7. Light conditions: _____

8. Optical equipment: _____

9. Distance to bird: _____

10. Duration of observation: _____

11. Habitat (be specific): _____

12. Description: (Include only what was actually seen, not what "should have been seen"). Include, if possible, body bulk, shape, bill, eye, plumage pattern, color and other physical characteristics. Describe voice, behavior and anything else that might help identify the bird.

_____

_____

_____

_____

_____

_____

_____

_____

—continued on next page—

13. How were similar species eliminated?

_____

_____

_____

14. Was it photographed? By whom? Attached?

_____

_____

15. Previous experience with species:

_____

_____

16. List any books or references used in identification:
    (a) at time of observation _____
    (b) after observation _____
17. This description written from:
    (a) notes made during observation _____
    (b) notes made after observation   _____
    (c) memory   _____
18. Are you positive of your observation? _____ . If not, explain: _____

_____

_____

19. Signature of reporter along with date and time of writing this
    account:

_____

ADDITIONAL NOTES (Please use extra sheets if necessary)

Appendix B

LIST OF BIG BEND BIRDERS

Peg Abbott, Ken Able, Peggy Accord, Marjorie and Red Adams, J. Adkins, Hilka Ahlers, Carl Aiken, Garrett and Kathie Albright, Lynne Aldrich, Betty and Tom Alex, Cathy Alger, Phillip F. Allan, C. Phillip Allen, Michael Allender, Cornelius Alwood, Dean Amadon, Guy Anderson, Kirk Anderson, Laura Anderson, Robert Anderson, Ben Archer, B. H. Armstead, Burl Armstrong, Johnny Armstrong, Nanatte and Rich Armstrong, T. and L. Army, Ron Arnberger, Keith Arnold, J. J. Arnold, John Arvin, Audrey Ashcroft, Gail and Jack Askew, Brooks and Lyn Atherton, Ansel Atkins, Stanley Auker, Mike Austin, Ann Ayers, Jeanne Ayers, Joan Babbitt, Mrs. Cleve Bachman, Paul Baicach, Jim and Natalie Baines, Peggy Baker, Larry and Martha Ballard, Jon Barlow, J. A. Barnes, J. R. Barnwell, Nancy Baron, Patricia Baron, Alma Barrera, Fred and Geneva Barry, Dominic Bartol, Benton Basham, Ken Bass, Albertine Bauguess, Gordon Baumgartner, Eleanor Beal, Mark Beaman, Dan Beard, J. Beard, Marjory Beaty, Richie Bechimiddleton, Travis Beck, Mary and Milford Becker, C. Edgar Bedell, Elliott Bedous, Don and Judy Bell, Anne Bellamy, Jim Bellamy, Charles Bender, Cris Benesh, Mabel N. Bendixen, Paul Benham, Dan Bennack, Karen Bennack, Jean Bensmiller, R. Benton, Dean Berg, Gary Berg, Byron Berger, Clair Berkman, Doug Bernard, Lynn C. Berner, Mark Berrier, J. R. Bider, William Biggs, Warren Bilkey, Donald Billiard, Millie Bilotta, Leon Bishop, Mike Bishop, John and Mary Bissonette, K. Bizak, James Black, Lorie Black, Richard and Susan Black, Gene Blacklock, ? Blackmore, Mac Blair, Mike Blaskiewicz, Byron Blend, Bill Bluhm, Kathy Blumig, Gary Blythe, Jerry Bock, Walter Boles, D. Boling, Addie and Joe Bolser, Bill and Jan Bolte, Patrick Bolton, T. Paul Bonney, Craig Booth, Karen Boucher, Robin Boughton, Albertine and Walt Bouguess, Bill and Sarah Bourbon, Bill Bouton, Martin Bovey, Jesse Boyce, Richard Boyden, Tom Boyle, Donald Bradburn, Bob and Myra Braden, A. Branden, Ken Branges, Karten

Bricher, Glenn Britt, Harold Brodrick, Bill Bromberg, Donald Brooks, Bernard Browerhand, David and Roy Brown, Gerald Brown, Marcia and Ron Brown, Virginia Brown, Dick Brownstein, Carol Brubaker, Tim Brush, J. P. Bryan, Kelly Bryan, D. Buck, Katie Buck, Joe Buckanan, R. J. Bullock, Cole Bunnell, Walt Burch, Byron Burger, John Burkhart, Jan and Robert Burnett, Deva and Jim Burns, George Burns, Jane Burns, Jim Burr, Sheriton Burr, Don Burt, Scott and Sylvia Burt, Bill Butler, Charles and Georgia Callagan, Jim Cameron, Mary Candee, Beverly Carlisle, S. Carmen, Buck and Linda Carpa, Larry Carpenter, Ginny and Jim Carrico, Scott Carroll, Steve Carroll, Dorothy and Jonathan Carter, Ruth Carter, Robin Carter, Barb and Ron Cavin, Don Chalfant, S. Chamberlain, Jim Chambers, George and Helen Champtax, Ansil Chapin, Henry Childs, Betty and Ken Christopher, Judith Christrup, Stephen Churchill, Eunice and Jeff Chynoweth, A. G. Clark, Jeremy Clark, James Clarke, John Clarkson, Ed Claypoole, Robert Coalston, Robert D. Cohen, Caroline H. Coleman, Patricia Collins, W. V. Combs, Jeff Connor, John Coons, Duck and Linda Cooper, Dave Cornman, Clarence Cottam, Ginger Coughran, Jim Court, Danny Covos, Mary E. Cowder, David Cox, Charles and Betty Crabtree, Glenn and Maryjane Crane, Lynda Cremer, Phyllis Cremorini, John Crim, Al Crockett, M. S. Croft, Mark Crotteau, Jewel Cummings, K. C. Cummings, Glenn Cureton, Wesley Cureton, Ed and Martha Curry, Richard C. Curt, Pete Cuthbert, Carolyn and Ray Cuthbertson, Lyn Dahl, David Dais, Fred Dalbey, Thelma Dalmas, Lee Daniel, Sandra Darby, Doris and Julian Darden, Ward Dasey, Cliff and Maryjane Davenport, Vidal Davila, C. Davis, Don Davis, Roberto Dean, Stuart Dechke, Frank Deckert, Bill Degenhardt, Deborah DeKeyzer, Billie Demant, L. DeMarsh, Richard Derdeyn, Murl Deusing, L. A. Deveutt, Robert DeVine, John H. Dick, D. Dickson, Julias W. Diekert, ? Dingus, James Dixon, Keith Dixon, N. Dobbins, Warren Dodson, J. Doherty, Joyce Dolch, Mary Doll, Louis Dombroski, Ward Dorsey, Dixie Douglas, Jean Dow, Don Dowde, Barbara and Tom Driscoll, Del DuBois, Edwin S. Duerr, J. W. Duffield, Joyce Dulch, Elizabeth and Lewis A. Dumont, John Duncan, Jon Dunn, Barbara Duplisea, James and Sheri Durden, Elvin and Lois Dusseau, Charles Easley, Dave and Patty Easterla, Roger Eastman, Marge Eaten, Doug Eddleman, Carol Edwards, John Egbert, Marc Eisdorfer, Mrs. F. P. Elby, David Elkowitz, Hugh M. Ellison, Walter Ellison, Bruce Ellsworth, Charles Ely, Victor Emanuel, Gary Emerson, DeeRenee Ericks, Ann and Carl Erickson, Keith Erickson, W. L. Erwin, Sterling Essenmacher, G. W. Ethridge, Ted Eubanks, Dale Evans, Doris and Doug Evans, Maxilla Evans, Michael Evans, Bruce Fall, Jeanne Farmer,

Bernard Fay, Victor Fazio, L. Feazel, Brooke Feeley, Ronald Feischer, Charles C. Fellars, Ben Feltner, P. Fieffer, Bob Fieney, Dean Fisher, Gordon Fitch, Curt Fitrow, J. M. Fitzgerald, Hal Flanders, Raymond Fleetwood, Carl and Florence Fleming, Mark Flippo, Lona and Steve Flocke, Nancy Flood, David Flowers, Norris Follett, Joseph Ford, Dorothy and James Forenof, Jeanne Forman, John Forsythe, Diane Foster, Robert Foster, Kathy Fox, Thelma Fox, Russ Fraker, Phyllis and Tony Frank, R. C. Frankenburger, Andrew and Rene Franks, Dr. and Mrs. J. Howard Fredrick, Rick Frederick, Stephanie Frederick, Howard and Ruth Fredrick, Bobbie Fredricks, Frank Freese, Frances Freet, Margaret Frick, Sam Fried, Bobby Friedricks, Jerry Frielich, Ned Fritz, W. H. Fritz, Stan Fulcher, David Fuller, W. R. Furley, Otta Gagel, Kim Galdler, John Galley, Gladys C. Galliger, Tony Gallucci, Charles and Louise Gambill, Klause E. Gampel, Cecil Garrett, Stephen Gast, Maurice Gatlin, Susan L. Gawarecki, John Gee, Fred R. Gehlbach, Klause E. Gempel, Mike Gerber, Paul Gerrish, Daryl and Margaret Giblin, M. E. Gibson, Doris Giewald, Ed Gildenwater, Charles Gill, P. A. Ginsburg, Clyde Glastetter, Vicki Glen, V. Lee Glover, Frank S. Goldberg, A. Gomez, Jennifer Gongaware, Janet Goodland, David Goodson, Dave Goodwin, Phil Gordon, Wayne Gordon, Peter Gottschling, Bill Graber, Cynthia Grant, Jesse Grantham, Helen and Gene Graves, Jane Gray, Pat Grediagen, Joel Greenberg, Laura Greffenius, Brete Griffen, Byron Griffen, George Griffen, Arch C. Griffith, Jr., Mary Griffith, Molly Grinkavitch, Marguerite Gross, Sharon and Tom Gruber, Joe Grzbowski, Richard Guillett, Gene Guinn, Lula Gullett, Dieter Gump, Roxanne Gunter, Burk Gurney, M. Gustafson, Hilton Hagan, Pat Hagan, Dorthy Hagewood, Bryan Hale, C. E. Hall, Terry Hall, Karl Haller, Bruce Hallett, Eunice Halm, Nicholas Halmi, Kathleen Hambly, Jane Hamilton, Bob Haney, ? Hanlon, J. Hansche, Doris Harden, Tyrrel Harden, Adele Harding, H. T. Hargis, Beverly and John Hargrave, Robert Harms, Fred Harris, Steve Harris, Joe Harrison, Eric and Mildred Hartman, Jim Harvey, Thomas Harvey, Tyrrell Harvey, Dave and Ginger Harwood, Herb Hausman, Steve Hawkins, Jim Hayes, Michael Hayes, N. C. Hazard, Kevin Head, William Hechroell, Harold Hedges, Herb and Lee Heger, Ray Heitmann, Michael and O. R. Henderson, Richard B. Henderson, L. Henley, Gene Henricks, Burt Hensel, Elizabeth Henze, Greg Heppner, Mark Herberger, Bonnie Herdel, Felix Hernandez III, Ray Hertman, Rod Hesselbert, Mr. and Mrs. R. N. Hewitt, Janet Heywood, Burnell Hill, Chuck Hill, Harold and Myrtle Hill, Julia Hill, Catherine Hillman, Barbara Hines, Jim Hines, Janet and Stephen Hinshaw, Barbara and Joe Hirt, Larry Hobkins, Robert Hobkinson, Gail Hodge, ? Hoefflinger, Mark Hoffman, Steve Hoffman, D. Holcomb, James Holdsworth, Margaret Holler, J. Hollingsworth, Eunice Holm, Harold Holt, Jimmy Homer, Bob Honig, R. L. Hooper, Barb Hosea, Julia and Ty Hotchkiss, Bill and Jean Hough, Barbara and Sam House, W. Householder, Jack and Norma Howard, Joan Howard, George Howarth, Henry Howe, Wilhelmania Howe, Charles Howell, Jean and Ron Hudson, Robert Huggins, P. D. Hulce, John Humphrey, Pete Hunt, Chuck Hunter, Gloria Hunter, E. B. Hurlburt, Florence Hurst, Jim Hurst, K. H. Husmann, Marlene Igo, Paul Ipsem, Peter and Ruth Isleib, J. Ivey, Nick Jackson, Linda Jarvis, Tom Jarvis, Richard Jeffers, Joan and Robert Jefferson, Malcolm Jenkins, Tim Jenkins, S. Jennings, Calyn and Tom Jenns, Bill Jensen, Carolyn and Tom Jervis, Ruth Jessen, Gloria Jewel, Cappy Johnson, Cheryl Johnson, David Johnson, Kathy Johnson, Max and Marian Johnson, Bob, Karen, and Ted Jones, Mrs. John Jones, Mary G. Jones, Morgan Jones, P. Kabal, Joanne Kangas, Wolf Kappes, Impe Karafaith, Dale and Kevin Karlson, Joanne Kaugos, Brooke Keeley, Greg Keiran, Nancy Kelley, Mike Kelly, Gary Kempf, E. Kendall, Gordon Kennedy, Steve Kerr, S. Kilpatrick, William King, Steve Kingswood, Jack M. Kiracofe, Jeffrey W. Kirk, Mark Kirtley, Joe Kleiman, Dan Klug, Peter Koch, Forest Koefe, Nancy Kohls, Kinki Koi, Mark Korducki, Ron Korosick, Randy Koroter, Chris and Ted Koundakscan, Danny Kovos, Paul Krapfel, Mary and Paul Krausmann, Carol Kruse, Essie Kruse, Joe Kuban, Tom Kursar, Ed Kutac, Steve LaForest, R. Lambgrton, Bill Lamond, Dr. and Mrs. J. M. Langham, H. P. Langridge, Scott Lanier, Kristin Larson, Greg Lasley, Rod Laslie, Christina and Renee Laubach, Richard Laursen, Robert M. Lavall, Orval Lawler, J. W. Leach, W. Leavens, Ken Lebo, Fred Lebseck, Jeanne and Mark Leckert, Gwenda Ledbetter, Tim Lehman, Dennis Lenston, Robin Leong, R. D. Leopold, Ann LeSassier, Peter Lesica, Rod Leslie, B. Leske, Charles W. Letcher, G. T. and M. Letis, Jay and Debbie Liggett, Earl Likes, Jim Liles, Cindy Lippincott, Margaret Littlejohn, A. C. Lloyd, Rick LoBello, Mark Lockwood, Ramon Lorgaria, D. R. Love, Glenn Lowe, Jr., John Lowley, Gail Luckner, Phyllis Lund, Joe Lunn, Bill Luparoos, Gil Lusk, Dennis Luton, Barry Lyon, Cliff Lyons, Willem Maane, John MacDonald, Bob Machover, Bruce Mack, Maurice MacKey, Deborah Macmillan, Doris Maguire, Gerald Maisel, Rudy Mancke, David Mandell, M. F. Marchase, John Marsh, Thompson G. Marsh, Joe Marshall, John Martin, A. L. Masley, Phil Mastrengelo, Steve Matherly, W. C. Matthews, Donn Mattsson, George E. Maxon, Joe Maxwell, Terry Maxwell, Larry May, Robert Mayer, Bill and John May-

nard, Florence and Roy Mazzagatt, Lena McBee, ? McCarroll, Guy McCask-
ie, Jim McChristal, Jones C. McConnell, Ian McCord, Mike McCormick,
David McCorquodale, P. A. McCoy, Carroll and Lucy McEathron, M. D.
McGhee, Ian McGregor, Millie McGuiness, Bruce McHenry, C. McIlroy,
G. Craig McIntyre, Annie McKelvey, Bonnie McKinney, Brad McKinney,
Barbara and Daniel McKnight, Ernest McLean, Roger McNeil, Bill Mealy,
Don and Ruthie Melton, Bob Merrill, Bob Metzler, Tom Meyer, Richard
Michael, Tommy Michael, Martha Michener, Jacob Miller, Jeff Miller,
Jody Miller, Lauri Miller, Roger Mitchell, Dave Mobley, Cathy Moitoret,
Betty Moore, Eric Morey, Janet Morgan, N. A. Morgan, James Morlock,
Harold Morrin, Vaughn Morrison, Robert Morse, B. Moscatello, Patty
and Paul Moser, Paul Motts, Robert Moyer, Garrett Moynihan, John
Muldrow, John Muller, D. R. Mullins, Steve Munden, JoAnn and Linda
Murray, Derek Muschalek, Roger Muskat, David Muth, Patti Muzny, Jean
Nance, Kenneth Nanney, David Narins, Ron Naveen, Sandra Naylor, Bon-
nie Neathery, Abbot and Ava Nelson, Dick Nelson, Helen and Tom Nel-
son, Kent Nelson, Charles and Ella Newell, Coleman Newman, Skip
Nichols, Manfred Noepel, Wendy Noomah, Don Norman, B. Norris,
Katie Northrup, Fran Nuebel, Keith and Peggy Nusbaum, Frank Oatman,
Allan and Bruce O'Brian, John O'Brien, G. V. Oliver, Leonard and Mary
Olmsted, Keith Olsen, Joseph Ondrejko, Noberto Ortega, Susan Ortiz,
Glenn Ory, June Osborne, Greg Oskay, Bruce Ostyn, Malcom Otis, Glen
Otteson, Doug Overaeber, Karl Overman, James Owen, Mrs. James
Owen, Ed Pace, H. Paish, Bruce and Chris Palmer, Jody Palmer, Richard
Palmer, A. Palmes, Marcos Paredes, Helen and Max Parker, Ted Parker,
Warren Parker, Janette Parks, Mike Parmeter, David Pashley, Sonja Paspal,
J. Pauley, Mike Pawlick, Dick Payne, Mary Ann Payne, G. B. Pearce, Larry
Pearler, John Pearson, Rob Pearson, Tina Pearson, Larry Peavler, Doyle
and Helen Peckham, Peter Peischbacher, Mike Perkins, Barbara and John
Perry, Kat and Steve Perry, Stephan K. Perry, Barbara Peterman, James
Peters, H. and R. Peterson, John Peterson, Pete Peterson, Barbara Pettit,
Victor Petty, Larry D. Pharris, Bud Phillips, P. Phillips, ? Pierce, Randy
Pinkston, Tom Plant, H. E. Poindexter, Bryant Pomrenke, John Ponds,
Maxwell Ponds, Jr., Georgia Porter, Richard D. Porter, C. G. Potter,
Josephine Potter, Dave Powell, Jeanne Pratt, Angie Price, Art Prickett,
Dennis Pritchard, Warren Pruess, Rich Pruett, Rick Prum, Ken Prytherch,
Warren Pulich, Warren Pulich, Jr., Bill Pulliam, R. Dan Purrington, Roy
Quillen, Bob Quinn, Ralph Raitt, Kevin Ramsey, L. E. Ramsey, Cynthia
Rankin, Dick Rasp, Darryl Rathbun, Bill Read, Bob Reid, Edward Regan,

J. Reinoehl, Vic Reister, Van Remsen, A. J. Revels, Katie and Tina Reynolds, Barbara and John Ribble, Jeff Rice, Esequiel Richard, Peter Riesz, David Riskind, Jan and Will Risser, S. Rivers, David Roark, C. Robbins, A. Robert, Craig Roberts, Len Robinson, Scott Robinson, Mary and Max Rodell, Alice and William Roe, Dennis and Jim Rogers, Glen Rogers, Jerry Rogers, R. Rogers, Aline and Forrest Romero, Cricket Rose, Judith Rose, Gary Rosenberg, Rene Ross, Robert and Joan Rothe, S. Rotroff, ? Rowe, J. Mark Rowland, Forrest Rowlands, John Rowlett, Rose Ann Rowlett, William Hart Rufe III, Vermille Ruff, Dick Russell, Kathlyn Rust, Kent Rylander, C. L. Sackett, Jr. , Bob and Marge Sakol, Ric Samulski, Maryann Santos, Starr Saphir, Paul Saraceni, Nancy Saulsbury, R. M. Saunders, D. Sawyer, Gloria Saylor, Richard Schaefer, Laurie Schaetzel, Don Schaezler, Madge Scharber, Bert and Millie Schaughency, Lillian and Roberta Scherer, Hank Schmidt, Terry Schmidt, Richard Schneider, H. Schultz, Michael Schwitters, Bruce Scoggins, Peter Scott, Norman Scott, Paul Scraceni, Betsy and John Searight, Elizabeth Seaunght, Alan See, E. J. Seedge, Ed Seeker, Steven Segal, Jean Segerstrom, Chris Seifert, Willie Sekula, John Selle, Jeff Selleck, L. E. Sellers, Chuck Sexton, Bernard Shandoin, Charlie Shannon, Mary Shannon, Devi Sharp, Don and Martha Shearer, E. and J. Shelton, Napier Shelton, William M. Sheperd, Jim Shields, George Shier, James Shifflet, David Sibley, Roger Siglin, R. Siebert, Martha and Vince Sikora, David Simmon, Cynthia and Rich Simmons, George Simmons, Virginia Simmons, Betty, Jerry, Leo, and Marion Simons, Thelma Sims, Shirley Sink, Jeff Skevington, Ray Skiles, C. L. Skulski, Jeffrey Smallwood, Bill Smith, E. Smith, Glenn Smith, Kaithe Smith, P. William Smith, R. C. Smith, S. Stovall Smith, Connie Snapp, Bill Snebold, Gerald Sneed, Dave Snyder, Linda and Ruth Snyder, Ken Soltesz, Tex Sordahl, Ben and Sally Sorensen, Hope Spear, Fred and Joyce Speer, I. Speer, Garry Spence, Charlotte and Phil Spencer, Theodore M. Sperry, Ron Spomer, Clare and Harold Spore, Alexander Sprunt, Jr., Ed Stackpoole, Cliff Stagner, Dale Stahlecher, Andrea Staley, Rich Stallcup, Richard B. Starr, Verma Starts, Bob Staub, David W. Steadman, David Stealman, S. A. Stedman, Roger Steeb, Harry Steed, Mrs. Cambell Steketee, Lee Sterrenburg, Carolyn and Jim Stevens, Andrew Stewart, Bruce Stewart, James Stewart, Kathaleen Stewart, Mary Louise Stewart, Susie Stewart, Brad and Elton Stilwell, Ken Stinnett, John St. Julien, Suzanne St. Onge, Byron Stone, Rose Marie Stortz, James Stovall, E. G. and J. H. Strauss, Jerry and Nancy Strickling, Paul Strong, C. Sturm, Bob Stymeist, George M. Sutton,

Steve Swanke, James Swartz, Andy and C. Swash, Carl Swenson, Paul Sykes, Dora Sylvester, Bruce Talbot, Robert Tanhope, Phil Tanimoto, G. S. Taylor, Joe Taylor, Ira Taylor, Ross Taylor, John and Ted Tedford, ? Tempel, Lynn Tennefoss, Clark Terrell, Ann Tews, Drew Thate, Timothy Thaws, Beverly and Gerhard Thiem, Helen and P. L. Thigpen, Doug Thomas, Timothy Thomas, Dale and Judy Thompson, Doug Thompson, Patty Thompson, Elise Thrasher, Ron Tibball, Stuart Tingley, Doyle and Judy Townsend, Rick Toomey, Elliot Tramer, Ben and Joan Trimble, John Trochet, Marilyn Troxel, Don Troyers, Betty and Bull Trumbauer, Jim Tucker, Dale Tuttle, Mark Tuttle, Jack Tyler, Ted and Sue Ulrich, Jim and Joann Unruh, Heraldo Ureste, Beverly Van Dyke, A. F. Van Pelt, Steve Van Pelt, Alan Van Valkenburg, Brad Vaughn, Al Velasco, Peter Vennema, Alfred and Joy Viola, Ellen Vogal, Jim and Lola Vukonich, Billi Wagner, George Wagner, Warren Wagner, Homer and Jamie Waite, Jim Walker, George E. Wallace, Richard and Wendy Wallace, Susan and Tim Wallis, ? Walstrom, Teresa Walters, Susan Ward, Gene Warren, Mike Warren, Anne and Vernon Waters, Teresa and Zeke Waters, Wendy Watson, Andy Weaks, R. C. and S. A. Webb, Jim and Teresa Weedin, Chris Weeks, Ted Weems, Jeffrey Weigal, Barbara Weintraub, Sharon Weiss, Roy Welch, Harold Wellander, Lee Wesson, Henry West, Steve West, Jack Whetstone, Chris White, Donald H. White, Ed and Geth White, Mel White, Lovie May Whitaker, Bret Whitney, Sarah Whitson, Lloyd Whitt, Chris and Ira Whitton, C. C. and Iris Wiedenfeld, Carl Wiedenfeld, David Wiedenfeld, Iris Wiedenfeld, Sue Wiedenfeld, Hal Wierenga, M. J. Wiggington, G. Wigington, Jan and Keith Wigger, Jack and Phyllis Wilburn, Roddy Wilder, Tom Will, Barbara and Dan Williams, Frances Williams, Harvey and Ruth Williams, Jo Williams III, Margery Williams, McRae Williams, Michael C. Williams, S. O. Williams III, Lorn Willingham, S. Willmot, Marian and Russ Wilson, Cecille and Gene Wilton, Susan Winkler, A. R. Winshall, Eric and Louis Winston, E. Winters, Doyle Wise, David and Mimi Wolf, Gerry and Vicki Wolfe, Libby and Ron Wolfe, R. A. Wolinski, Cynthia Womack, Fred Wong, Barbara Woods, Bryant Woods, Harriet and Joseph Woolfenden, Albert H. Worl, Alan Wormington, Brian Wylie, Mitch Wyss, Laurie Yorke, David Young, Ruth Young, Dick Youse, John C. Yrizany, James Zabriskie, Steve Zachary, Albin Zeitler, Marlene Zichlinsky, Barry Zimmer, Kevin Zimmer, and Dale and Marian Zimmerman.

INDEX

bold = illustrations

Robin, American: 140,
247; Clay-colored,
245; Rufous-backed,
X, XII, 245–246
Robinson: Carl, VI; Len,
245; Scott, 166, 250
Rodell: Mary, 60;
Max, 60
Roe: Alice, 100; William,
100
Rogers: Jerry, 205; R., 133
Romero: Aline, 174;
Forrest, 174
Rooney, Walter: 64
Rose: Cricket, 171;
Judith, 119
Rosenberg, Gary: 214
Ross, Rene: 180
Rothe: family, 61, 93, 115,
144, 171, 190; Joan,
172; Robert, 118,
119, 172, 192, 193,
214, 227, 241
Rowe: 55
Rowlands, Mr. and Mrs.
Forrest: 122;
Forrest, 197
Rowlett, Rose Ann: 54,
120, 131, 146, 164,
173, 182, 195, 251
Ruff, Vermille: 228
Russell, Dick: 88
Rust, Kathlyn: 174
Rylander, Kent: 88

Sakol: Bob, 107;
Margie, 107
San Antonio Audubon
Society: 172
Sandpiper: Baird's, 11,
61; Buff-breasted,
240; Least, 11, 61;
Pectoral, 239;
Semipalmated, 239;
Solitary, 8, 11, 58;

Spotted, 8, 11,
58–59; Stilt, 239;
Upland, 59–60;
Western, 60–61;
White-rumped,
XI, 239
Saphir, Starr: 214, 248
Sapsucker: Red-naped,
96; Williamson's,
15, 96–97; Yellow-
bellied, 96
Saraceni, Paul: 190
Saulsbury, Nancy: 251
Sawyer, D.: 46
Saylor, Gloria: 192
Scaup, Lesser: 32
Schaafsma, Harold: 3
Schaefer, Richard: 171
Schaetzel, Laurie: 182
Schaezler, Don: 33
Schaughency: Bert, 54,
59, 115, 120, 159,
238; Millie, 115,
120, 159, 238
Scherer: Lillian, 232;
Roberta, 232
Schmidt, Terry: 52
Schneider, Richard: 101
Schultz, H.: 193
Scott: Norman, 92;
Peter, 24, 27, 36, 60,
85, 93, 112, 120,
141, 149, 155, 159,
164, 178, 181, 184,
201, 209
Screech-Owl: Eastern, 13,
14, 73, 74; Western,
13, 14, 73, 74
Scudday, Jim: 64
Searight: Betsy, 178;
John, 178
Seaunght, Elizabeth: 171
See, Alan: 60, 72
Seedge, E.J.: 174
Seifert, Chris: 170

Sekula, Willie: 41, 90,
108, 112, 118, 136,
164, 193, 246
Selle, John: 214
Selleck, Jeff: VI, 4, 20, 21,
23, 32, 82, 118, 150,
184, 215, 219, 227,
229, 234
Sellers, L. E.: 83
Semple, John B.: 2
Sexton, Chuck: 40, 41,
48, 80, 90, 107, 120,
132, 136, 141, 173,
178, 181, 192, 234
Shandoin, Dr. and Mrs.
Bernard: 247
Shannon: Charlie, 60;
Mary, 182
Sharp, Devi: 35
Shearer: Don, 141;
Martha, 141
Shelton, Napier: 21, 238
Shepherd, William M.:
28, 190
Shields, Jim: 104, 184
Shier, George: 138
Shiflett, Jim: 92, 138,
166, 172
Shoveler, Northern:
8, 30
Shrike, Loggerhead: 14,
149–150
Sibley, David: 90, 216
Siebert, R.: 172
Siglin, Roger: 20, 24, 31,
36, 66, 71
Simmon, David:
131–132, 170, 180
Simmons: Cynthia, 20,
24, 27, 30, 31, 38,
54, 57, 62, 114, 115,
124, 136, 140, 159,
173, 212; George,
21, 34, 60, 238, 239;
Rich, 21, 24, 27, 31,